New Media and the Nation in Malaysia

In the four decades or so since its invention, the Internet has become pivotal to how many societies function, influencing how individual citizens interact with and respond to their governments. Within Southeast Asia, while most governments subscribe to the belief that new media technological advancement improves their nation's socio-economic conditions, they also worry about its cultural and political effects. This book examines how this set of dynamics operates through its study of new media in contemporary Malaysian society.

Using the social imaginary framework and adopting a socio-historical approach, the book explains the varied understandings of new media as a continuing process wherein individuals and their societies operate in tandem to create, negotiate and enact the meaning ascribed to concepts and ideas. In doing so, it also highlights the importance of non-users to national technological policies.

Through its examination of the ideation and development of Malaysia's Multimedia Super Corridor mega project to date and with reference to the seminal socio-political events of 2007–12, including the 2008 General Elections and the Bersih and Hindraf rallies, the book provides a clear explanation for new media's prominence in the multi-ethnic and majority Islamic society of Malaysia today. It will be of interest to academics working in the fields of Media and Internet Studies, and Southeast Asian Politics.

Susan Leong is an Early Career Research Fellow at Curtin University, Australia. Her research focuses on the implications of new media for nations, and her latest project examines the effects of new media for the relationship between diaspora, home and receiving nations.

Routledge Contemporary Southeast Asia Series

1. **Land Tenure, Conservation and Development in Southeast Asia**
   Peter Eaton

2. **The Politics of Indonesia–Malaysia Relations**
   One kin, two nations
   Joseph Chinyong Liow

3. **Governance and Civil Society in Myanmar**
   Education, health and environment
   Helen James

4. **Regionalism in Post-Suharto Indonesia**
   Edited by Maribeth Erb, Priyambudi Sulistiyanto and Carole Faucher

5. **Living with Transition in Laos**
   Market integration in Southeast Asia
   Jonathan Rigg

6. **Christianity, Islam and Nationalism in Indonesia**
   Charles E. Farhadian

7. **Violent Conflicts in Indonesia**
   Analysis, representation, resolution
   Edited by Charles A. Coppel

8. **Revolution, Reform and Regionalism in Southeast Asia**
   Cambodia, Laos and Vietnam
   Ronald Bruce St John

9. **The Politics of Tyranny in Singapore and Burma**
   Aristotle and the rhetoric of benevolent despotism
   Stephen McCarthy

10. **Ageing in Singapore**
    Service needs and the state
    Peggy Teo, Kalyani Mehta, Leng Leng Thang and Angelique Chan

11. **Security and Sustainable Development in Myanmar**
    Helen James

12. **Expressions of Cambodia**
    The politics of tradition, identity and change
    Edited by Leakthina Chau-Pech Ollier and Tim Winter

13. **Financial Fragility and Instability in Indonesia**
    Yasuyuki Matsumoto

14. **The Revival of Tradition in Indonesian Politics**
    The deployment of *adat* from colonialism to indigenism
    Edited by Jamie S. Davidson and David Henley

15. **Communal Violence and Democratization in Indonesia**
    Small town wars
    Gerry van Klinken

16. **Singapore in the Global System**
    Relationship, structure and change
    Peter Preston

17. **Chinese Big Business in Indonesia**
    The state of capital
    Christian Chua

18. **Ethno-religious Violence in Indonesia**
    From soil to God
    Chris Wilson

19. **Ethnic Politics in Burma**
    States of conflict
    Ashley South

20. **Democratization in Post-Suharto Indonesia**
    Edited by Marco Bünte and Andreas Ufen

21 **Party Politics and Democratization in Indonesia**
Golkar in the post-Suharto era
Dirk Tomsa

22 **Community, Environment and Local Governance in Indonesia**
Locating the commonweal
Edited by Carol Warren and John F. McCarthy

23 **Rebellion and Reform in Indonesia**
Jakarta's security and autonomy polices in Aceh
Michelle Ann Miller

24 **Hadrami Arabs in Present-day Indonesia**
An Indonesia-oriented group with an Arab signature
Frode F. Jacobsen

25 **Vietnam's Political Process**
How education shapes political decision making
Casey Lucius

26 **Muslims in Singapore**
Piety, politics and policies
Kamaludeen Mohamed Nasir, Alexius A. Pereira and Bryan S. Turner

27 **Timor Leste**
Politics, history and culture
Andrea Katalin Molnar

28 **Gender and Transitional Justice**
The women of East Timor
Susan Harris Rimmer

29 **Environmental Cooperation in Southeast Asia**
ASEAN's regime for trans-boundary haze pollution
Paruedee Nguitragool

30 **The Theatre and the State in Singapore**
Terence Chong

31 **Ending Forced Labour in Myanmar**
Engaging a pariah regime
Richard Horsey

32 **Security, Development and Nation-Building in Timor-Leste**
A cross-sectoral assessment
Edited by Vandra Harris and Andrew Goldsmith

33 **The Politics of Religion in Indonesia**
Syncretism, orthodoxy and religious contention in Java and Bali
Edited by Michel Picard and Remy Madinier

34 **Singapore's Ageing Population**
Managing healthcare and end of life decisions
Edited by Wing-Cheong Chan

35 **Changing Marriage Patterns in Southeast Asia**
Economic and socio-cultural dimensions
Edited by Gavin W. Jones, Terence H. Hull and Maznah Mohamad

36 **The Political Resurgence of the Military in Southeast Asia**
Conflict and leadership
Edited by Marcus Mietzner

37 **Neoliberal Morality in Singapore**
How family policies make state and society
Youyenn Teo

38 **Local Politics in Indonesia**
Pathways to power
Nankyung Choi

39 **Separatist Conflict in Indonesia**
The long-distance politics of the Acehnese diaspora
Antje Missbach

40 **Corruption and Law in Indonesia**
The unravelling of Indonesia's anti-corruption framework through law and legal process
Simon Butt

41 **Men and Masculinities in Southeast Asia**
Edited by Michele Ford and Lenore Lyons

42 **Justice and Governance in East Timor**
Indigenous approaches and the 'New Subsistence State'
Rod Nixon

43 **Labour Migration and Human Trafficking in Southeast Asia**
Critical perspectives
Michele Ford, Lenore Lyons and Willem van Schendel

44 **Population Policy and Reproduction in Singapore**
Making future citizens
Shirley Hsiao-Li Sun

45 **Political Change and Territoriality in Indonesia**
Provincial proliferation
Ehito Kimura

46 **Singapore Malays**
Being ethnic minority and Muslim in a global city-state
Hussin Mutalib

47 **Southeast Asia and the Cold War**
Edited by Albert Lau

48 **Legal Pluralism in Indonesia**
Bridging the unbridgeable
Ratno Lukito

49 **Building a People-Oriented Security Community the ASEAN way**
Alan Collins

50 **Social Activism in Southeast Asia**
Edited by Michele Ford

51 **Chinese Indonesians Reassessed**
History, religion and belonging
Edited by Siew-Min Sai and Chang-Yau Hoon

52 **Parties and Parliaments in Southeast Asia**
Non-partisan chambers in Indonesia, the Philippines and Thailand
Roland Rich

53 **Journalism and Conflict in Indonesia**
From reporting violence to promoting peace
Steve Sharp

54 **The Technological State in Indonesia**
The co-constitution of high technology and authoritarian politics
Sulfikar Amir

55 **Party Politics in Southeast Asia**
Clientelism and electoral competition in Indonesia, Thailand and the Philippines
Edited by Dirk Tomsa and Andreas Ufen

56 **Culture, Religion and Conflict in Muslim Southeast Asia**
Negotiating tense pluralisms
Edited by Joseph Camilleri and Sven Schottmann

57 **Global Indonesia**
Jean Gelman Taylor

58 **Cambodia and the Politics of Aesthetics**
Alvin Cheng-Hin Lim

59 **Adolescents in Contemporary Indonesia**
Lyn Parker and Pam Nilan

60 **Development and the Environment in East Timor**
Authority, participation and equity
Christopher Shepherd

61 **Law and Religion in Indonesia**
Faith, conflict and the courts
Melissa Crouch

62 **Islam in Modern Thailand**
Faith, philanthropy and politics
Rajeswary Ampalavanar Brown

63 **New Media and the Nation in Malaysia**
Malaysianet
Susan Leong

New Media and the Nation in Malaysia
Malaysianet

Susan Leong

LONDON AND NEW YORK

First published 2014 by Routledge

2 Park Square, Milton Park, Abingdon, Oxfordshire OX14 4RN
711 Third Avenue, New York, NY 10017

Routledge is an imprint of the Taylor & Francis Group, an informa business

First issued in paperback 2017

Copyright © 2014 Susan Leong

The right of Susan Leong to be identified as author of this work has been asserted by her in accordance with sections 77 and 78 of the Copyright, Designs and Patents Act 1988.

All rights reserved. No part of this book may be reprinted or reproduced or utilised in any form or by any electronic, mechanical, or other means, now known or hereafter invented, including photocopying and recording, or in any information storage or retrieval system, without permission in writing from the publishers.

Notice:
Product or corporate names may be trademarks or registered trademarks, and are used only for identification and explanation without intent to infringe.

British Library Cataloguing in Publication Data
A catalogue record for this book is available from the British Library

Library of Congress Cataloguing in Publication data
Leong, Susan (Susan Mee Mee), author.
  New media and the nation in Malaysia : Malaysianet / Susan Leong.
    pages cm. – (Routledge contemporary Southeast Asia series ; 63)
  Includes bibliographical references and index.
  1. Internet–Social aspects–Malaysia. 2. Internet–Government policy–Malaysia.
  3. Digital media–Social aspects–Malaysia. 4. Digital media–Government policy–Malaysia. I. Title.
  HN700.6.Z9I565 2013
  302.2309595'1–dc23
                              2013012002

ISBN: 978-0-415-81981-7 (hbk)
ISBN: 978-1-138-57555-4 (pbk)

Typeset in Times New Roman
by Out of House Publishing

for Silverius and Claire

Contents

List of figures xiii
Acknowledgements xiv
List of abbreviations xv

Introduction: of nations, technologies and non-users 1

1 Social imaginaries 14

2 The nation, race and religion 33

3 Nation and Internet 50

4 Malaysia and new media: the Multimedia Super Corridor 69

5 Users and non-users in the Malaysian social imaginary 90

6 Malaysia and the Internet: new configurations? 109

In closing 127

Glossary 133
References 134
Index 159

Figures

1 Theory of social imaginary – Cornelius Castoriadis vs. Charles
  Taylor 18
2 Social stock of knowledge – Alfred Schutz 26

Acknowledgements

My deepest gratitude as always to Michele Willson, Matthew Allen and Wanning Sun, who have all been mentors at different stages of that long trek from study and research to publication. I am indebted to Brian McNair for his expert guidance and advice in the art of authorship.

Various people have been a part of the team that helped me put this book together over the years. I want specifically to thank Kristen Philips, Sasha Mackay and Angela Kuga Thas. My thanks are also owed to the two anonymous readers who reviewed the manuscript for their insightful advice and comments.

I am grateful to Queensland University of Technology for granting me professional development leave in the first half of 2012 to work on the manuscript.

Abbreviations

ASAS	Islamic Academy of Science
Bersih	'The Coalition for Clean and Fair Elections' – a political campaign that rallied for the cause of clean and fair elections on 10 November 2007, 9 July 2011 and 28 April 2012
BN	Barisan Nasional: National Front – the dominant political coalition in Malaysia
ETP	Economic Transformation Programme
FDIs	foreign direct investment
FOSS	Free and Open Software movement
Hindraf	Hindu Rights Action Force
ICTs	information and communication technologies
IPTN	Indonesian aircraft industry company
JARING	Joint Advanced Research Integrated Networking, Malaysia's first Internet service provider which became available in 1990
MDeC	The Multimedia Development Corporation that was formed to manage the MSC
MSC	Malaysia's Multimedia Super Corridor mega project, launched in 1996
MUIS	Majlis Ugama Islam Singapura – Islamic Religious Council of Singapore
NEM	New Economic Model – Malaysia's current national policy framework which shapes the nation's economic direction. The NEM was initiated by Malaysia's sixth Prime Minister, Najib Razak
NIC	newly industrialized countries
NITC	National Information Technology Council
NPPA	Singapore's Newspaper and Printing Presses Act, 1974
NSTB	National Science and Technology Board (in Singapore)
PAS	Pan-Malaysian Islamic Party
PKR	Pakatan Keadlian Rakyat, People's Justice Party – opposition party led by Anwar Ibrahim
PR	Pakatan Rakyat, People's Alliance – the opposition coalition in Malaysia's government

PPPA	Malaysia's Printing Presses and Publications Acts 1984
RTM	Radio Television Malaysia
SIC	The Printing Permit
SINDA	Singapore Indian Development Association
SIT	The Publishing Permit (which, along with SIC, were predecessors to SIUPP)
SIUPP	The Press Publication Enterprise Permit
STEP	Science, Technology and Enterprise Plan 2011–2015
UMNO	The United Malays National Organisation – the ruling coalition party of Malaysia's government

Introduction
Of nations, technologies and non-users

When I first started to look seriously into the Internet in Malaysia, much of what turned out later to be pivotal events and developments had yet to occur. For example, few had any idea that the day would arrive when blogging would be a platform from which two Malaysians would be elected Members of Parliament at the 2008 General Elections – the GE08.[1] The story of new media's role in the minor opposition parties' triumph over the long-serving *Barisan Nasional* (National Front) government in five out of thirteen states has since been rehashed many times. Following then Prime Minister Abdullah Badawi's admission that his 'biggest mistake' was to neglect online campaigning (*Abdullah: Big mistake to ignore cyber-campaign*, 2008) and the dubbing of the upset as a 'political tsunami' (K. S. Lim, 2008), the idea that the election results were due to the overwhelming force unleashed by new media was planted.

Such a view has, for example, gained sufficient ground that pundits from the majority party of the ruling coalition, the United Malays National Organisation (hereafter UMNO), are now convinced that the deployment of 'cybertroopers' and social media content would determine the outcome of the nation's next election (Darwis, 2012). This is despite the World Bank's estimate of the proportion of Internet users in Malaysia at 55.8 per cent in 2008 (*Internet users (per 100 people)*, 2011), and the many nuanced accounts subsequently published that stress the multiple other factors involved in the GE08 results (Welsh, 2008; W. Case, 2010; Moten, 2009; Lian and Appadurai, 2011).

It would not be wrong, then, to say that new media occupy a front-stage position in Malaysian society today. This book is dedicated to understanding how new media are imagined and experienced within this nation. How, for example, do we explain the dominance of new media in a society where a significant proportion of the population are still non-users of the Internet? It is my proposition that understandings of new media in Malaysia such as those mentioned earlier have their roots in how the Multimedia Super Corridor mega project (hereafter MSC) was conceived and implemented.

Inaugurated in 1996 by Malaysia's third and longest-serving Prime Minister, Mohamad Mahathir, the demands of the MSC are the reason Malaysia still holds a stance unique to nations in the region, i.e. the guarantee to keep the Internet free from censorship (*MSC Malaysia 10 Point: Bill of Guarantees*, 2008). In a region where states such as Singapore and Burma, for different reasons and through various mechanisms, maintain vice-like grips on information flow within their territories, this is a distinction of note. Yet broadcast media ranging from newspapers and television to radio within Malaysia remain rigidly controlled. The Malaysian nation is unique in the contradictions between its policies on mass and new media. As later chapters will argue, the incongruities have since inflected how the Internet is experienced in Malaysia and have, in turn, created broader implications for the nation beyond the economic and the technological.

To be clear, the Malaysian government is not unusual in its approach towards technology. It is common practice for nations from Nigeria and India to the United Kingdom to have some variation of a policy that spells out a whole-government approach towards science, technology and innovation. Access to new media is so strongly linked to life opportunities in these policies that it is assumed individuals cannot but eventually become users if they do not wish to stagnate or lose out to others. As such, in most cases where non-usage is addressed in these policies, it is often regarded as a problem of access, education or age that can and should be overcome. Put simply, many of these policies equate technology with positive change. It is taken as read that the introduction of technology will result in the acquisition of knowledge, the flowering of innovation, and the creation of new and better-paid jobs that will eventually lead to economic growth. Thus, a common criticism of such policies is that they are technologically deterministic in how they ascribe the ability to create difference to technology rather than humans.

According to Williams (2003: 6), the defining characteristic of technological determinism is the isolation of technology from society in order to set it apart as an agent of change. Williams argues that the changes associated with media cannot be detached from the social histories of their use or the various conditions that surround their usage. Additionally, Williams contends that media technologies are cultural forms (ibid.: 2–3) and as such, the account of television as a cultural form he relates incorporates two social histories – of television as a technology and of the use of television.

Proudly declared by the Internet's early adopters as a separate realm free of regulation, nations and borders (Barlow, 1996), new media are doubly susceptible to being cast as a lone-standing agent of change. States bent on seizing the advantage of early adoption or leapfrogging their nations from developing to developed status have utilized versions of technological determinism in their introduction and promotion of the benefits of the Internet to their people. The nations of Southeast Asia are no different.

In *The Shock of the Old*, Edgerton (2006) argues that our collective fascination with new technologies stems from the tendency to create histories of technologies based on inventions and innovations rather than everyday use. From a national perspective, nations proudly claim inventions that emerged from their shores, and countries vie to outdo each other in the numbers of patents filed. Patent league tables and innovation indices compiled and published by various bodies valorize these achievements and hold them up as dividends of governmental investments in technologies, training and education. The habit of 'innovation-centric' records has led to certain technologies receiving greater cultural visibility than others (Edgerton, 2006: 3–4). Of these, the accounts fuelled by 'digital optimism' (G. Turner, 2009) ensure new media stay in the spotlight of public attention.

In contrast, Edgerton asserts that unheralded technologies such as corrugated iron play as important a role in societies' interaction with technology as the famous technologies of the steam engine and the atomic bomb. Further, Edgerton maintains that analysis based on the use of technologies 'is not enough' because significance cannot be equated with usefulness. Usefulness, in this sense, is not about 'what [technologies] do, but how well they do it, and what they can do that cannot be done otherwise' (2006: 7). Yet, despite both Williams' and Edgerton's emphases on uses of everyday technologies, the fact is that non-users remain a significant portion of many societies around the world.

The privileging of the user's viewpoint as the one that matters assumes that as long as individuals do not adopt a technology they remain untouched and shielded from it. Nonetheless, the effects of technologies on societies do not inhere only in the capabilities that technologies enable, but also in how knowledge of technologies informs and inflects individual world-views. For example, many people in contemporary societies do not drive cars, preferring instead to use public transport, walk or cycle. Aside from cost considerations, their decision not to drive might be due to the desire for a healthier lifestyle or to avoid contributing to the greenhouse gases emitted by car exhausts. At the same time, knowing that cars exist means that whenever they are on the road whether as a passenger, pedestrian or cyclist, they know they have to take the dominance of cars into consideration and shape their behaviour accordingly. Not only do non-users of cars know about cars, their actions, decisions and reactions are inflected by that knowledge.

The same might be said of the 39 per cent of Malaysians who, as of 2011, still did not use the Internet (*Internet users (per 100 people)*, 2011). They might not desire to communicate via the Internet, be able to afford a computer or indeed, deem their time better spent elsewhere than online. Nonetheless, the knowledge that new media exist in all their forms within Malaysia must have penetrated even the most sheltered of existences. That awareness means that whilst their own options may not include new media for various reasons and motivations, their actions, practices and decisions must allow for and accommodate the views and knowledge of those who do use these technologies.

Since the lives of non-users are fundamentally affected by technologies even though they appear to have no use for them, it seems logical that non-users should be considered in analyses of the implications of the Internet for a nation. Unfortunately, with the exception of only a handful of studies (Wyatt,

2003; Wyatt et al., 2002), research on the Internet revolves largely around users. The omission is even more apparent when it comes to research on the Internet's implications for the nation. Even when non-use is addressed, the tendency has been to treat non-use as a pathological condition, the origins, causes and cures of which are in need of explication, if not outright eradication (Chia et al., 2006; Selwyn et al., 2005; Jung et al., 2001).

The exception comes mainly from those who argue that non-users matter as much as users of scientific and technological products because they are co-constructors of these technologies (Oudshoorn and Pinch, 2003, 2008). They contend that the rejection, demands and dislike of non-users for certain technologies provide at least some of the impetus for designers and manufacturers to change and improve their products. Kline, for example, contends that the resistance of American farmers to the 'prescribed use of the telephone' led ultimately to the redesign of rural telephony in America (Kline, 2003: 58). Still, the dominant approach is to cast the non-user as the exception to the rule at best, or simply lagging.

Broadly speaking, then, this volume asks: what position should national technology policies take with regard to non-users? Is it safe to assume the issue of non-use will diminish as new media technologies become available and affordable to more of the world's population? Or that the networked nature of the modern world will turn even the most stubborn and incapable of non-users round to adopt new media platforms and devices? A few signs indicate both assumptions are hasty.

Earlier research on those who 'refuse to assimilate' into a social-networked world (Zeynep, 2008) have led to more recent work on 'media refusal' as an ascetic practice of a technology of the self (Portwood-Stacer, 2012a, 2012b, 2012c). At the same time, revived demand for simple mobile phones such as John's Phone[2] with its plain and single-featured interface suggests that although many covet smart phones, others are quite content to only be able to communicate whilst out and about. Together, these trends reveal that firstly, even where access, affordability and media literacy are not obstacles, non-use and discriminate selection of features continue to be an option preferred by some. Secondly, that there exists various degrees of non-use that are not captured by the user/non-user binary. It is evident that non-use of technology is not to be dismissed, especially when it comes to national policies that concern the interactions between society and technology. Still, there are few frameworks that include the role of non-users alongside that of users.

Taking my cue from Williams and Edgerton, I aim to arrive at a proper understanding of how new media interact within Malaysian society through the consideration of the social, cultural, political, economic and regulatory conditions surrounding their introduction, implementation, use and non-use. In the interests of feasibility I have elected to focus on one technology policy: the MSC. Few technologies have received higher cultural visibility in Malaysia than new media. The continuing rollout of new programmes, training grants and development schemes from the MSC ensure new media retain their high profile. Notably, since the MSC also incorporates special technological zones, the policy has been manifested in rather more tangible fashion through the urban design and architecture of the various precincts of government (Putrajaya), technology (Cyberjaya) and business (Cybercities). Additionally, given that over 15 years have elapsed since the MSC was first initiated, it seems fitting that the longer-term implications of one of Malaysia's most ambitious and far-ranging technology policies are reviewed in order to illuminate the interactions that occur between new media and nation.

It is a fact that all nations exist within the global system of nation-states and gain some part of their validity through the recognition of their counterparts. The call for broader contextual understandings demands, then, that some of the regional histories related to Malaysia are included here. The two nations whose histories and economic political development parallel those of Malaysia are Indonesia and Singapore. The obvious reasons for this are geographical proximity and common histories of colonization. However, where their inclusion here makes most difference is in the divergent paths Indonesia and Singapore took towards nationhood despite early colonial commonalities, and their experience of Japanese rule during the Pacific War.

Like Malaysia, Singapore was once a British settlement and it shares many of the legal and administrative structures set up by the colonial government. Yet, since its expulsion from Malaysia in 1963, Singapore has successfully leveraged its interactions with technologies to make the transition from postcolonial nation and newly industrialized country to developed nation. Along the way both governments have co-opted the media to the project of nation-building and continue to demand compliance with this objective (T. Lee, 2010; Nain, 2000; Kitley and Nain, 2003; *Media must work for a united Malaysia: PM*, 2010).

By contrast, former Dutch colony Indonesia and its mediascape (Appadurai, 1990: 9) has only recently emerged from a period of intense reform begun in 1998 after the overthrow of President Suharto. Indonesia is home to the world's largest Muslim population but unlike Malaysia, which considers itself a moderate Muslim nation, since the 1998 reforms Indonesia's policy approach towards mass and new media is consistently liberal (M. Lim, 2011). In 1996 where Malaysia had less than one Internet user per 100 persons and Indonesia just 0.05 of one, Singapore had an average of just eight. In 2011 the Internet penetration across the board has risen so that it sits at 61 per cent for Malaysia, 18 per cent for Indonesia and 75 per cent for Singapore.

Such figures are, of course, relative to the size of the population and no one can deny that there are major disparities between those of all three nations. However, there are sufficient similarities in the conditions within which Malaysia, Indonesia and Singapore formed into nations and developed their economic and technology policies to believe that insights into the issues examined here can be found. Hence, in order to provide broader contextual information on Malaysia's formation as a nation and its technology policies, similar developments in Indonesia and Singapore are drawn on throughout this book and most heavily in Chapters 2 and 3.

The framework I have elected for the task of understanding the interaction between new media and nation in Malaysia is that of social imaginaries. Broadly speaking, there are two parts to this framework. The first part explains how individuals within a society come to hold common expectations and assumptions of phenomena and still retain the ability to enact a range of acceptable social practices. This section of the framework is critical to understanding how non-users might also be considered when it comes to national technology policies like the MSC. The second part explicates how appropriate responses are generated in the first place and how, once formed, certain responses are absorbed into a society's stock of knowledge even as other responses are not. Using the social imaginaries framework, four of the ideas central here – the nation and technology/new media, as well as race and religion and the relationships between them – are explored and explained.

Before launching into the final section on social imaginaries, a few definitions of the key terms used are needed. The nation is defined here as *a sociopolitical community under the administration of a single state system whose people share the commonalities of history, destiny and future*. In most instances where the nation is mentioned here, the state is its silent partner. This conflation of nation with state is quite common in everyday understandings of the nation where the state is either implicit or taken for granted. In many instances of everyday life when the nation is mentioned, what individuals mean to discuss is the nation-state. As this book is concerned with the nation as lived experience, it seems only right that this everyday conflation be maintained. Within the context of this book, then, nation is short for nation-state.[3]

The Internet is defined as *the set of technologies enabled by the global system of computer networks*. At this point in time, it includes platforms such as the World Wide Web (WWW), email, blogs (web logs), online multimedia ranging from audio and video to animation and photographs, as well as instant messaging (IM) and Twitter but this is a highly mutable and growing list. This is thus a moving definition tempered by the awareness that the list of applications and platforms that comprise new media will continue to multiply, as will the type and number of devices by which the Internet is accessed. The current gamut includes mobile phones, desktop, notebook and tablet computers, as well as game consoles and global positioning systems. The definition of the Internet is, thus, deliberately broad in recognition of the fact that rather than a single, monolithic notion, the Internet is many things to many people. For example, within a cybercultural context the Internet can be defined as an anti-establishment, anarchic understanding of the world such as that typified by The Hacker Manifesto (Mentor, 1986). Why and how so many different possible understandings of the Internet and for that matter, the nation, come to exist and how one version comes to dominate within any one society is part of what the social imaginaries framework will help us understand. What follows is a brief outline of the social imaginaries framework, included to give an indication of the theoretical orientation that applies in this book. A more detailed explanation and analysis of the framework is to be found in Chapter 2.

The social imaginaries framework

The definition of social imaginary used here is *the body of loosely co-ordinated significations that enable our social acts and practices by making sense of them*. This is adapted largely from Taylor, who defines social imaginaries as 'the ensemble of imaginings that enable our social acts and practices by making sense of them' (2004: 165). The full framework draws too from Castoriadis' theorization of how significations, as opposed to Taylor's imaginings, constitute social imaginaries and is also informed by Schutz's research on the social stock of knowledge (Schutz, 1972; Schutz and Luckmann, 1974).

In pulling together these various works from different traditions of study, I am aware of the fact that the synthesis may not, on first appearance, be entirely compatible. For example, the concept of social imaginaries in Taylor's work explains the emergence of the atomistic individual in Western society as a result of the 'great disembedding' (2004: 49–67) from the monotheistic, Christian framework of the pre-modern world. Taylor's primary objective is to argue for the presence of an 'orientation to the good' (1989: 47) in the history of Western societies and the void that the lack of a strong direction (accompanied by the proliferation of possible directions) concerning this deeply basic need leaves in contemporary society (Taylor, 2007). In contrast, for Castoriadis, the social imaginary is a meta-theoretical explanation for how societies function and relate to the individual (Castoriadis, 1987: 147).[4] Castoriadis' project is to reveal the potential for political autonomy (Joas, 1989; Kalyvas, 2001). Finally, Schutz's phenomenological studies are directed at revealing through close examination the processes of knowledge transmission between individuals within societies.

With each of the theorists mentioned above – Taylor, Castoriadis, Schutz – the central issue they seek to address is how cultural knowledge is socially acquired, shared, distributed and transmitted from one individual to another, one society to another and one age to the next. My reading of their work is that they hold in common a concern for the potential within social acts and practice for socio-political change. Additionally, whilst their approaches range from the socio-historical and psychoanalytical to the phenomenological, their focus remains everyday lived experience. These reasons suggest that the social imaginaries framework synthesized here is not without basis.

For those who wonder why Actor Network Theory, or indeed Deleuze and Guattari's work on rhizomes and assemblages are not considered appropriate theoretical frameworks, my own reasoning is that although these are powerful analytical tools used by many to understand technology and new media, their emphasis on actors, social and non-social, means that non-actors and, by inference, non-users, remain largely outside of these frameworks. Further, whilst assemblages might conceivably be used to shed light on how non-users figure in societies, none of these frameworks account satisfactorily for how societies manage to broadly cohere in how and what they understand and expect of the nation and the Internet. In contrast, the social imaginaries framework used here not only offers a way to study the everyday interaction between technology and society; it also includes non-users within its structure.

To recap, the social imaginary is the body of loosely co-ordinated significations that enable our social acts and practices by making sense of them. The social imaginary is thus that which enables individuals to know what is acceptable, expected and unacceptable in social life. The social imaginary acts as a map by which individuals navigate and negotiate the intricacies of life with others (Taylor, 2004: 23–30). It is, as Castoriadis puts it, by the constitution and articulation of their social imaginary that one society distinguishes itself from another (1987: 149). Social imaginaries, therefore, lend both coherence and meaning to our social worlds.

How individuals comprehend the world they live in is not always a result of direct experience. Often, social actors rely on second-hand knowledge passed down from their predecessors through hearsay, custom, tradition, rituals and historical record. At other times, individual pictures of the world comprise information gleaned and inferred from the experience of those with whom they share a space and time, even if they are not personally acquainted with each other. The accumulation and acquisition of the tacit knowledge that tells individuals what is appropriate and expected within societies is profoundly social in nature and not usually explicit in form. This is why individuals who move away from their usual social milieu, like migrants, visitors and strangers, feel lost and vulnerable, reduced again to social novices. They have not had the opportunity to acquire the necessary social grammar from a new group of contemporaries and are thus unable to draw on this to inform them how their new social environment functions, or what its denizens consider acceptable.

A significant portion of how individuals make sense and derive the meanings of their world originates from those with whom they share that world: their contemporaries. As a term, contemporary is understood here as 'one whom I know coexists with me in time but whom I do not experience immediately' (Schutz, 1972: 180–1). Contemporaries share the same temporality but do not occupy the same space. Hence, relationships between contemporaries occur primarily 'in imagination' (ibid.: 180–1). The many members of a nation who live within the bounds of the same territorial nation-state and share its values and systems yet do not know each other personally is a prime example of this kind of relationship (Anderson, 1991). The passions that national belonging and nationalism provoke also illustrate the strength of these imagined connections. Within the social world, then, second-hand knowledge garnered via the experience and accounts of contemporaries are important influences on how individuals behave and act socially, and are essential to how they understand the world around them.

Why this matters now

As mentioned earlier, Malaysia's twelfth general election was held in early 2008. The results when returned were the realization of long cherished dreams in the eyes of many (Ooi et al., 2008). Whilst the ruling coalition, Barisan Nasional (National Front) retained federal government, its historical political dominance was greatly diminished when the long-held advantage of a two-thirds majority in Parliament was vanquished 51 years after independence. The smaller opposition parties then governed five out of 13 states in Malaysia. The change of political fortunes has been attributed to the exercise of People Power and the use of the Internet by the opposition parties during the election. The current moment is important not only because of the 2008 election or its results; it also matters because of the events and developments that surrounded it and others that have occurred subsequently. There are too many events and associated developments to discuss here but two sets that led up to the election are noteworthy for the insights they bring to the status quo in Malaysia and the issues confronting the nation.

Despite years of representation by the Malaysian Indian Congress (MIC) party working within the ruling coalition of the Barisan Nasional (BN), many Malaysian Indians are still victims of systemic discrimination. This is evidenced in the demolition of Hindu temples by the state and the absence of assistance to address multi-generational issues of poverty and lack of opportunities. The need of the Malaysian Indian community to air deeply felt grievances found expression in November 2007 through the work of the Hindu Rights Action Force (hereafter Hindraf), which amassed one of the largest gatherings to their protest rally (*30,000 Hindraf protesters rally in KL streets*, 2007). The ethno-communal approach that Hindraf took has since been critiqued (Devadas, 2009; S. Leong, 2009) but their attempts have brought to the forefront the limitations of the established pattern of ethno-political representation in Malaysia.

Divided amongst the three main ethnic groups (Malay, Chinese and Indian), ethno-communalism has been in place since the earliest days of Malaysia's independence. Its embedded-ness is also why Malaysians are accustomed to framing their dissatisfaction with the state's performance in ethnic terms. Viewed alongside the cow head protest, so dubbed because of the unfortunate choice of a gruesome cow's head as a prop at a protest against the proposed re-siting of a Hindu temple by residents of a Malay-majority neighbourhood (S. Leong, 2012), this first set of events highlight what is at stake for the various parties. The need for certain Muslims to reassert their primacy in the face of encroachment on their rightful place in Malaysia springs from their belief that Malay paramountcy is a core part of Malaysia's formation as a nation. Such thinking, in turn, calls for all the markers of Malay-ness distinctive to Malaysia due to its constitutional definition of what a Malay is – the Malay language, the religion of Islam and its practices and customs – to be placed above that of other languages, other religions and their practices and demands.

Ultimately, the question being posed is twofold. Firstly, can the foundational myth of Malay paramountcy continue into the twenty-first century; and if so, how might it be upheld without disadvantaging the non-Malays in Malaysia? If not, what are the viable alternative foundations?

The second set of events revolves around a series of rallies organized by a coalition of non-government organizations banded together under the banner of *Bersih* (clean and fair). Bersih's cause is reform in the nation's electoral system, which they decry as flawed, corrupt and riddled with fraud. The first Bersih protest took place in November 2007, the second in July 2011, and the third in April 2012. Like the rally organized by Hindraf, the Bersih events also have a narrow agenda (*Bersih People's Gathering, 10 November 2007*, 2007; *Press statement: Launch of Perhimpunan BERSIH 2.0*, 2011). Where they differ from the Hindraf rally is in their point of focus, which draws its impulse not from the wrongs inflicted on an ethnic community, a religious group or a disadvantaged minority. They are, in fact, refreshingly devoid of any mention of race or religion. The organization, therefore, differs in that its appeal is addressed to the broad spectrum of Malaysian citizens. Bersih's demand for reform is framed as the active request of a people to its governmental representatives.

Taken together, these two developments are symptomatic of the nature of the issues that are currently at stake in Malaysia. Stripped back to its most basic, this moment is one that is witnessing the struggle of a postcolonial, Southeast Asian nation to define its own contours and futures. The narrative of racial difference as the basis for affirmative action is deeply embedded in the history of Malaysia's formation as a nation. To abandon these foundational imaginings the nation needs to establish new footings. Exactly what they might be is unclear, though some of the possibilities are discussed here.

In this task new media can be said to play a dual role. The first role is as a discursive space for the discussion that has to take place if the foundations of the Malaysian nation can be recast. The other role new media play is as an indicator of attitudinal change. In other words, how the nation comes to understand and treat technologies like the Internet is emblematic of the approach it adopts towards nation-building. To continue the view of new media technologies as a near autonomous agent of transformation is to relinquish some part of the responsibility for change to technology. To understand new media as a suite of cultural technologies whose place in Malaysia is determined by the complex relationships between situational contexts, applications, users and non-users is to acquire a more active and nuanced grasp of how technologies can be wielded to confront the issues confronting the nation.

In light of the results of the twelfth general elections in Malaysia, it is tempting to reduce the situation to a contest wherein one side seeks to define the nation free of the nineteenth-century European ideas of race and nation on which Malaysia was founded, while the other seeks to retain the cornerstone of racial/religious/communal difference on which its power structure is constructed. Globally, most have dismissed the theory of race as a primordial category so it seems the race-blind modernists' struggle is certain of eventual victory. Even more seductive is the argument that the Internet empowers the cause of civil society that seeks to redress the imbalance of power. Malaysia's censorship-free Internet does invoke visions of emancipation especially when considered alongside its mass media environment.

Given the many popular movements that have prompted protests that threatened the Iranian government in 2009 and forced out rulers in Tunisia, Yemen, Libya and Egypt in the Arab Spring, the Najib administration is understandably wary of the much-hyped revolutionary potential of new media (Aw, 2011b, 2011d; Stephen and Rose, 2011). Accounts of each of these events have valorized the role of new media platforms like Facebook, Twitter and blogs. Some governments, such as that of China, have even acted to stop online movements like the Jasmine Revolution well before it could amount into a movement with mass appeal (*Mandarin News Australia*, 2011). East against West, the oppressed against the oppressor, the weak against the powerful; it is easy to be seduced by the romance that new media bestow agency, which can then be used to voice dissent that might gain sufficient momentum to mobilize a society to revolt. In reality, the trajectory is never as linear, and the field within which new media operate in any national context cannot by any means be described as uncluttered. Aside from regulatory conflicts, media illiteracy and infrastructure issues, obstacles such as historical mistrust and entrenched differences may impact upon new media use and its potential for activism.

The battle is hence as much about whose vision of the new foundations of Malaysia should prevail as it is about the content of this re-envisioning. The Internet opens up the contest to social actors who previously had no space and sometimes no ability for public expression, but existing theories make little room for those who continue for whatever reason not to use the Internet. What are their avenues of expression and participation? Where, indeed, are their voices to be heard and who do they listen to amidst these struggles? How are they affected by the struggle when so much emphasis is given over to online debate? When, where and how are the flows of information in this contest over the nation inflected by its direction through the Internet? Somewhat counter-intuitively, it is precisely because so much of the online conversations on Malaysia feature so prominently within the public discourse that a framework that includes non-users of the Internet is needed.

Finally, it would be remiss to forget that such space as is opened up by the Internet in Malaysia is equally accessible to parties interested in maintaining the status quo. In the period of initial investigation, the powers-that-be had yet to wake up to the furious pace and intensity of online deliberation over the nation in Malaysian civil society. Since the 2008 elections this has been rapidly corrected. Prime Minister Najib Razak, for example, now has two Facebook accounts – an official one where he interacts with the general population, and another specifically created to woo Chinese Malaysian voters where he is addressed as Ah Jib Gor (Brother Najib). In 2012, for example, an informant told me the ruling coalition has also taken to sending regular SMS (short message services) texts to individual citizens on red letter days such as Merdeka Day, Christmas and New Year and – somewhat more intrusively – on the occasion of individual citizens' birthdays (Anonymous, 2012).

The tensions and possibilities that confront Malaysia at this point mean the current moment taking shape is an exhilarating but precarious one. The potential for creating meaningful and sustainable change lies within reach but the dynamics between the overlapping, interpenetrating understandings of nation and Internet as well as the conditions that engender and surround them are complex. What I have done so far is merely to outline the crude shape of the argument of this book. The chapters that follow will flesh it out further.

In total there are six chapters to this book. The first chapter consists of the synthesis of the social imaginaries framework touched on very briefly here. The second chapter traces the development of the nation as a concept within a Southeast Asian context. Continuing within the same context, the third chapter examines the role of technology in nation formation. In Chapter 4, an examination of the ideation and execution of the MSC explains why and how new media are understood and experienced in Malaysia. Chapter 5 is a discussion on non-users of new media, why they continue to matter and the role they play in Malaysia. In the final chapter, I discuss possible new configurations thrown up by the interaction of new media and nation in Malaysia today and the likely development of three outcomes: monitory democracy (Keane, 2009), sousveillance (Mann et al., 2001) and trans-ethnic sodalities (Gabriel, 2011). Throughout the book, examples of relevant policies and approaches taken by the Indonesian and Singaporean states will be offered to provide contextual information on the regional conditions within which decisions and changes took place.

Nations do not exist in isolation. Tasked with providing a comfortable standard of living for their citizens, governments have a duty to learn from, emulate and compete with each other. They assiduously study instances of success, eager to pick out the factors that created these accomplishments and attempt to recreate the same conditions in their countries. Given the extremely high cultural visibility of new media and technology giants like Google and Apple not just in the United States but also across the world, it would be negligent of governments not to attempt to stimulate similar technology-inspired activity.

It is a central tenet of this book that when technologies are introduced into societies, they bring with them extant meanings and practices that touch even those who do not take up them up. At the same time, it is also the case that societies will add their own interpretations and inflections to these same acts and practices. With Malaysia as an example, the aim of this book is to create a nuanced understanding of the interactions between new media and nation. It is envisioned that the social imaginaries framework synthesized and applied for this purpose will be useful in studies of interactions between other nations and different technologies.

Notes

1 The two elected were Jeff Ooi, who became the Member of Parliament for Jelutong, Penang, and Tony Pua, Member of Parliament for Petaling Jaya Utara, Selangor. Ooi's blog, Screenshots, at http://jeffooi.blogspot.com.au/, is no longer active. Pua has three blogs that can be found at http://tonypua.blogspot.com.au/, http://educationmalaysia.blogspot.com.au/ and http://puakiamwee.blogspot.com.au/, written in Chinese.
2 This is a no-frills mobile handphone whose main feature is a simple and highly visible keypad. See http://www.johnsphones.com/
3 I recognize that this is, in many instances, a simplification for it is also possible to interpret the nation-state as containing many (sub-)nations. Examples include the many Aboriginal nations contained within the nation-states of Canada, the United States of America and Australia.
4 Castoriadis describes the social imaginary as a society's self-articulation. For him, the social imaginary of a society is its elucidation. Accordingly, every society is distinguished by its social imaginary as it defines that society's relations to the world and the objects within it, its needs and its desires (1987: 147).

1 Social imaginaries

How does the average Malaysian walking into any of the eating places along Jalan Bukit Bintang in Kuala Lumpur know what kinds of behaviour and acts are appropriate and which are not? Generally, menus of some kind inform customers what is on offer and the odd sign prohibiting smoking might remind them of what is now illegal, but otherwise there are few obvious instructions that tell individuals how to conduct themselves in the social practice of eating in company. Yet, most people know without being told that neither conducting one-sided conversations loudly over mobile phones nor leaning over to pick food from another customer's table is acceptable. If such knowledge is attributed to good training and social etiquette, the question follows, how did social etiquette come to be? Who decided what is acceptable in the Malaysian context and how did they go about it?

On a day-to-day basis, we take our cue from those around us but nothing of what we read from how acts and practices are performed by others is written down anywhere. By and large this material remains in the background, unspoken except when we explain to children that 'this is not how things are done here'. We take comfort from our skill in not drawing attention to ourselves through inept behaviour and take care to pass that ability on to our young. This same bank of knowledge also helps us to recognize when acts and practices previously considered appropriate, like the habit of using the spittoon or smoking in public places, become taboo.

The above examples may seem too trivial to require theorization but everyday social life is no simple matter. It is through these 'fragments of social reality' that 'we are able to glimpse the meaning of the whole' (Göle, 2002: 179). There are many bits of knowledge that people within the same social context carry that allow them to fit in with others and feel at home. The term used to describe the conventions governing acceptable as well as unacceptable patterns of behaviour as well as the various habits of speech and gestures that make up social life is public culture. Public culture is necessarily a function of the social space individuals inhabit. Therefore, it obviously differs from place to place and era to era, yet the processes by which public culture are formed remain unclear.

Public culture guides not just our modest, individual actions; it is also the foundation of our social practices. At every level, from the humble acts of everyday life to the broad ideas of political practice, tacit knowledge shared by individuals enables, guides and lends meaning to social life. To take another example from contemporary Malaysia, let us consider the eight demands of the Bersih movement: a clean electoral roll, postal ballot reform, the use of indelible ink, a minimal 21-day campaign period, free and fair access to media, stronger public institutions and a stop to both corruption and 'dirty politics' (*Bersih 2.0's 8 Demands*, 2011). Where do these demands stem from and on what understandings are they founded? The demand of electoral reform rests on the notion of an acceptable electoral process that accurately represents the wishes of the Malaysian people.

Delving to a further level, the idea of an acceptable process can be said to be based on the concept of popular sovereignty where the legitimacy of a state and its government is derived from the general will of its people. A fraudulent, unfair and corrupted electoral process places said legitimacy in jeopardy. The eight demands of Bersih are a Malaysian interpretation of the broader concept of popular sovereignty. How did the concept of popular sovereignty, so deeply associated with the European origins of general will and consent (Rousseau, 2001), make its way into Malaysian society and gain enough relevance to move thousands of people to participate in three controversial rallies on three different occasions in 2007, 2011 and 2012? Those better schooled would point to their education but that is a privilege reserved only for some and as has been proven, participation in Bersih actions have cut through socio-economic and educational as well as ethno-communal differences in Malaysia. Still, that leaves the question of where everyday understandings of popular sovereignty originate from.

We seldom pause to reflect on how we know what to do every day repeatedly in multiple different situations without consciously having to reach for an instruction manual of some kind. Indeed, if we did consider too often, we might well feel paralysed by the options open to us. On the occasions we do wonder at the source of public culture, our reflex is to attribute it to custom, tradition, convention and norms. Does what passes for common wisdom evolve through happenstance or is there a system by which public culture is accumulated, habituated and then transmitted? What are the processes involved? At what point do ingrained habits become unsuitable within a social context and give way to new forms? Is this system a conscious or haphazard process? Who takes part in this process of evaluation? And finally, why does it matter at all?

It matters because what we understand of the system and processes by which we gain tacit knowledge frames our views of the world. Frameworks are broad structures that colour our individual and collective actions and the attitudes we take towards life. If, for example, we adopt a Marxian framework the assumption is that the rich and powerful are ultimately the ones who determine what passes into public culture. Such a framework would then compel an approach that analyses the relationships between new media and nation, the topic of this book, in terms of power.

Yet, as Prime Minister Najib Razak's appeal to the Malaysian constituency that 'street demonstrations must not be made a part of the Malaysian culture' (Anis and Rahim, 2011) makes clear, agency – or the capacity to act – is not solely the privilege of the rich and the powerful. How elections have been conducted in the past in Malaysia and what, according to the Bersih movement's conditions, they should be in the future also highlight that social practices are multiple in their enactment. On different occasions and under different conditions, for example, elections in Indonesia during the period of President Sukarno's administration were vastly different from those during the administration of his offspring, Megawati Sukarnoputri (Leifer, 2000: 167). Although the idea of elections is common to many societies it takes on localized forms in accordance with the period and context of enactment. Within the 'shared collective' that 'we invent together out of common experience' (Arthurs, 2003: 582) to guide our social acts and practices, then, dwells a certain degree of flexibility.

To return to the issue of why frameworks matter, they matter particularly here because they lay the foundation of the approach taken in this study of the interaction and relationships between new media and nation in Malaysia. The theoretical framework on which this book is constructed is that of social imaginaries. The concept is developed here from the work of three theorists: Charles Taylor (1989, 2004), Cornelius Castoriadis (1987, 1997) and Alfred Schutz (1972, 1974). Put simply, the framework posits that each society possesses a unique social imaginary that informs its denizens' actions and practices. The social imaginary is unique in the sense that the collection of knowledge that holds a specific society together differs from that of another. The Malaysian social imaginary, for example, would be different from the Indonesian one and despite certain similarities in history, distinct to that of Singapore. I define the social imaginary as the *loosely co-ordinated body of significations that enables individual social acts and practices by making sense of them.*

This chapter explains and develops the overarching framework for this book. It begins by laying out broadly what the social imaginaries theoretical framework is and then explains how it is synthesized. The framework lays the groundwork for the socio-historical approach taken up in later chapters for the analysis of the nation and new media in Malaysia. This then paves the way for the ideas, actions and practices associated with nation and new media to be regarded as products particular to the history and social, political, economic, cultural and other conditions specific to the Malaysian context.

Social imaginaries are basic and vital to all societies as they explain how public culture is produced, reproduced, transmitted and undergoes change. They perform the essential homogenizing role of helping individuals identify with their societies. At the same time, social imaginaries act like a store of customary solutions that individuals can turn to when they meet with problems that are typical to their society. In this sense, they relieve people of the burden of having to solve a problem anew each time they encounter it.

As developed by both Taylor and Castoriadis, the social imaginaries concept excels at explaining the world at the societal level. By virtue of being meta-theories, their connection with the minutiae of everyday life is limited. Nonetheless, in order to properly understand whence concepts such as nation and new media emerge from the socio-historical processes of Malaysia, it is necessary 'to go back and forth between micro- and macro- levels of analysis, between empirical practices and theoretical readings' (Göle, 2002: 179). This is where Schutz's phenomenological approach to the structures that make up individual social worlds comes into its own. It brings to the framework a careful account of the processes that drills down to create an appreciation of how individual acts and experiences spring from our connection to the social world. Schutz's work is revisited again in Chapter 5 where the relational matrix of predecessors, contemporaries, consociates and successors helps to explain the complex interactions between users and non-users of new media.

In a special issue of *Public Culture* published in 2002, various theorists published a set of articles themed around the idea of new imaginaries (Gaonkar and Lee, 2002). Their shared concern was with how we might grapple with the variances that develop in our world despite the seemingly homogenizing effects of globalization (Gaonkar, 2002: 18). One of the key ideas that emerged from Taylor's contribution was the notion of multiple modernities, which was further fleshed out in the monograph *Modern Social Imaginaries* through the historical example of North America (2004). The basic argument behind the multiple modernities thesis is that each society creates a modernity that is conditioned by its particular historical circumstances and dominant moral order and is, as such, different. Rather than a singular modernity that sweeps across the whole world, then, the thesis explains each society via the context of its development.

In the same special issue of *Public Culture*, Gaonkar acknowledges the deep association of the social imaginaries concept with the work of Castoriadis (2002: 6–9). At the same time, Gaonkar finds Castoriadis' psychoanalytical approach overly abstract in its preoccupation with ontology and for a meta-theory, problematically Eurocentric. Given Taylor's critique of psychology as attempting to strip the self of the need for 'strong, qualitative discriminations' (1989: 32), it seems as though the work of Taylor and Castoriadis cannot be reconciled (Gaonkar and Lee, 2002).

I think otherwise and argue that commonalities do exist between the two. I have already pointed to their common societal approach. Additionally and importantly here, despite the difference in the language, grammar and process Taylor and Castoriadis use, for both, the individual is a production of the social. Ontologically, for each theorist, the notion that the individual emerges from rather than constitutes society is fundamental. Hence, although there is no doubt that extending such a framework to 'nonclassical, non-Western, real-life contemporary' Malaysia 'thrusts theory into difficult new ground' (Arthurs, 2003: 582), the possibility of gaining a better understanding of how a multiply divided society like Malaysia 'holds together' despite the 'pervasive raggedness' (Geertz, 1998) of the contemporary world is, by my reckoning, well worth the trek through tricky terrain.

In what follows, I detail how Taylor and Castoriadis conceive of social imaginaries and the insights I draw from them to synthesize the framework used here. I draw mostly on Taylor's work to construct the broad framework with some support from Castoriadis. The latter's work informs the process whereby the constituents of social imaginaries, i.e. significations, are translated into acts and practices. Along the way I explain why I call the various elements that make up a social imaginary significations, and how Schutz's work sheds light on the processes whereby significations enter into social imaginaries and are subsequently reviewed, renewed and discarded. Diagrams are introduced in this chapter to aid in the visualization of the connections made between the work of Taylor, Castoriadis and Schutz. They are crude simplifications of the theories and should not at any point be understood to properly represent the complexities of their work.

Theories of social imaginaries

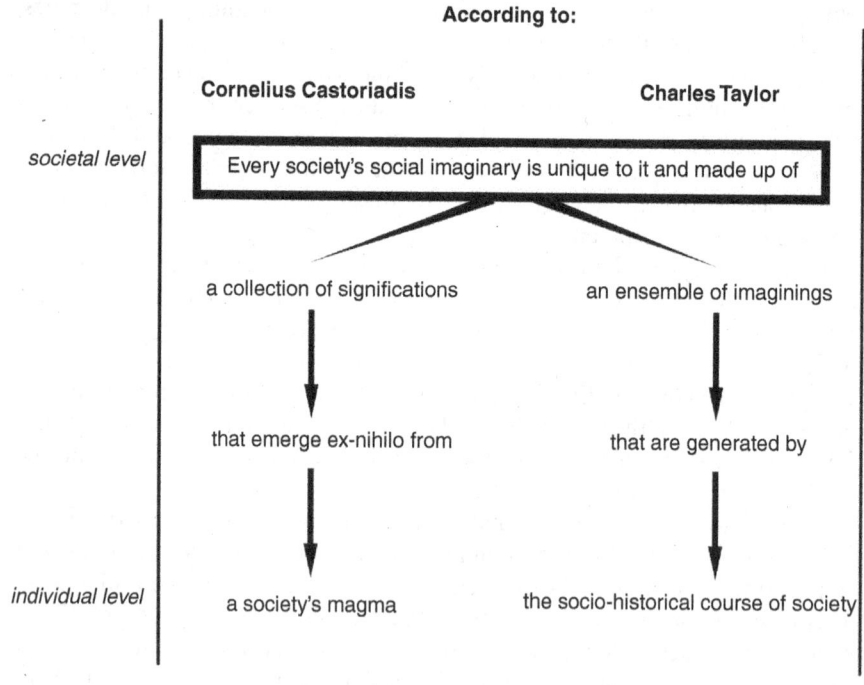

Figure 1: Theory of social imaginary – Cornelius Castoriadis vs. Charles Taylor

Social imaginaries 19

According to Taylor, the social imaginary is 'the ensemble of imaginings that enable our social acts and practices by making sense of them' (Taylor, 2004: 165). Taylor explains the use of 'imaginings' (as opposed to visualizations and concepts) as the term most suitable to denote the ways in which ordinary people use images, symbols, stories and legends to imagine their daily existence and their relations to others (ibid.: 23). To illustrate, Taylor employs several political processes such as elections, demonstrations and protests as examples. The argument is that – like many socio-political practices – elections, demonstrations and protests only make sense and hold significance because individuals within a society share a common understanding of what is expected of them and each other, and both the norm and the ideal form of which a democracy consists. The Malaysian Bersih movement's call for 'clean and fair elections' is based on another of the ideals associated with democracy, i.e. popular sovereignty. Towards the end of the last century, thousands of Indonesian protesters and demonstrators called on the egalitarian ideal of democracy when they ousted dictator President Suharto from his 30 years in office (P. Smith, 1999). In other words, some form of common if unspoken understanding always animates collective action. That same understanding, of living in or desiring democracy, also underlines everyday social relations between individuals in the same society.

Of course, it is possible that this kind of knowledge is formally taught in early life but subsequently absorbed, adapted and incorporated into an individual's stock of tacit knowledge. In Western liberal democracies, for example, prior to an election, political rallies, blogs, televised debates, weekly media reports and polls are produced and conducted to allow candidates standing for election to disseminate information on their proposed policies and persuade voters to vote in favour of them. The classic example would be the US presidential elections held every four years. During the election, with the exception of postal votes, most individual voters turn up on the predetermined day, stand within a private booth or enclosure and make marks on an electoral form to indicate their choice of candidates and leave after slotting their folded votes into sealed ballot boxes. The ways of conducting an election campaign and casting and tallying votes vary in actuality from election to election (social media, for example, are a recent phenomenon first introduced as more populations access the Internet as a source of information), and they do not always operate in an ideally democratic manner. Yet, that is exactly where the power of the social imaginary as a concept manifests itself most clearly, for it not only guides the proper conduct of the election process, it also enables the recognition of improprieties, as per Bersih's claims in Malaysia, in the enactment of what is jointly imagined and held as ideal. Once imagined, these imaginings can be enacted throughout a society.

For Taylor, 'the social imaginary is that common understanding that makes possible common practices and a widely shared sense of legitimacy' (Taylor, 2004: 23). It is the overall image contained within their shared social imaginary that provides participants in the election with the factual knowledge they need to stand for election, campaign and cast their votes as well as the normative knowledge which informs their awareness of what is acceptable in a democratic election and what is not. The social imaginary also allows individuals to make sense of their exercise of voting as constitutive of the employment of collective agency as a people, community or nation to choose a government by common consent. Coherence, meaning and legitimacy are thus lent to such a socio-political practice through social imaginaries.

Consider further the ideal of democracy in Malaysia. The Bersih movement is a major factor in the shift in the appreciation of what constitutes an acceptable election, but the model extends further than national, general or by-elections. This is evidenced in the lead-up to the 2012 campus elections at Malaysian universities where highly visible contests over how these institutions should be run were fought by students insistent on the need for transparency, independence and non-interference from political parties (Koh and Zulkifli, 2012). These events demonstrate how, once part of a society's social imaginary, a concept such as democracy can take many forms and be enacted across various socio-political arenas and lend both meaning and legitimacy to socio-political practice.

However, Taylor makes the point that these occasional socio-political practices are not the only ones that social imaginaries enable. For Taylor, the social imaginary is 'the "repertory" of social actions at the disposal of a given group of society' (Taylor, 2004: 25). Acting as 'social maps', social imaginaries lend individuals an overall implicit understanding of their social existence by providing 'background' to daily life (ibid.: 25–6). So not only does the social imaginary make sense of our occasional socio-political acts, it also allows us to make sense of the everyday, mundane acts and practices that make up daily life: knowing, for example, when it is appropriate to strike up a conversation with strangers in a lift.

Profound or quotidian, social acts and practices such as general elections and crossing at traffic lights are only possible when a society generally abides with the tacit rules and indeed, only work when these social acts and practices become an acceptable part of the social imaginary. In that sense, then, according to Taylor, the social imaginary can be said to consist of two facets. The first is the repertoire of social acts and practices that a society must accumulate in common. The second is the meanings that they ascribe to these acts and practices. These two facets must be agreed to and held in common. Without the legitimacy of common meanings, i.e. action and meaning working in tandem, social acts and practices fail to become part of the social imaginary (Taylor, 2004: 115).

Aside from distinguishing societies from each other, social imaginaries also serve the important function of coalescing those within a given society. As they are primarily composed of tacit rather than explicit knowledge, there are few ways that outsiders, strangers and newcomers to a society can quickly and easily access a society's social imaginary. Acquisition is largely a matter of spending time living within and becoming part of that society.

Access to a social imaginary is, hence, an indication of one's belonging to and inclusion within a society. Those who share a social imaginary have common understandings and expectations that inform them as to what is appropriate and acceptable to any given social situation within that society, as well as what is not. Possession of this inside knowledge imparts a sense of coherence, commonality and meaning to individual members of their social acts and practices and bonds them further to that society.

Like Taylor, Castoriadis argues that every society is to be distinguished by its social imaginary as it defines that society's relations to the world and the objects within it, its needs and its desires (Castoriadis, 1987: 147). Accordingly, it is the social imaginary that makes a signifying whole of all that a society encompasses (ibid.: 149). The social imaginary holds a society together as it describes, prescribes and circumscribes society for every individual, orientating them in each case within their society, world and universe (ibid.: 145–7). According to this interpretation, individuals derive their understandings of what matters and what does not within their society, what is of value and what is not, from their social imaginary. As an overall image of how things should be within the society, the social imaginary allows individuals to conceive of their societies as a coherent, convergent whole and to possess a certain sense of the order in which they, their society and their world relate to each other (ibid.). Castoriadis understands social imaginaries to be constituted by 'significations'.

The flip side to the inclusionary function of social imaginaries is, of course, what happens when individuals do not possess the social imaginary of the space they inhabit. In such instances, social imaginaries serve an exclusionary function as those who do not have the same prevalent social imaginary are quickly marked out as not fitting within a society. Indeed, individuals who do not have access to a society's social imaginary are singled out as not belonging to that society. Their lack of access to that society's social imaginary renders them vulnerable to gaffes and ineptitude and often makes life within that society awkward, if not difficult. This is because typical customary solutions and practices vary from society to society. Idioms of speech are a common example of this variance but other examples include customs such as bowing, which still have the relevant function of denoting respect for others in societies like the Japanese and Korean, but are more readily associated with a bygone era of male chivalry in Western societies. In most instances, no signs or cue cards would inform new arrivals to Malaysia, for example, that many Muslims regard dogs as unclean animals and that they should not expect the warm reception their pets might receive in dog-loving cities like Melbourne or Perth.

Social imaginaries, thus, both identify and delineate societies. In the interests of ensuring continuity and stability, each society – or rather, the members of the society – takes care to sustain and transmit its collective pool of knowledge from one section to another, one generation to the next, much as was pointed out at the beginning of the chapter. Consequently, social imaginaries often assume an aura of permanence and fixity that belies both their vulnerability and potential to change. Nonetheless, it would be a mistake to think of social imaginaries as explicit sets of instructions. Though the occasional book on social etiquette might form part of it, most if not all of a society's social imaginary consists of tacit, unspoken and unwritten information. No definitive manual exists that the social novice can use for reference. It is to their tacit nature that social imaginaries owe their malleability and flexibility but it is also the reason behind their occasional, lamented elusiveness. It is the failure to grasp the social imaginary of a society that sometimes makes an adult feel like a helpless infant in unfamiliar situations.

Additionally, although many significations are common to societies, the understandings that underpin their enactment can vary widely. While the de facto couple, for example, is both legally and socially recognized as a family unit in Australian society, this is not as readily the case in many Asian societies such as Singapore and Malaysia. Newcomers to either society might not immediately be cognizant of the differences and may find themselves disadvantaged on occasion. Social imaginaries, therefore, perform an essential homogenizing role in that they help individuals identify with their societies and relieve those who encounter typical problems of the burden of trying to solve them anew by supplying them with customary solutions. In doing so, social imaginaries bind and circumscribe societies, including those in the know and excluding those yet to know and those who do not know.

For the synthesis of social imaginaries developed here, I substitute Taylor's ensemble with the phrase 'loosely co-ordinated body' and borrow Castoriadis' use of 'significations' to refer to the constituents of social imaginaries. My intention, in using the phrase 'loosely co-ordinated body' rather than ensemble, is to convey two main characteristics of social imaginaries. The first is that though tacit and mostly unwritten, social imaginaries are not arbitrary collations of random information but rather the result of the socio-historical consequences of societies. There is also no deliberate (or explicit) overall organization involved in their compilation, which the term ensemble implies, and social imaginaries are regarded and retained as unitary.

Social imaginaries are, hence, loosely co-ordinated in the sense that no deliberate (or explicit) co-ordination is involved in their constitution but they are, nevertheless, regarded as and retained as unitary by social actors. The second characteristic of social imaginaries that the substitution of the word ensemble with the phrase 'loosely co-ordinated body' is meant to convey is that of their continuously shifting meanings and stage of development. The substitution of significations for imaginings serves to emphasize the role that social imaginaries play in communicating public culture. At the same time it is hoped that in adopting the term 'signification' rather than imaginings, the model developed here would suffer less from the common perception of imaginings as fabrications.

For Taylor, for a society to deem certain acts and practice 'to make sense' is to articulate what makes issues such as justice, respect for human life and well-being, as well as the meaning and fulfilment of life itself, appropriate. As such, making sense is a moral response, as it is tied to what the notion of a good life, and a life worth living and defending is about. Taylor's notion of making sense is borrowed but broadened in this book in order to understand social imaginaries as having the function of informing individuals as to when a social act or practice is ethically as well as morally appropriate within any given social milieu. My intention in doing so is not to impoverish Taylor's formulation but to maintain the possibility that decisions as to what is right or wrong, appropriate or inappropriate, may not necessarily be a moral response in all societies.

Social imaginaries are a product of a society's socio-historical continuum. That is to say, every society's social imaginary is the accumulated result of the particular intersections of events, history and coincidences that occurred, actions and reactions taken and omitted, as well as ideas and theories pondered, discarded and lived by its members. The contents of social imaginaries continue to grow and contract, shift and change even as individuals and groups employ them. This is because social imaginaries are not structures imposed from outside a society but dynamic, relational formations that are shaped, informed and reformed by the sayings and doings of the social actors that put social imaginaries into practice.

Take, for example, the signification known as citizenship in Malaysia. Since 2002 the Malaysian citizen's duty to vote was deemed to have been suspended once they step foot outside the nation's borders, for apart from military personnel, public servants, students and their spouses, all other Malaysians living overseas were denied the right by law (Elections (Registration of Electors) Regulations, 2002). Right or wrong, good or bad, this is a feature specific to the conditions and developments that occurred in Malaysia. However, starting in 2010 the regulations dictating that only the four above-named categories stationed away from Malaysians are eligible to vote has been contested, particularly through the advocacy of the group named Myoverseasvote (see their website at http://myoverseasvote.org). This challenge to the Malaysian Election Commission's interpretation of the signification of citizenship gained sufficient ground (Yoga, 2011) within the expatriate community for six of its members to file a suit against the Commission (*Overseas Malaysians file suit against EC*, 2011). Though they failed to win the suit, their feedback – for indeed one might consider their persistent campaign as such – appears to have had some effect on how citizenship is to be enacted in Malaysia. At the time of writing, the country's Election Commission had issued a public undertaking that the franchise would soon be extended conditionally to those who had 'returned at least once to Malaysia in the last five years' once they submitted a certain Form A (*Overseas M'sians can apply to vote by post in next GE soon*, 2012). From this example, we can see that individuals and their social imaginaries have a symbiotic relationship in the form of a feedback loop, with each relying on the others to define and refine their existence.

Broadly speaking, Taylor and Castoriadis share similar understandings of how social imaginaries operate but differ in the term they use to denote the elements that constitute social imaginaries. Instead of Taylor's 'imaginings', Castoriadis calls them 'significations' and describes them as society's de facto set of answers to questions of identity and life. This difference springs largely from the start-points of their approaches to the formation of social imaginaries. Taylor sees the emergence of social imaginaries as a consequence of 'the long march' (Taylor, 2004: 30),[1] which he describes as a socio-historical process of infiltration whereby practices or sets of practices, both new and modified, are developed, improvised, launched or evolved by 'certain groups and strata of the population' so as to gain new meaning(s) for people and in so doing, become part of and alter the social imaginary (ibid.).

Castoriadis employs socio-psychoanalysis to explain the individual's gaining of a social imaginary as part of the processes of socialization and language acquisition. In answer to the question of where social imaginaries originate, Castoriadis introduces the notion of the radical imaginary. In doing so, he explains that he uses the term 'radical' (as arising from the root or source) to distinguish radical imagination from the kind that reproduces or combines what already exists (Castoriadis, 1987: 369). According to Castoriadis, the radical imaginary is imagination that 'exists before the distinction between "real" and "fictitious"' (Castoriadis, 1997: 321). Castoriadis credits the radical imaginary with the *ex nihilo* creation of all figures, forms and images (Castoriadis, 1987: 369). By *ex nihilo*, he means that the radical imagination creates out of nothing, without cause, external agitation or excitation.

Castoriadis' approach amalgamates psychoanalysis with social theory and breaks new ground in that sense (Elliott, 2002: 157–8, 167). However, it is beset with flaws and for some, Castoriadis' formulation of the theory of the radical imaginary is 'an unaccounted-for conception' that remains 'an ungroundable project' (Joas, 1989: 1197). For this reason, I continue in this and subsequent chapters to adopt the more widely accepted socio-historical approach used by Taylor to explain the interactions and relationships between new media and the Malaysian nation.

How do significations come to be and how do they work?

We arrived at the definition of the social imaginary as the loosely co-ordinated body of significations that enable social acts and practices by making sense of them in the previous section. However, this still leaves the question of how significations actually function within social imaginaries. Taylor's concept of social imaginaries has been accomplished 'largely through historical example and evidence' (Arthurs, 2003: 582). To gain a clearer understanding of the course whereby significations emerge, which Taylor refers to as the 'long march' (2004: 30), I now turn to Schutz's theory on the social stock of knowledge and then to the process of objectivation. The main difference between the concept of the social stock of knowledge and that of the social imaginaries springs from Schutz's phenomenological concern with lived experience. Nonetheless, I argue that there are also many similarities that connect the social stock of knowledge theory with the concept of the social imaginaries. What follows is a brief discussion that outlines these connections.

Schutz argues that individuals bring a social stock of knowledge to every encounter with others, which is added to from moment to moment. This social stock of knowledge consists of information on the other that is both specific and typical, including the interpretive schemes the other is likely to use, their habits and their language. It also includes more or less taken for granted information about the reasons or motives behind their social action (Schutz, 1972: 168). It is this stock of knowledge that enables individuals to anticipate what is expected of themselves as well as of others.

Accordingly, for Schutz, there are countless variations that can be applied to each social situation and even these can change depending on context. Nevertheless, there is usually sufficient predictability within each situation for the social stock of knowledge to provide individuals with some notion of how to act and react. For example, a typical reaction to being introduced to a stranger at a wedding is to introduce oneself with a handshake and some relevant information on how one is related to the bride or bridegroom. A specific situation, such as attending a wedding in a place where one does not speak the local language, might require one to vary one's behaviour accordingly. However, sufficient similarity exists for the social stock of knowledge to provide some assistance as to how one should act.

Schutz theorizes that the primary function of the social stock of knowledge within a society is to relieve the individual from having to independently acquire knowledge on myriad everyday problems and allow them to draw instead on existing social stocks of solutions that others have arrived at and shared or passed down (Schutz and Luckmann, 1974: 297). In other words, like the social imaginary, the social stock of knowledge provides individuals within a society with a background or social map, a working proposition, as it were, on what to do and expect in that society.

Similarly, like the social imaginary, the stock of knowledge of any one society is never fixed nor is it ever entirely homogeneous. Fundamentally, for Schutz, all the elements that make up the social stock of knowledge originate from experiences and reflections of individuals. The social stock of knowledge itself is the 'result of the sedimentation of subjective experiences of the life-world' (Schutz and Luckmann, 1974: 123). The diversity of elements within the social stock of knowledge is, therefore, a result of the diversity of events by which 'lifeworldly knowledge is acquired' (ibid.).

Yet, while all elements of the stock of knowledge are made up of independently acquired subjective knowledge, not all independently acquired subjective knowledge ends up as part of the social stock of knowledge (Schutz and Luckmann, 1974: 262). Certain preconditions determine which independently acquired subjective experiences are selected to become elements of the social stock of knowledge. Hence, the social stock of knowledge should never be understood simply as the 'sum of subjective stocks of knowledge' of a society (ibid.: 263). Schutz uses the term 'objectivation' to denote the process by which elements are selected for inclusion in the social stock of knowledge. Objectivation, for Schutz, is the 'embodiment of subjective processes in the objects and events of the everyday life-world' (ibid.: 264). Figure 2 depicts Schutz's explanation in simplified form.

According to Schutz, objectivation begins when an individual faces a problem for which they have no ready solution. In an era where the Internet provides quick answers within easy reach for so many in developed nations, to speak of such a process might seem quaint. Yet, the Internet itself was a response to several newly perceived problems articulated in the post-Second World War years (Naughton, 2000; Abbate, 1999) that in turn produced new situations that invited solutions.

Examples of the latter include the World Wide Web (WWW) developed by Tim Berners-Lee (Berners-Lee and Fischetti, 1999). We tend to think of the Internet and the WWW as inventions because of their strong associations with technology and new media today. However, at a basic level, both the Internet and the WWW were first and foremost solutions to problems. In the case of the WWW, it was the growing amounts of scientific and academic

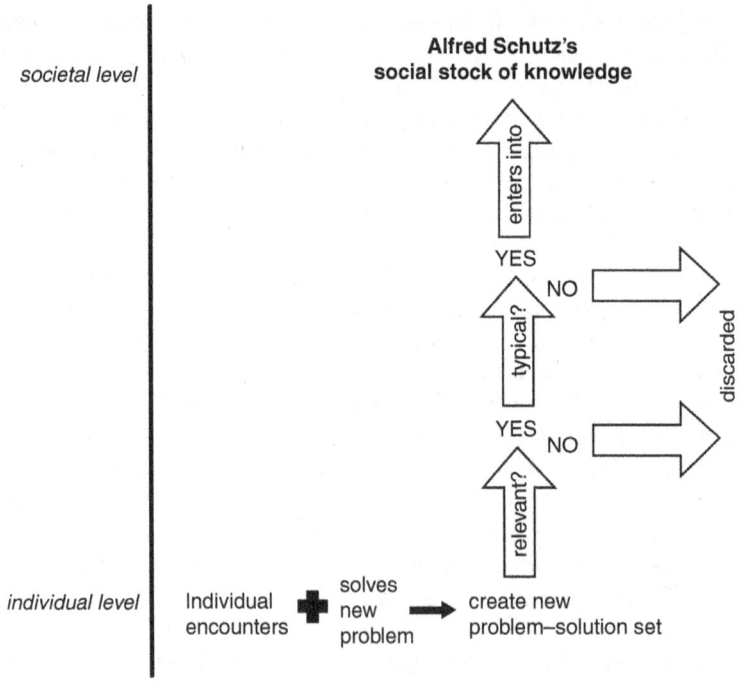

Figure 2: Social stock of knowledge – Alfred Schutz

information that prompted Berners-Lee to search for a system that would facilitate the broader sharing of information for discussion among colleagues spread across the world (Berners-Lee and Fischetti, 1999). More often than not, the problem–solution sets formed through the objectivation process are not always as globally momentous as either of the above. Oftentimes they are simply responses to new situations.

An indigenous tribe of Sabah in East Malaysia, for example, might have to trek across one of the fast-flowing rivers formed by a heavy monsoon season. The problem is new because the river is new and as yet, unknown. To find a route that the rest of the tribe could safely negotiate, a member of the group might consider a series of steps according to their priorities, ranging from speed and safety to staying dry. These steps would include testing the depth of the river at various points and assessing the obstacles and ease of passage at the various potential crossing-points to determine which is best. Part of the solution might involve the use of props in the form of a handy log, stepping-stone or a guide rope.

It is only after having ascertained the right starting point and successfully negotiating the crossing that an acceptable solution can be said to have been found. Once manifested, knowledge about how to cross such a river becomes part of the socially shared common knowledge of the group. At a later period it might be abstracted from its situational context of said river to become the solution to the problem of crossing bodies of water with similar characteristics. To use Schutz's terms, thus anonymized and abstracted from its original context and application, this element of knowledge is objectivated. The problem–solution can now be shared through various means of dissemination amongst others who were not present at the initial situation. It can also be handed down through generations to eventually be part of a wider pool of information.

Schutz further explains that before elements of knowledge like the above about river crossings and the WWW as an information-distribution system are absorbed into the social stock of knowledge, they are assessed for two qualities. Firstly, it must be considered relevant to the social structure to which the stock of knowledge accrues. Secondly, it must be typical of problem–solution sets that exist within that society. If the problem was not typical of that society or indeed, relevant, the element of knowledge would not form part of its stock of knowledge. As such, the question of what enters into the social imaginary is always an issue of social structure. For example, the sharing and discussion of knowledge might be relevant for inhabitants of developed nations but it might be irrelevant to those who live in developing nations where shelter and water supply problems still loom large.

Generally, in most societies the question of what 'typical problems are, whose typical problems are involved, who has to transmit the solutions, and to whom the solutions are transmitted are for the most part pre-determined' (Schutz and Luckmann, 1974: 293). In practice, subjective stocks of knowledge are predominantly derived from the extant material stock. Indeed, although it is always possible to add to the elements of the social stock of knowledge, few of these are actually independently acquired or entirely new. It is often the case that these additions are improvements or modifications of existing elements rather than truly independently acquired subjective experiences (ibid.: 263).

Under what conditions then do elements remain within the social stock of knowledge? Clearly, to remain, the element must retain its relevance and typicality or be discarded. Accordingly, it is usually when changes occur in social structures that the relevance and typicality of the problem–solution set addressed by an element is reconsidered. Both objectivation and the judgement of what the typical problem–solution sets are in a society are processes deeply anchored in a society's social structure. Hence, societies do not stop assessing the relative obsolescence of significations within their social imaginaries. The ongoing nature of the assessment process is one of the main reasons why social imaginaries should be understood as dynamic rather than static depositories of significations.

It would be a mistake, though, to understand objectivation to be a deliberate process carried out by a carefully selected panel composed of a society's elite and powerful. While it is true that certain ideas and theories may originate with the elite and the intellectuals of a society to infiltrate into social imaginaries, many significations may also emanate from the grassroots level.

Objectivation is an ongoing process of negotiation and contestation conducted by a society at the same time as it goes about its daily business. The state and its many institutions, public and private corporations, communities, groups and individuals are all participants in the process. It is, therefore, the society as a whole, all of the social actors, their actions and the dynamics of a society that determine exactly which significations are included as part of its social imaginary and which are excluded. The reasons why a signification that carries little weight in one society holds great import in another are contained within the course of each society's history and are as much cultural as they are socio-political. The point is that the collection of significations selected, retained and assembled by a society throughout its socio-historical continuum is unique to that society.

To recap, we now have an understanding of how, once devised, solutions to problems – or, to use the terminology specific to the framework being developed here, significations – are evaluated before they become part of a social imaginary. However, it will be fairly obvious that all around us there are hundreds of significations that have a plurality of interpretations. How do individuals choose which of the potentialities to enact at a given time? Castoriadis offers insight into this through his theory that every signification is made up of two parts: its 'condition of possibility' and its enactment (1987: 143). It is this characteristic two-part makeup that makes it possible for every signification to consist of multiple potentialities, of which one is selected and lived by individuals and groups when they enact a signification. Indeed, it is in the pause between potentiality and enactment that much of the strength of social imaginaries as a framework inheres. Though infinitesimal, the pause allows social actors to exercise their agency in the selection of the potentiality they put into practice.

The degree of play between potentiality and enactment explains how heterogeneity is possible even within the most conformist of societies, and it also admits room for creativity in social acts and practices. Hence, although social imaginaries perform an overall homogenizing role, they are never rigidly enforced but rather, always flexibly employed by social actors. The choice of which potentiality is enacted differs from person to person as well as from one occasion to the next. Even when a particular potentiality of a signification is dominant within a society, neither its enactment nor its interpretation can be foisted wholesale on individuals. The multiple possibilities of interpretation, their appropriation, persuasion and subversion make that extremely difficult. Still, it is not implausible for a dominant signification or a dominant potentiality of a signification to have considerable inflections within a society, influencing how the majority within a society embody the said signification.

The nation is a classic example. Generally speaking, the nation can be lived in many different ways – as a concept, an ideological construction, a discourse, a political doctrine and even as a pseudo religion. The nation can be embodied communally as a theocracy, a democracy and a dictatorship, or individually through the choice of language, dress and cuisine. An example of this is evinced in Singapore's Economic Development Board, which makes explicit its mission to actively '[c]reate sustainable GDP growth for Singapore with good jobs and business opportunities for its people' (*Port Set to be World's Busiest*, 2004). The different themes that Malaysian political parties and their supporters chose to celebrate Merdeka Day in 2012 are another example. While the ruling BN coalition rolled out '*Janji Ditepati*' (Promises Fulfilled) as the official theme, the opposition coalition opted to set up the alternate theme of '*Sebangsa, Senegara, Sejiwa*' (One Nation, One Country, One Soul) (S. K. Ahmad, 2012). The embodiment of a signification can correspond to its rational, perceived or imaginary aspects (Castoriadis, 1987: 139).

At each instance of embodiment, whether communal or individual, the nation is lived by social actors as one of its multiple potentialities is imagined and enacted. Hence, whatever form the nation takes is never permanent. While the idea of the nation might seem eternal, how it is experienced is always in flux, formed and reformed at each juncture of time and space. Nonetheless, this does not mean that everything is relative and that the nation is dependent on individual whim and defined at will. To be at all, the nation must exist for a collection of people. If a group of people, however aggregated, do not commonly embrace a nation it ceases to exist.

This is most vividly illustrated by the example of the Achuar Indians who regard the conception of themselves as a body politic an absurd, exotic idea (Descola, 2005). Consequently, for the Achuars the nation is impossible to contemplate and cannot be a signification of their social imaginaries. For this reason, despite the threat of reprisal from the Ecuadorian state, few Achuars vote in a country where voting is compulsory (ibid.). At the same time, it is important to remember that the nation is not lived only through grand gestures made *en masse*. As Billig points out in *Banal Nationalism* (1995), it is as possible to enact the nation with heedless banality as it is with intense profundity. The nation of Singapore is, hence, just as thoroughly enacted when individuals speak Singlish (Singaporean English) than it is when they sing the national anthem, *Majulah Singapura* (Onward Singapore).

How an individual embodies any signification varies from one occasion to another and from one person to another. But all this is not to say that social actors pause to ponder which potentiality of a signification they wish to enact on every occasion. The minute pause between potentiality and enactment is, in most instances, glossed over and significations are practised with little ceremony or mindfulness. As tacit knowledge, significations are akin to second nature and only very rarely deliberated over, plotted in detail or pondered at great length. If that were the case, many people would be suspended in paralysis as significations are encountered with every social act and practice. At that frequency, extended deliberation as to which potentiality and how to enact them would render social intercourse near impossible. Yet, complete spontaneity is precluded, as there is no possibility of embodying a signification if it does not exist within one's social imaginary. The choices an individual makes about which potentiality to enact are based on a finite number of possibilities determined beforehand by their social imaginary. If a signification does not exist within a social imaginary, it cannot be embodied. This, in the end, is what Castoriadis meant when he stated that every society is distinguished by its social imaginary (1987: 147).

Significations, like social imaginaries, are never entirely external or internal but rather integral to societies and individuals. Hence, it is a mistake to think one can arrive at an average, total or general meaning of a signification such as that of the nation by adding up all the various connotations, meanings and inferences that accrue to it (Castoriadis, 1987: 143). Though the various enactments of a signification feed back into and inflect on how it is lived, the signification itself can never be completely encapsulated by any one of its potentialities.

Significations can neither be defined by nor dependent on the various potentialities, shades and meanings put to them but they do develop in response to their embodiments. The characteristic malleability and nebulosity of significations is the chief reason why it is futile to insist that any one enactment of a signification is the only correct one. While one potentiality might prevail under certain conditions, significations are always subject to change. As a socio-political institution and as a signification, the nation and its potentialities will continue to shift, increase and change as long as it is retained within social imaginaries as relevant and typical. The same is true of all significations until deemed obsolete and consigned to the scrap heap of social imaginaries. Though it would be an exaggeration to consider significations alive, it is right to think of them as possessing a dynamic and evolving nature. This is another reason why 'body' is a much better collective term for significations than ensemble.

Additionally, in the same way that the type and range of significations that exist in a society's social imaginaries is a matter of its socio-historical development, so is the range of potentialities that each signification holds. The specific conditions and circumstances that surround each society mean that in the process of its development, each society gathers a unique collection of potentialities to every signification it holds.

In sum

The types of social acts and practices that social imaginaries inform range from acts as banal as the understandings and expectations that, for example, prevent huge numbers of people stuck in gridlock on a freeway from descending into chaos during peak hour traffic, or as intense as the sense of belonging that enables a diversity of individuals within a nation to participate in the rites and ceremonies of patriotism and war. As collective depositories of knowledge, social imaginaries 'enable our social acts and practices' by transmitting the elements that constitute the public culture of each society. This transmission occurs between individuals and those immediately present to them, their consociates, and those who coexist with them but are not immediately present, such as their contemporaries, predecessors and successors. Individuals derive meaning for their social acts and practices, as well as a sense of connection to their societies through the tacit knowledge contained within social imaginaries.

Societies of all kinds, contemporaneous and ancient, differ widely in the significations that constitute their social imaginaries. The concept of the large extended family, for example, might still resonate in subcontinental Indian society today but find little purchase in the coexisting American society. At the same time, social imaginaries can also distinguish one generation of a society from its earlier and later incarnations. For example, while nation as a signification is of great relevance in today's China, it would have been of little consequence to those who lived in second-century Chinese society.

Social imaginaries are, hence, markers of distinction that identify a society as such. It is the type, number and varieties of significations contained within its social imaginary that set one society apart from another. This does not mean though that social imaginaries are free of contradictions. The fact that there are multiple potentialities open to each signification, whose interpretation and enactment can differ from one point to the next, means considerable tensions must exist within social imaginaries. These tensions exist in large part due to the numerous subtle and not so subtle negotiations that occur when the decision as to which potentiality to enact is deliberated over by individuals and groups.

At the heart of many of these decisions are contests of power and agency that manifest themselves as issues of individual freedom, social pressures and political debates. Hence, though power is not the theoretical framework here, its exercise remains a strong undercurrent. 'Power', according to Foucault, 'exists only when it is put into action' (Foucault, 1982: 788). As such, it is not so much a quality possessed by the few at the apex of a pyramid as a quality that the individual may choose to exercise or not. This understanding of power underpins the analyses done here. At the same time, it aligns with the theoretical framework of social imaginaries in that power, like all significations, remains no more than a set of potentialities until enacted.

In the next chapter we apply the framework and begin to examine the Malaysian social imaginary through three significations that are strongly interrelated within its context: nation, race and religion. These significations and their enmeshing within Malaysia are products of the course of Malaysian history and as such, are particular to this social imaginary. To illustrate and emphasize this, the examples of Indonesia and Singapore will be brought into the discussion, for despite the similarities in history, socio-cultural influences and geographic proximity, each of these societies enacts the significations of nation, race and religion in distinctively different ways. This will lay the groundwork for the discussion in Chapter 3 on nation and technology.

Notes

1 Perhaps Taylor intends some connection to China's historical event but he makes no explicit reference to it in his texts.

2 The nation, race and religion

This chapter is mainly an account of the nation as a signification in the Malaysian social imaginary. In the previous chapter we established social imaginaries as the theoretical framework and know from that that social imaginaries are made up of collections of significations that are unique to each society. Additionally, the collection of significations that make up a social imaginary and its various potentialities and enactments are products of a society's historical, political, socio-cultural and economic development. A different political outlook during a period, for example, could see the same signification take on different possibilities in one society than another despite similarities in history. Using this understanding as a frame here we examine three significations – nation, race and religion – to shed light on why and how they are commonly imagined and enacted in Malaysia as they are today.

The inclusion of three rather than one (nation) signification is necessary due to the prominence given to race and religion in the formation of the Malaysian nation. To make the point about how differently significations can turn out, the Indonesian and Singaporean examples are brought in here. Partly as a result of geographic proximity, these three countries share many major influences and historical experiences, which at different periods have included Islam, intense trade flow, European imperialism, mass Chinese (and to a lesser extent Indian) migration, Japanese occupation during the Pacific War and the Communist threat. Yet, each former colony has received different inflections from these common experiences to interpret and enact the signification of nation in a unique fashion. This chapter interweaves the interactions between these inflections and nation formation in Malaysia, Indonesia and Singapore.

Of the three significations discussed here, nation and race are commonly regarded as having been introduced by Europeans to the Southeast Asian region (B. S. Turner, 2007; Hirschman, 1986). Religion itself pre-dates colonialism but its enmeshment with race in Malaysia is an offshoot of colonial administrative practices (Aziz and Shamsul, 2006; R. L. M. Lee, 2004: 125–31). The point to take from the movement of significations across social imaginaries described above is this: that social imaginaries are not rigidly bounded spheres of tacit knowledge but supple, loosely co-ordinated and interpenetrated bodies of significations. One of the reasons social imaginaries are such abundant sources of information is because they overlap and interpenetrate each other. Hence, individuals are seldom restricted to the singular social imaginary of the societies they inhabit but actually draw from and contribute to the compound influences of everyday others and their social imaginaries. Such an overlap of social imaginaries has always been the modus operandi of human life.

Shamsul describes the overlap of social imaginaries differently and argues that colonialism was also a form of 'cultural invasion' that involved the 'conquest of the native "epistemological spaces"… so that the local order of things was replaced by a foreign one' (Shamsul, 2001: 357). Much like the social imaginaries framework, such an explanation exposes the origins of ideas as external and reveals concepts such as 'Malayness' to be mutable and fluent rather than fixed and unchanging (ibid.). The nation is a prime example of such a 'conquest'. Though the nation was itself a new signification introduced into Asian social imaginaries, its impact across the region was not so much to replace as it was to displace an older 'order of things' in favour of the nation.

Turner explains that Western colonialism such as that practised by the British and the Dutch is based on the Westphalian model of nation-state wherein the separation between church and state had been fought over and settled upon after the Thirty Years War of the 1600s (B. S. Turner, 2007: 408). In the nineteenth-century social imaginaries of the British and Dutch colonials, then, religion was deemed 'subordinate' to politics and rightly to belong to the private sphere. As a result of the bitterly long and costly experience of the war, the colonial powers were convinced that separation between church and state was 'necessary to avoid communal conflict' (ibid.). Such a stance was contrary to many Asian cultures where 'the religious constitutes the political, or at the very least is deeply woven into its institutional fabric' (ibid.: 412). Notwithstanding that, Malaysia today is a federal constitutional monarchy where Islam is the official religion, while Singapore is a republic run along a racialized system and Indonesia is a unitary, secular state with the world's largest Muslim population.

In what follows my intention is to offer an explanation for why the nation is predominantly realized as it is in Malaysia based on the intersecting developments of the three significations of religion, nation and race. It needs to be emphasized that while they appear in linear order here many of the historical events and influences did not occur in neat, consecutive fashion. Rather, sometimes they overlapped and other times they intersected with each other but they took place within different social imaginaries and their effects moved across multiple social imaginaries via the flow of people and the exchange of cultures. The focus here is with the early developments of the nation as a signification and its crossover, introduction, absorption and adaptation into Malaysia. This mapping begins with religion as the major influence and signification in Southeast Asia before the arrival of European colonialism. It continues with a brief discussion of race as it was introduced, understood and enacted during the colonial period. It ends with the a brief tracing of understandings of the nation from the period when it first dominated Western social imaginaries and theorizations of it as a construction of modernity through to how the nation is imagined and experienced in Malaysia.

To reduce confusion and simplify matters I use the modern label of Malaysia in all references to the nation except where specific historical instances such as the Treaty of Malayan Union demand otherwise. I want to stress that although the account reveals the trajectory of these significations and some of the misunderstandings that have led to the current state of affairs in Malaysia, nowhere does it imply that once revealed these can be corrected so society can start from scratch. Even flawed and problematic as they are, it is clear these significations are already embedded within the prevalent social imaginary. However, there is no reason to believe that new, less contradictory interpretations of the significations cannot nudge them into irrelevance.

Religion

Centuries of interaction with foreign traders and travellers, especially for those who lived along the coast, had exposed the peoples of the Southeast Asian region to many religions, foreigners and their ways. So even before the arrival of the British, Malaysians were aware of and practised a multiplicity of religions. These included Animism, Buddhism, Christianity, Hinduism, Islam and Taoism. Malaysians were highly receptive to new ideas and equally capable of adapting alien ideas and practices to their local conditions and environment (Andaya and Andaya, 2001: 18). They were, to use the idiom of the social imaginaries framework, adept at filtering and adding new significations and interpretations to the Malayan social imaginary. Prior to the thirteenth century, the dominant influence in the Malayan peninsula and, indeed, the entire Southeast Asian region, was Indian (SarDesai, 2003: 83; Ryan, 1962). All areas of life from the material to the spiritual received some Indian inflection. It is, for example, to the Indian culture that Malaysia owes its forms of medicine, literature, alphabet, political system, law and religion (Winstedt, 1966: 24–31).

It was also the Indians who introduced both Hinduism and Buddhism to Malaysia (Ryan, 1962: 12–13; Winstedt, 1966: 24–31). In turn, Malaysians themselves interpreted and enacted the beliefs and practices of Hinduism and Buddhism in their own fashion. Despite the complicated but similar animistic beliefs that prevailed in Southeast Asia before their advent, Buddhism and Hinduism were both able to make inroads in the region because of their ability to accommodate and blend with the existent religious systems (SarDesai, 2003: 83; Turnbull, 1989: 11). It is still possible, for example, to witness some of this synthesis in the echoes of Hindu ritual present in the enthronement ceremony and regalia of Malay rulers (Ryan, 1962: 30; Winstedt, 1966: 24–31; Andaya and Andaya, 2001: 16). India's people and culture can, therefore, be said to have introduced new potentialities of religion as a signification to the Malaysian social imaginary.

When a Muslim dynasty came into power in 1208, India itself came under Islamic influence (SarDesai, 2003: 58). Likewise with Hinduism and Buddhism, it was the Indians who introduced Islam via Malacca (also known as *Melaka*) (ibid.: 83–4), which was then amongst the most important and busiest ports along the Straits of Malacca. Many Malays were converted in that period (ibid.: 66). Islamic ideas, law and mysticism all 'coming from India and tinged with Indian ideas' were studied in Malacca and spread from there to other parts of Southeast Asia, i.e. Sumatra, Java and Borneo (Winstedt, 1966: 38–9). That Islam arrived via Indian rather than Arabic influence was crucial, for while Indian Muslim missionaries destroyed the symbols and idols of Hinduism in India itself (as per Islam's anti-idolatry teachings), in Malaysia they were content to leave the customs and traditions of cultural life alone (Ryan, 1962: 21).

Indeed, it is argued that it was precisely because Islam was absorbed rather than enforced in Malaysia that it was able to adapt local traditions and rites including those of animist beliefs and Hinduism (Ryan, 1962: 13–15; Turnbull, 1989: 110). The same is true of the Javanese of Indonesia who accepted Islam in the sixteenth century without abandoning many of the traits of their 'pre-Islamic religious system' (Reid, 2011: 3). Of the many colonists who left their mark on Malaysia, the Portuguese were the only ones motivated by religious zeal as well as trade in the sixteenth century (Andaya and Andaya, 2001) and the Catholic faith many of their present-day descendants profess is one of their most abiding legacies. Importantly, as McGregor describes, due to the flow of people and information contained on the watercraft plying the India–China trade route between port cities, Southeast Asians were kept abreast of 'technological advancements and enmeshed in world economies' (McGregor, 2008: 23). These cross-currents were stemmed during the early period of colonialism when Southeast Asia was 'slowly excluded from trade and technological innovations taking place in other parts of the world' as European powers devised exclusive agreements with local rulers as the Dutch United East India Company (VOC) did in Indonesia (ibid.: 24–5).

Turner argues that the Westphalian system of nation-states introduced into Asian imaginaries by Europeans favours 'Protestantism as the model of religion', which was individualistic and private (B. S. Turner, 2007: 409). This underlying assumption of religion as a matter for the private rather than public domain raises problems for Hinduism as well as Judaism. However, it proved to be a relatively smooth transition for Singapore, the only nation in Southeast Asia with a majority Chinese population that practised religions ranging from Buddhism and Taoism to Christianity. With the notable exception of efforts by groups organized along ethno-religious lines such as MUIS (*Majlis Ugama Islam Singapura*, Islamic Religious Council of Singapore) and the self-help group SINDA (Singapore Indian Development Association), religious concerns rarely feature in the island-state's public sphere.

However, for Malaysia and Indonesia and their majority Muslim populations, the assumption of separation between politics and religion was to be the cause of great strife because 'the relationship between religion and politics in Islam is very different from that relationship in other civilizations' (B. S. Turner, 2007: 409–13). Turner continues:

> [m]odern commentators on Islam have assumed that the problem of incorporating Islam into the modern Western polity lies in the fact that Islam does not recognize the separation of church and state. Islam has no 'church' as such, Islamic law (*Sharī'ah*) is not merely a law of private status, and the Islamic community (*ummah*) is a transnational social system.

Precolonial Islam admitted no such separation because within its teachings religion and politics were not separate entities. Aziz and Shamsul make a similar point about Islam in Malaysia in the distinction between *KERAJAAN* and *kerajaan* where the former denotes 'a fused state and nation' and the latter denotes 'a separated church and state' (Aziz and Shamsul, 2006: 345). This disparity between two different ways of understanding the world became crucial when ideas such as nation were carried over from one social imaginary to another and underlying notions were imposed alongside. According to Aziz and Shamsul, the disparity also springs from the British misunderstanding of Islam as a religion (ibid.: 346). Still, this is the view that has been cemented in the centuries since and is by and large accepted as the norm, so much so that for a world entrenched in the Westphalian system of nation-states, the prospect of 'political Islam' is looked upon with horror whilst a modern, moderate Islam is preferred. In Southeast Asia this bifurcation finds expression in the struggle within Islam between the moderates and the conservatives to which various labels are ascribed: liberal, moderate versus radical, and political Islam (Macdonald and Lemco, 2002).

This is problematic because Islam remains the dominant religion in Malaysia and Indonesia today. In fact, Muslims constitute 60.8 per cent of Malaysia's (Saw, 2007: 77) and 88 per cent of Indonesia's 205 million-strong population (*Muslim Population of Indonesia*, 2010). All Malays are constitutionally deemed Muslims in Malaysia (Laws of Malaysia: Federal Constitution, 2006) but members of many other races are also Muslims (Saw, 2007: 79). The relationship between race and religion and the divisiveness it has engendered between Malays and non-Malays is a complex one and much of that complexity derives from how race as a signification travelled from Europe through colonialism and filtered into Malaysia's social imaginary.

Race

The port-state of Malacca located mid-way along the west coast of Malaysia, about 148 kilometres south of present-day Kuala Lumpur, had been an important centre for trade with China since the fifteenth century (Ryan, 1976; Turnbull, 1989). Much of early European rivalry centred around the control of this coveted trading centre. Several European powers including the Portuguese, the Dutch and the British were later to rule over parts of Malaya at different periods but on the whole, Western influences in the peninsula prior to the nineteenth century and the arrival of the British were largely limited to the port of Malacca (Ryan, 1976).

It was during the thirteenth century that the scattered tribes of the Malaysian peninsula began to identify themselves as Malays (Winstedt, 1966: 16). However, up to the nineteenth century there remained in Malay writings themselves vagueness as to whether *Melayu* (Malay) was a general reference to all the subjects of the various peninsular sultanates or a specific reference to the people of Malacca (Milner, 1998: 154). In its earliest usages, the term was used to denote a line of kings and a style of language and manners originating and developed in Malacca (Reid, 2009).

In 1511, the Portuguese arrived to rule Malacca for 130 years (Ryan, 1976), until 1641 when the Dutch successfully routed them from Malacca. With the signing of the Treaty of London Malacca lost its primary role as a trading centre and declined in importance (SarDesai, 2003). The 1824 treaty divided the two areas of imperial influence between the British and the Dutch (entailing the exchange of Dutch Malacca for British Bencoolen) and left the British supreme northeast of an imaginary line drawn through the Strait of Malacca, while the Dutch retained control of the islands southwest (Harper, 1999). In 1826, the three trading settlements of Malacca, Penang and Singapore were combined by the British to form the Straits Settlements (Winstedt, 1966; Reid, 2009).

Beliefs and understandings about race were already widely circulated in Victorian social imaginaries of the nineteenth century (Bolt, 1971: 217). The British blend of understandings about race and commercial *nous*, though, lent the signification of race a greater emphasis in the Malayan social imaginary (Hirschman, 2004: 393–4). Once introduced, the European understandings of race fused with indigenous beliefs about lineage and descent to become entrenched in both the colonized and non-colonized populations (ibid.: 396).

Stamford Raffles, the founder of Singapore and Straits Settlements, was amongst the chief proponents of the definition of the Malays as a distinct race and such views were given great credence by the English-speaking public (Reid, 2009: 91). For example, in an early essay published in 1809, Raffles asserted that the Malays should be thought of as 'one people, speaking one language' (ibid.: 92). Influenced by eighteenth-century Enlightenment and German romanticism (Lund et al., 1962), Raffles applied the familiar signification of a people (*volk*) to what he witnessed in Malaysia. In 1821 when the Malacca royal chronicle was discovered and translated by fellow Briton John Leyden and printed for the first time in 1821, Raffles named it *The Malay Annals*. Importantly, he also gave it an equivalent Malay title: *Sejarah Melayu* (the history of the Malays) (Milner, 2009: 92; Reid, 2009: 119). In doing so, he implicitly transformed the contents from an account of a line of kings to the story of a people, replacing, to use Shamsul's phrase, a local order of things with an alien one. Long after his death in 1826, Raffles' views on ethnolinguistic categories remained a major influence on British Empire makers (Andaya and Andaya, 2001: 126).

The example of Raffles illustrates what can happen when social imaginaries overlap and significations are transferred and applied across societies. There was no guarantee that any signification thus transferred, in this case, from the British social imaginary would filter down to take root in the Malaysian social imaginary. Some part of the success or failure of this process is thus owed to the stature and power of the individual(s) who first employed the signification in such a fashion. In this sense, Raffles' political prominence can be said to have been translated into discursive influence.

Noor uses the term 'racialised capitalism' to describe the style of enterprise the Europeans brought to Malaysia (Noor, 2009: 83). Certainly when the British took over Malaya from the Dutch, their intent was to utilize Malaysia as a base for their capitalistic endeavours. Indeed, their aim was to 'guard British interests while avoiding direct commitment' (Andaya and Andaya, 2001: 126). The signification of race was employed to enable the enumeration and organization of labour necessary to the activities of mining, agriculture and trade on which their earnings rested. This is why scholars now maintain the overwhelming colonial legacy is the ideology of race (ibid.). Nonetheless, it must be said that the Malays were known to possess 'great pride of race – due perhaps, as much to his Islamic religion as to a past he has forgotten' (Winstedt, 1966: 19). The Chinese had long been racially conscious and wary of the barbaric hordes besieging the borders of their homeland, the Middle Kingdom (Aihwa Ong, 1999: 56). Reid suggests that it was more the Chinese than the Europeans in the centuries before the British and Dutch arrived that introduced 'Southeast Asians to distinctiveness otherness' by way of their 'own continuum of shifting and overlapping identities' (Reid, 2009: 54).

Nagata argues that there was little concept of a wider Malay unity or 'collective consciousness transcending state boundaries' because there was perceived to be no political necessity for it (Nagata, 1979: 52). Further, that what eventually endowed the Malays with a sense of race and welded them into a people were subsequent political developments, many of which first manifested during the period of British administration (ibid.). Under British rule, Malaysia was administered through formalized institutional governance that introduced many concepts alien to the Malayan social imaginary. Many of these were rather more rigid in nature than the customs of old.

For example, where impermanence was formerly the accepted condition of life and a good reputation via service to the Sultan the only form of permanence (Milner, 1991: 115), under the British, impermanence was considered disruptive and unconducive to effective administration. As such, settlement and social cohesion were preferred and encouraged by the British administrators. The enumerative characteristic of European rationalism combined with the institutional governance of the colonial state to underline many aspects of life (ibid.: 121). From the legal and the educational to the financial and bureaucratic, European regimes and methods of accounting for rights, debts and obligations were implemented. 'The Europeans', according to Reid, 'did not seek to create communities of belonging between the state and its subjects' but one of the consequences of the structures of administration they created was a level of new-found homogeneity that 'laid a firm basis for anti-imperial nationalism' (Reid, 2009: 37).

The second major influence in the development of race consciousness in Malaysia was the mass migration of Indian and Chinese workers that colonial administrators welcomed to colonial Malaysia. Commercial enterprise in Malaysia was confined to the upper classes, who dealt primarily with trade in an administrative capacity. Native Malaysians were not indolent but reluctant to engage in the style of labour the British required for their colonial prosperity (Alatas, 1977). As a result, rather than employing indigenous labour for enterprises such as mining and plantations, it became customary to have this kind of work performed by immigrant workers, like the Chinese and the Indians (Turnbull, 1989: 110, 176). The practice of importing labour to tackle undesirable work was to add greatly to the Malaysian population but such growth was not to be had without tensions developing between the native and the migrant communities.

According to Reid, the Chinese were one amongst a multitude of commercial minorities in Southeast Asia but by the start of the eighteenth century, they had become 'the pre-eminent' one (Reid, 2011: 238). The significations of race or ethno-linguistic categories became much more evident as the migrant populations in Malaysia expanded. For example, in 1826, the Chinese population in Malacca was only 4,124 (Ryan, 1962: 17). The Chinese only began migrating to the peninsula in large numbers during the nineteenth century when dissatisfaction with conditions in China motivated their dispersal to all parts of Southeast Asia (Andaya and Andaya, 2001: 140). Encouraged by the British who needed willing labourers to mine tin, a major export commodity of the time, the size of the Chinese population swelled, eventually to form as much as 46 per cent of the population in the 1921–31 censuses (Nagata, 1979: 17).

Chinese migrants were a source of both labour and revenue through taxes exacted on their habits of opium, pork, pawnbroking and spirits (Andaya and Andaya, 2001: 140). So pivotal was Chinese labour to mining and commerce, they became a significant force in the balance of power among rival Sultans as 'the ubiquitous middlemen' (Ryan, 1962: 19). As noted earlier, despite their openness to new ideas and flexibility, native Malayans never quite adapted Chinese culture into their precolonial social imaginary. This continued even in colonial times. The Chinese brought with them their own culture, language and religion, and due to the above reason and by virtue of their numbers, they were able to remain a separate and self-sufficient community (Ryan, 1962: 19).

The numbers of migrant workers from India were smaller but their presence also helped to consolidate the idea of distinctive races. The majority of those who migrated from India were from South India and of the Hindu faith (Ryan, 1962: 19). Many others, mostly Hindu, joined them from then Ceylon (Sri Lanka) and Malabar but there were also many Sikhs among them (Winstedt, 1966: 18). As late as 1910, many Indians were still arriving as indentured labourers, engaged by agents (Ryan, 1962: 19–20). Unlike the Chinese, however, the Indians remained relatively mobile and their numbers in Malaysia small. Intermarriage, a common feature of life in earlier times, was frowned upon in the late nineteenth century as increasing awareness of racial differences – or, to use the idiom of social imaginaries, of race as a signification – saw 'each ethnic group seeking to preserve its own identity' (Turnbull, 1989: 192). Hence, at the same time as a consciousness of themselves as a separate race was cultivated and reinforced by the colonial administration, the Malays were also introduced to the notion of the Chinese and Indian migrants as Others.

The Dutch also invited the Chinese to their colony in Indonesia but employed them differently, to farm the collection of state revenues (Reid, 2011: 241). Despite the less menial nature of their roles, the Chinese in Indonesia were officially classified as '"foreign Orientals (*Vreemde Ossterlingen*)"' (Thung, 2012: 375). Like the British during the nineteenth century, the Dutch in Indonesia kept the Chinese legally distinct from the native population in terms of residence, land ownership, education and dress (Reid, 2011: 244). The task of brokering between the colonials and the local population and controlling the influx of their compatriots from China fell to them.

To efficiently manage the colony, the British divided the population neatly into three racial categories – Malay, Chinese and Indian. They also developed and applied stock descriptions and understandings to their perceptions of Malaysians. The Malays were, hence, considered to be traditional, loyal, rural agrarians with a relaxed attitude towards life. The Indians were servants of the colonies and the Chinese deemed clannish (Reid, 2009: 93). In less complimentary terms, the Indians were labelled drunkards, the Chinese, thieves and the Malays, idlers (Warnford-Lock 1901, cited in Noor, 2009: 68). These standardized perceptions had the effect of emphasizing differences and characterizing them as racial distinctions within the colonial government, but more importantly, there is little doubt that British interpretations of race as a signification filtered through into the Malaysian social imaginary via the administrative system.

With their nineteenth-century European ways of understanding, the British were convinced that as lesser, savage and weaker races, the Malays were subject to auto-genocide (Noor, 2009: 71) and held back from material advancement by historical and cultural tradition. By contrast, British perceptions of the Chinese were as economically aggressive 'locusts of commerce'

(Winstedt, cited in Harper, 1999: 228). These views coloured much of the British's administrative approach so that colonial policy towards the Malays became 'couched in the language of Protection' (Harper, 1999: 228).

During the mid-nineteenth century this sense of anxiety increased as Malaysia experienced an influx of Chinese, Indians and Ceylonese, drawn there by the prospect of employment in the tin mines and plantations of rubber, pepper, coffee, sugar and gambier (Turnbull, 1989: 2). While many of the migrant workers had originally travelled to Malaya for employment probably with little intention of permanently settling down, many did eventually do so. The majority of these workers were from mainland China and many decided to settle in the then Straits Settlement of Singapore. Over time, Singapore grew to become the Chinese enclave of the region.

Both the British and the Malays viewed the overwhelming presence of the migrant Chinese with unease. This was all the more so as these workers organized themselves into various support groups and associations even as they broke off ties with the Chinese homeland. This unease grew as the organization was taking place along increasingly distinct communal lines. That most of the Chinese, unlike the Malays, were not of the Islamic faith but rather Buddhists and Taoists only deepened the lines of division between the Malay and the Chinese. Additionally, under British influence early nineteenth-century Malaysians of Malay, Chinese, Indian and European descent grew more concerned to preserve their own identities and actively discouraged the intermarriage and mixing among the races of earlier periods (Turnbull, 1989: 192). As a signification, race began to loom even larger in the Malaysian social imaginary as the Malay community grew progressively more anxious about the perpetuation of their own race within Malaysia (Milner, 1998: 157).

Through the application of an administrative style infused with their Victorian understandings of race, the British further exacerbated these ethnic divisions. For example, whereas the 1891 census of the various Malay States grouped the various communities by their nationalities, the 1911 census of the Federated Malay States used race as the primary category of belonging (Harper, 1999: 27).

Thus, race increasingly came to occupy a central position in the Malaysian social imaginary through its multiple embodiments in the administration. Writing specifically of the emergent new states of Africa and Asia of the mid-twentieth century, Geertz argues that the ethnic bonds of blood, kinship and belief are experienced as primordial (Geertz, 1963) even if, intellectually, few people confronted with the evident multiplicity and mutability of contemporary identities can sustain such a belief on intellectual grounds.

That this keenly felt experience of ethnic bonds resulted in a majority–minority discourse that shaped how the signification of nation is enacted in Malaysia, as a constructed multicultural society, is an observation often made of Malaysia (Shamsul, 1998: 137). What is often left unsaid is how such a perception might also be understood as a reciprocal process that occurs between earlier and contemporary claims and counter-claims of identity and not entirely a discourse derived and constructed by the British (Milner, 1998: 168). Reid provides the most vivid illustration of such a process in the words of A. C. Vlieland, the chief administrator of the 1931 census, who lamented that '"[m]ost Oriental peoples have themselves no clear conception of race, and commonly regard religion as the most important, if not determinant, element"'(Vlieland, cited in Reid, 2009: 33). Tasked with the responsibility of assigning race to a population careless of the category, Vlieland resorted to a '"judicious blend ... of the ideas of geographic and ethnographic origin, political allegiance, and racial and social affinities and sympathies"' (ibid.).

The second major influence on the development of the nation as a signification in Malaysia as well as Singapore and Indonesia is the occupation of the Japanese during the Pacific War from 1942 to 1945. Both Malaysia and Singapore fell because the British failed to defend them against the Japanese aggressors (Abshire, 2011: 83; Andaya and Andaya, 2001: 257). In Malaysia, the Japanese administration continued to emphasize ethnic differences through their better treatment of Malays over the Chinese, whom they associated with the anti-Japanese movement in Communist China (Andaya and Andaya, 2001: 258). Japanese support for Pan-Malayan organizations also strengthened the Malay sense of community (ibid.: 259). Similarly discriminatory treatment was meted out to the various races of Singapore; the Malays and Indians received rather kinder handling than the Chinese who were, for example, subjected to a 'brief but brutal' purging campaign, the *sook ching* (Abshire, 2011: 102).

After Malaysia and Singapore were surrendered, the Dutch did not attempt to defend Indonesia. Welcomed as liberators from the Dutch, the Japanese had a more solicitous attitude towards the local population to begin with, even if they maintained their harshness towards the Chinese (Reid, 2011: 154–5). Crucially, the Japanese introduced Indonesians to political theatre and propaganda and also importantly, imparted a sense of discipline, toughness and 'a spirit of sacrificial patriotism' to the pre-war elite via their military-style training regimes (ibid.: 23–7). Courtesy of the Dutch's 1901 Ethical Policy, this very small elite had received the benefits of a European education (ibid.: 10) and was by 1942, 'sensitive to Dutch power and arrogance on one hand, and anachronistic aristocratic pretension on the other' (ibid.: 15). The grooming they received at the hands of Japanese trainers and teachers gave this small but influential elite confidence and lent greater urgency to their agitation for independence from the Dutch.

That the British and Dutch were both defeated by the Japanese in the space of three short months had a profound effect on the Southeast Asian countries. The 'collapse of imperial authority' previously thought mighty meant that Southeast Asians were no longer cowed by the assumed superiority of European knowledge and technologies (Mehta, 1958: 93). Equally, it also affected the British and transformed their post-war approach to demands for independence in Malaysia (Harper, 1999: 56). In the years immediately after the war, the British were keen to divest themselves of the responsibility and expense of governance in British Malaya. The Dutch were more reluctant to relinquish their colony but after the Japanese surrender were confronted with the declaration of independence that a young Sukarno proclaimed on 17 August 1945. A four-year struggle ensued before independence was won (McGregor, 2008: 38).

The retreat of the Japanese set the stage for the early formation of nations in many former colonies in Southeast Asia. Writing in *Nationalism in Asia* (1976), Wang argues that Asian nations such as Malaysia, Indonesia, and Singapore are largely a result of a wider reaction to Western dominance in the region (Wang, 1976: 83). The stout defence of the principles of freedom, democracy and liberty during the Second World War led to these same values being cherished and desired by the people of Asia as well (ibid.). How the various countries in the region took the form of nations was undoubtedly influenced by the differing reactions of the colonials, whose views were themselves coloured by the overriding European conception of the nation.

Nations in Southeast Asia

According to Kumar, although modernists generally associate the development of the nation with the French Revolution in the late eighteenth century, the idea of the nation did not attain canonical status until the nineteenth century (K. Kumar, 2006: 9). Indeed, as James points out, while nations existed before the nineteenth century, they were not then nation-states, nor were they territorial states (James, 2006: 375). Prior to the nineteenth century, there were two dominant understandings of the nation. The first was that of the nation as tribe or *ethnie*, defined as 'a named and self-defined human population sharing a myth of common ancestry, historical memories and elements of culture ... and a measure of solidarity' (A. D. Smith, 2006: 172). The second understanding was of the nation as communities of people who 'found common purpose with each other under conditions of being lifted out of their locales into new settings of face-to-face *interaction*' (James, 2006: 375, original emphasis). Examples include the communities of the military barracks, universities and monasteries.

The point at which the nation came to dominate Western social imaginaries is also when it was increasingly associated with the state. This was because it was the development of the state with its growing powers of centralization, standardization and administration that facilitated the organization of populations into nation. Though the nation has 'older roots, it was shaped by the process of state making, including wars, as well as by markets and transport and communications infrastructures' (Calhoun, 1997: 10–11).

States did not create nations but they were instrumental to the nation's ubiquity from the nineteenth century onwards. To facilitate the exchange of goods and improve the economies from which they derived tax and other revenue, states developed standards, laws and contracts for trading; roads, routes and transportation to carry goods to markets; and they waged wars over lands rich with natural resources (Hall and Ikenberry, 1989). All these activities had the effect of consolidating the notion of collectivity that is now intrinsic to the idea of nationhood. This led, towards the end of the nineteenth century, to the nation being increasingly identified with the state.

The work of two theorists, Fichte (2001) and Renan (1990), typify the understandings of the nation dominant during the nineteenth century. Fichte regarded the nation as eternal in spirit, springing from the organic and natural love of the Fatherland (Fichte, 2001: 119–20). He understood all of humanity to be naturally divided into nations, each distinguishable by certain characteristics unique to them. As Kedourie (1993) subsequently argued, the essentialization of the nation as primordial and perennial is more political doctrine than undeniable truth. Scholars of today have largely discredited the understanding of the nation as primordial. Nevertheless, as Calhoun comments, it is a notion that still finds great favour with national ideologues and hence, an understanding of the nation that persists in many social imaginaries (Gellner, 1995, 1996). This is the form of nationalism commonly referred to as ethnic nationalism.

Renan argued the case for an alternative understanding of the nation: as a civic institution wrought by the will of the people (Renan, 1990). Rather than being grounded on racial characteristics, he argued that the nation was 'the historical result of a series of events, converging in the same direction'. For Renan, the nation was 'a living soul, a spiritual principle' whose strength rested on the remembrance of 'a long past of efforts and sacrifices, and devotion' (ibid.: 19) and the shared oblivion of differences. As 'the daily plebiscite' the nation was, he asserted, to be lived and relived each day through the deeds of its people, in their remembering and forgetting (ibid.: 11–12). Renan's ideal of the nation as a political communion of people founded on common will is typical of the civic model.

The two different models of the nation, the ethnic and the civic, remain dominant in contemporary social imaginaries. The ethnic–civic binary has also, over the course of time, become associated with other ways of categorizing nationalism, most notably that of the Eastern and Western forms. Many, if not all of the nations of today base their reason for being on one or the other of the above understandings. However, that the ethnic or non-Western model is often treated like a 'corruption' (A. D. Smith, 1991: 11) of the Western model is symptomatic of the preference, since at least the latter half of the twentieth, for the Western, civic model.

Reid argues that:

> [t]he modern states which introduced state nationalism in its modern form were alien imperial states. They were able to establish their authority in Southeast Asia in the late nineteenth century in large part because they embodied, to a much greater extent that their local opponents, that homogeneous amalgam of ethnie and state nationalism which proved so successful in the nineteenth century. (Reid, 2009: 37)

To facilitate the gradual handover of self-administration to a multi-racial Malaya after the Second World War, the British came up with the Malay Union proposal in October 1946 (SarDesai, 2003: 197). In it, the British proposed the conferment of common citizenship on immigrants equal to that of the Malays, totally failing to appreciate that the notion of Malay paramountcy as being vital to the economic advancement of Malays had become an ingrained feature of the Malayan social imaginary. As 'Muhammadan monarchies' (Turnbull, 1989: 236), the Malaysian states were by now always and forever part of a Malay country. Hence, the Malay Union proposal was widely interpreted as an attempt to deprive the Malays of power (SarDesai, 2003: 197).

To the majority-Malay population by then convinced that Malays needed protection, the British divestment of their colonial responsibilities created much anxiety. Handed independence by the retreating British, Malaysia saw 'the survival of the [Malay] rulers' as the 'crucial ingredient' of nation formation and elected to adopt a federal model 'retaining nine monarchs within a single state' (Reid, 2011: 213). The compromise in the form of the 1948 Federation of Malaya meant that automatic citizenship was granted only to the Malays, whilst special rights and privileges such as preferences in public education and employment in the civil service were reserved for *Bumiputeras* (sons of the soil) (SarDesai, 2003: 197–8).

As Harper points out, there was always a disparity between the debatably benign British expectations and norms of how the nation should be enacted and how it was actualized in Malaysia (Harper, 1999: 358). In fact, Malaysia's very constitution is a compromise between Western-style nationalism and Malayan Sultanism (Milner, 1991: 110). Established alongside the pomp and ceremony of the Sultan monarchy, itself an amalgam of Malayan and Hindu rites, were the instruments of a constitutional form of government: a parliamentary government, an independent judiciary and an independent civil service.

Several attempts were made by Singapore to be part of the federation, yet it was only ever briefly included from 1963 to 1965 when the Federation of Malaysia Agreement of 1963 incorporated both Sarawak and Northern Borneo (subsequently renamed Sabah) and Singapore. However, Malay unease at Singapore's overwhelmingly Chinese population was never sufficiently quelled and on 9 August 1965, Singapore was expelled from the Federation of Malaysia to become an independent sovereign nation (Selvaraj, 2007: 23–4; Abshire, 2011: 131).

Although race and religion were equally important in the formation of the Indonesian nation they produced notably different results. As formed in Indonesia, the nation is unitary, secular, and since the 1998 reforms, democratic. Given its archipelagic geography, diverse cultures and languages, the federal model of nation that Malaysia took might have made more sense. According to Reid, it is because Indonesia had experienced an accidental revolution constituted by 'a series of autonomous but parallel uprisings in a dozen parts of the archipelago', that nation formation became 'an irresistible myth, sanctified by the blood sacrificed for it' (Reid, 2011:41). '[R]evolution', in Reid's view, 'has proven to be hostile to federalism in the name of the sovereignty of the people' (ibid.: 209). The fact the Dutch favoured the federal model made '[u]nitarism such an important part of the "victorious nationalist package" that any "people outside Java placing a high-value on their ethnic identity"' were deemed to be 'pro-Dutch' (Feith, cited in Reid, 2011: 217). Instead, the resultant unitary state eschewed the significations of race and religion in favour of the nationalist ideals of *Panca Sila* (Five Principles) 'freedom, natural harmony, culture, nationality and humaneness' as the bedrock on which the nation of Indonesia was built (ibid.: 14). The fact that the Javanese majority 'did not insist that theirs should be the "national" language, and educated Sumatrans ... played a prominent role in diminishing apprehension of Javanese dominance in the outer islands' is significant (Tarling, 2004: 107).

Singapore's majority Chinese and non-Muslim population means it has steered clear of the complications surrounding Islam. This has enabled the country to adopt the civic model of nation alongside a meritocratic style of governance that has delivered an enviable lifestyle to its population. However, race was retained as an organizing category of the administrative apparatus inherited from the colonial system. Despite the daily Pledge by school children of commitment to a republic of people united 'regardless of race, language or religion', an individual's race is still employed as a disciplining device that structures not only how Singaporean citizens live and where they may purchase government-subsidized housing, but also which public schools their children attend as well as what second languages they can undertake. Moreover, any meaningful dialogue about race itself is stymied by the state's determination of the subject as too sensitive for open discussion.

Unfortunately, how race and religion are enacted as significations continues to play a disproportionate role in how the nation of Malaysia is imagined and experienced. For example, since the Malay Reservations Act of 1913, the definition of a Malay person linked the race to the practice of Islam and the use of the Malaysian languages (Andaya and Andaya, 2001: 183). When Malaysia gained independence in 1957 and introduced its Constitution (Turnbull, 1989: 250), the foundational definition of a 'Malay' person as 'a person who professes the religion of Islam' who 'habitually speaks the Malay language' and 'conforms to Malay custom' was enacted as law and became further entrenched (Laws of Malaysia: Federal Constitution, 2006).

One effect of writing such a definition into the emergent nation's Constitution was to give rise to the population identifying itself either as Malay and hence, *Bumiputera*, or as non-Malay. When the special rights and privileges such as civil service employment and public education were subsequently accorded to *Bumiputeras* in later years, this distinction between the three main ethnic groups – the Malays, the Chinese and the Indians – grew in importance and became firmly lodged in the Malaysian social imaginary.

The tensions over perceived ethno-communal disparity between the Malays and non-Malays continued to fester until the breakout of racial riots on 13 May 1969 that started in Kuala Lumpur and spread to other parts of the nation (Heng, 1997: 262). Their main impact was to give rise to the National Economic Policy (NEP) when the Second Malaysia Plan was released in 1971. Based on similar grounds of pro-Malay affirmative action as the *Bumiputera* policy, the NEP was developed in response to the perceived cause of the riots, i.e. the resentment of the Malay majority at the prosperity and wealth of the minority Chinese.

Formulated in 1971 and effective until 1990, the NEP's original intention was to 'correct economic imbalance, so as to reduce and eventually eliminate the identification of race with economic function' (Second Malaysia Plan, 1971: 1); it singled out the 'creation of a Malay commercial and industrial community in all categories and at all levels of operation' as policy (ibid.). In doing so, the achievement of economic parity for the Malays was thus placed over and above that of other parts of the population like the Malaysian Indians (Heng, 1997: 269).

Though subsequently renamed and rebadged, the gist of the pro-Malay affirmative action that grew out of the NEP policy continues to apply today (The Ninth Malaysia Plan: 2006–2010, 2006: 3). The need to appease those disenfranchised by inter-ethnic tensions and economic inequity continues to be a primary concern of the Malaysian government (Heng, 1997). The placatory logic behind these policies is an entrenched part of the nation's socio-political foundation. Amongst other effects, it created a distinctive framework for the nation and expectations from certain sections of society that has had, and continues to have, many repercussions. The equation of ethnicity with economic status pushed the trait of 'inter-ethnic bargain and compromise' to the forefront of life in modern Malaysia (P. Ramasamy, 2004: 148). Another consequence is the setting up of a pattern of state interference in economics that remains to this day (Haque, 2003).

Conclusion

In this chapter, I have tried to demonstrate that in many ways, nationalists in Malaysia, Indonesia and Singapore began the task of nation formation with the same building blocks. Race, for example, was introduced and defined in essentialist terms by the European colonials in all three countries. Although initially introduced to these social imaginaries mainly for administrative purposes, this signification grew to occupy a dominant position in all three societies. And whilst religion as a signification pre-dated European arrival in Southeast Asia, it was heavily inflected by the interpretations Europeans brought to the relationship between church and state. Islam, in particular, has in Malaysia become almost inextricably imbricated with race, most famously through its Constitution.

At the same time, in the lead-up towards independence, Malaysia, Indonesia and Singapore underwent broadly similar traumatic experiences. These include mass migration from China, Japanese occupation during the Pacific War, the threat of Communism, civil unrest and inter-communal rioting. As significations in the social imaginaries of Malaysia, Indonesia and Singapore, race, religion and nation shared many common interpretations; how each country enacts nationhood today is markedly different.

Fashioned by former empires and agreed upon after three decades of war in Europe, the Westphalian system of nation-states was adopted eagerly by these Southeast Asian countries as a passageway out of colonialism. However, while similar significations were brought to the task of nation-building, the nations that ensued were vastly different. Having formed their nations, the governments of Malaysia, Indonesia and Singapore were faced with the responsibility of creating a viable future for their nations. Socio-economic progress was vital to the long-term survival of these new nation-states.

Towards this end, many nation-states have turned to the romantic belief that technology can bring about social, economic and political progress. The tendency towards techno-romanticism and hyperbole seems to multiply when it comes to the nation because of technology's historical reputation as the homogenizing apparatus *par excellence*. One has only to think of shipbuilding, timekeeping, land surveying and radio to realize the enormity of the effects the technological capabilities of large-scale expansion, centralization, standardization and dissemination have introduced to human coalitions. That these technologies sustain and reinforce much of the nation's hegemony is also clear when one considers the overt discursive power of the media and the underlying structure of the systems and institutions that are utilized on a daily basis, from railway stations and debit/credit cards to prime-time television.

In more recent times the rapid advance of Internet technologies has been viewed with awe and hailed by many as the herald of yet another phase of drastic adjustment to how the nation is lived (Katz, 1997). The 'cyberbolic' (Woolgar, 2002) tenor of these forecasts has a distinctively different tone because the Internet is, in contrast to older media and communication technologies, understood in these narratives to facilitate decentralization, fragmentation and individuation. The next chapter addresses the relationship between nation and technology and like this one, continues to bring in the Indonesian and Singapore examples where appropriate.

3   Nation and Internet

This chapter is about the relationships between the significations of the nation and the Internet. I have already discussed the nation as a signification in Chapter 2 and want to do the same for the Internet here. There are a number of ways to approach the study of the Internet. It is primarily perceived as a form of media by the public today, but in the broad context of this book, its implications for Malaysia nest within a set of relationships between nation and technology. So it is that this chapter begins from this perspective.

This approach is important for a number of reasons. Foremost of these is the sense of optimism that new technologies evoke within societies. Though often unwarranted, these attitudes nevertheless deeply influence the understandings and expectations of the relevant technology within social imaginaries. Such was the case with the telegraph, hailed by France's first chair of political economy as a technology with the potential to 'allow all the citizens in France to communicate their will, within a rather short time, in such a way that this communication might be considered instantaneous' (Mattelart, 2003: 22). A similar claim was made of the steam engine in the eighteenth century, anthropomorphized into 'an agent ... [capable of] triumphing over space and time ... to subdue prejudice and to unite every part of our land in rapid and friendly communication' (Fraser, cited in Quirk and Carey, 1989: 120).

Well into the twentieth century, the trope of national progress via technological means continued to flourish. Electricity, for example, was imbued in 1933 with the transformative power to 'yoke a whole continental economy into something like one unified machinery, one organic whole ... [and] give us universally high standards of living, new and amusing kinds of jobs, leisure, freedom and an end to drudgery, congestion, noise, smoke, and filth' (Chase, cited in Quirk and Carey, 1989: 129–30). The introduction and expansion of technology is so intermeshed with national development that the current Australian government's catchphrase in the rollout of its National Broadband Network is: 'connecting us to a better future' (NBNetwork, 2012).

Thus, this chapter begins with how technology was broadly understood and applied in Malaysia to the task of national development in the early days of independence. This is followed by a discussion on the role of technology in nation-building in Southeast Asian contexts. As with the previous chapter,

I refer to the Indonesian and Singaporean examples to lend regional context and provide information for comparison wherever possible. This leads finally to a discussion on the Internet as a signification.

In previous chapters it has been established that significations take on different potentialities in different societies, so in order to understand how and why the nation and the Internet are imbricated in the way they are in Malaysia, it is important that we continue to adopt a socio-historical stance in our examination of the Internet as a signification. We therefore trace the Internet's beginnings as a signification to its origins as an idea(l) and lived experience in Western social imaginaries before taking the examination to the Internet in Malaysia in the next chapter. As with the nation, the Internet has multiple genealogies, hence, whilst it is possible to attribute the development of crucial distributed networks, cables and nodes to US finance, the Internet's roots as an idea and way of thinking about the world runs across many social imaginaries (Naughton, 2000). There is, as such, no intention to claim this brief chapter to be a complete history of the Internet. It is one version of the stories we tell ourselves about cyberspace (Bell, 2001).

Technology and national development

To understand Southeast Asia's love affair with technology is to understand the conditions from which the region emerged out of colonialism. Nineteenth-century colonialism had been achieved by dint of superior weaponry and transport technology (McGregor, 2008: 26). And up until the arrival of the Japanese and the defeat of both the British and the Dutch, few in Southeast Asia thought Asian nations could gain the technological prowess to upset the status quo. When the Japanese occupied Malaysia, Indonesia and Singapore during the Pacific War, they not only dispelled these notions of European technological superiority, they also boosted indigenous technical education as well as industrialization in these nations (Edgerton, 2007: 31).

We have already seen in the previous chapter how race was central to the understanding and social organization of the colonial empires. According to Edgerton, European colonizers applied the same racialized logic to scientific and technological superiority (ibid.: 27). Edgerton explains that 'there was a profoundly racial economy of technology-in-use' that saw enclaves where technologies not generally available to the indigenous population such as motor cars, telephones, running water and electricity, were reserved for the 'European colonizers in colonies' (ibid.: 29). Everywhere 'white technology went, white technicians were in control' (ibid.: 29).

The British, for example, extended the logic of race to the type of education, technical and non-technical, available to local populations in India. In the decades immediately preceding independence in the early part of the twentieth century, technical skills, knowledge, training and occupations were, thus, also subject to a 'racial order' with the locally born whites at the top of the hierarchy, followed by those of mixed race and the local (ibid.: 30).

Unsurprisingly then, as 'nations emerging out of empires' Malaysia, Indonesia and Singapore had a burning desire 'not only to develop national technologists but national technologies too' (ibid.: 31).

Left with a nation pre-formed in administrative and legal terms and in the case of Malaysia and Singapore deeply underscored by the learnt categories of difference in race and religion, the newly elected governments of the time needed to unite their people and provide a means of living. Nineteenth-century colonialism had also successfully reoriented Malaysia, Indonesia and Singapore to the production and shipping of materials for European industrialization (McGregor, 2008: 32). In the process these nations were exposed to many of the new technologies that were responsible for European prosperity. However, they possessed few manufacturing capacities of their own and right up to independence had economies largely based on the export of commodities. However, once independent, these new nations were confronted with the unsustainable costs of continuing the late colonial practice of importing finished goods from Europe and the urgent need for economic growth.

According to McGregor, there were two main paths, the capitalist market-based development strategies and the socialist state-led approaches, taken by these new nations towards economic development and the 'economic diversity of Southeast Asia' today reflects these different choices (McGregor, 2008: 47). Post-independence Malaysia, Indonesia and Singapore were amongst those nations who adopted a capitalist-led development model (ibid.: 48).

As a nation, Malaysia deliberately chose industrialization 'as an instrument of ethnic nationalism'; there is, thus, an established history of causal relationship between nation and technology (W. F. Case, 2000: 147). In the immediate postcolonial period at the end of the 1950s, Malaysia's economic policy was based on protectionist import substitution policies. This was followed in the 1960s by export-oriented industrialization (Jomo, 1988: viii). In the 1970s, after the occurrence of the 1969 race riots and their prescribed underlying cause, Malay resentment at the prosperity of the non-Malays (mainly Chinese) led to an economic policy that was skewed towards correcting 'economic imbalance', and ultimately to eradicating 'the identification of race with economic function' (Second Malaysia Plan, 1971: 1). The Second Malaysia Plan covering the period 1971 to 1975 reveals the prominence of manufacturing technologies in the nation's 'New Development Strategy':

> [d]evelopment will be directed towards increased production for export, including new industrial and agricultural items, greater local processing of domestic raw materials, and further substitution of domestic production for imports. Economic growth will be facilitated by increased direct activities by the public sector and by new measures designed to ensure that the private sector will expand at a rapid rate. (Second Malaysia Plan, 1971: 6)

As a matter of course, to ensure the gainful employment of their citizens, these same states had to provide adequate education and training to transform their populations into suitable labour pools. In this respect, Malaysia was hampered by its ethno-communal divisions, which had penetrated to influence the national education system so much that ethnic minorities – such as the Chinese community – were insistent on maintaining their own schools, while state authorities continued to grant *Bumiputeras* preferred access to local universities (J. Lee, 2011: 7). The variations this created, from the language of instruction and style of delivery to curricula emphases, have been one of the sources of continued socio-economic differences, and as later chapters argue, is likely to continue to hobble efforts like the Economic Transformation Programme (ETP) – the master plan of the Najib administration (see http://etp.pemandu.gov.my).

Part of the orientation of an export-oriented industrialization involved the development of zones within which special conditions conducive to the injection of foreign capital into local environments were set up. Often purpose-built and equipped with necessary infrastructure such as transport and communication, these areas of exception were also commonly accompanied by a slew of favourable concessions in several areas from tax exemptions and relaxed tariffs to labour laws so as to ensure 'export efficiency for investors'. Many of Singapore's early successes stemmed from such strategies and at different stages other Asian nations have adopted the same model (McGregor, 2008: 50–1).

The emphasis on technology as a deliverer of economic progress must be understood within the broader context of the literature of that time. As a signification, technology became ever more deeply interpreted and entwined with national development and nation-building through the dissemination of views that identified 'the emerging role of technology as the master key of development' to such an extent that it seemed logical for 'development planning at the national and sectoral levels' to be 'reoriented throughout the developing world towards the utilization of a technology-based strategy' (Sharif, 1986: 363). Even then, the notion of leapfrogging where 'careful skipping of intermediate stages' of technology may be used by developing nations 'to skip over early developers' was already being mooted (ibid.: 371). The belief that playing 'technological catch-up' would enable developing nations to 'harness technology as a driver of economic growth' remains popular even today (J. Smith, 2009: 17).

In Malaysia, the development of heavy industries had been gaining greater emphasis since the late 1970s when Mohamad Mahathir was Minster of Trade and Industry. When Mahathir was appointed Prime Minister in 1981, heavy industries received a further boost (Jomo, 1988: vii). The nation was further distinguished from its counterparts when Prime Minister Mahathir announced and refined the 'Look East' policy over the course of 1981 and 1982 (Saravanamuttu, 1988: 4). Mahathir advocated that Malaysia turn towards the 'rapidly developing countries of the East' (Japan and South Korea) to advance the progress of the country. The East, as such, was praised for its emphasis on diligence, discipline, loyalty to the nation and the collective over individual interests, which Mahathir linked within the same breath to productivity, high quality, efficiency and their ability for 'narrowing differentials and gaps' between the various socio-economic groups (Mahathir, 1988: 1).

The Look East policy was based on the argument that as Pacific Rim nations, both Japan and Malaysia shared a 'common economic destiny' (Mahathir, 1988: 5) and there was much in the economic successes of newly industrialized countries (NICs) Japan and South Korea that Malaysia could emulate and benefit from. Importantly, it was hoped that the invitation for Japanese and Korean corporations to relocate their manufacturing bases to Malaysia and invest in joint ventures with local firms under favourable terms would result in the 'faster and wider transfer of technology' (Furuoka, 2007: 506).

This, as Furuoka argues, was motivated firstly by Mahathir's nationalism (Furuoka, 2007) and secondly, by a burgeoning anti-Western stance, itself fuelled by an earlier brawl with the British over the control of the Guthrie Corporation (Saravanamuttu, 1988: 4). However, it needs to be said that the strategy was never intended to be a total abandonment of Western ways (ibid.: 7). Unfortunately, at least two of the star outcomes of the Look East policy – the 'national auto project' Proton and the national steel plant, *Perjawa* – 'struggled to extract technology' from their Japanese partners (Felker, 2009: 482).

Like Malaysia, Indonesia began with a phase of protectionist import substitution with the added advantage of the local oil boom (Thee, 2006: 342). This later graduated to an emphasis on export-oriented projects predominantly of the labour-intensive manufacturing sector through into the 1980s. In the 1990s Professor B. J. Habibe, who had been appointed to the post of Minister of Research and Technology in 1978, successfully advanced the argument for a major impetus towards heavy industries vis-à-vis the sunset industries of manufacturing (Hill, 1995: 95).

Although Indonesia had no explicit 'technology policy' (Hill, 1995: 110), Habibe advocated 'an explicitly interventionist technology' direction (ibid.: 84). Ten high-technology industries were singled out as having the potential to 'promote indigenous technological capability' (Okamoto and Sjöholm, 2001: 17–18). These included aerospace, shipbuilding, railroad, telecommunications, electronics, explosives, steel and three industries in the field of machinery (ibid.). Thus, before the 1997 economic crisis and the resignation of President Suharto, Indonesia had 'two lanes of industrial policies: (i) a policy for strengthening and deepening the industrial structure' and '(ii) a policy for industrial transformation through high-tech application in strategic state-owned enterprises' (Aminullah, 2007: 6).

Amir (2004) describes an attempt by Indonesia to jumpstart an indigenous aircraft industry through the design and manufacture of a flagship product, the N25 airplane. A state-owned industrial enterprise, the Indonesian Aircraft Industry (IPTN) company was the brainchild of B. J. Habibe, a successful former aeronautical scientist trained in Germany (ibid.: 109). Started in 1976 and based in Bandung, IPTN was an important part of President Suharto's New Order government's bid to use sophisticated technology to 'leapfrog' national development (ibid.: 108). In the course of twenty years, the IPTN's growth and success with the N25 airplane was the source of much national pride. Finally launched in 1994 and touted as an aircraft '*entirely* designed and constructed by Indonesian scientists and engineers' (ibid.: 111, original emphasis), the company was later to flounder along with many other regional businesses in the Asian monetary crisis of 1997/8.

Interestingly, many observers note B. J. Habibe's championing of the latter policy and his influence with President Suharto to be an important factor in the formation of Indonesian economic and technology policies (Amir, 2004: 111; Hill, 1995: 84; Thee, 2006: 345). Amir further opines that Habibe's credentials as a scientist were also crucial to the project of national development under Suharto (Amir, 2004: 111). Given the argument I make in the next chapter regarding Malaysia's Multimedia Super Corridor and the influence of two individuals in the social imaginary – Malaysia's longest serving Prime Minister Mohamad Mahathir, and scientist Tengku Azzman Shariffadeen – this is an important point.

Similarly, Singapore aggressively pursued 'export-oriented industrialization' by deliberately creating conditions that would encourage foreign direct investment (FDI) (McGregor, 2008: 50). The nation's economic development had a fairly conventional trajectory moving from basic industrialization in the early days of independence (1966–1973), to a 'sophistication and broadening of the industrial base' between 1974 and 1978 and a 'restructuring of the economy to higher value-added industries and services between 1979–1984 (A. Lim, 2001: 182). According to Lim, the logic of 'evolution into a high-technology, service-based knowledge economy' emerged post the severe recession of 1985–6 (ibid.).

Singapore's first formal science and technology plan came into being in 1991 (Koh and Wong, 2005: 275) immediately following the formation of the National Science and Technology Board (NSTB) (Toh, 1998: 48). There was a similar focus to Malaysia's on technology transfer through industry-based research and development, and niche areas such as microelectronics, manufacturing technology, biotechnology and medical sciences were identified and specifically targeted (ibid.: 49). Since 1991 successive national plans have been implemented every five years with additional foci such as science added to the strategies. Unlike Malaysia, Singapore's technological direction does not have an East/West distinction. The metaphorical doors of business have always been open to all multinational companies ready to invest in the island state's economy. In the current Science, Technology and Enterprise Plan (STEP) 2011–2015 (Science, Technology and Enterprise Plan 2015, 2011), that emphasis on technology transfer has shifted to a focus on nurturing the innovative talents of locals, schooled at well-funded Singaporean institutes and both trained and employed at research collaborations with industry and local enterprises (ibid.: 2).

In the years leading up to the early 1990s, many Asian nations newly independent in the 1950–60s turned their embryonic economies around through export-oriented strategies (McGregor, 2008: 55). By the end of 1995, the 80 per cent of commodities that Malaysia exported fifteen years previously in 1980 had been successfully turned around to become an equal proportion of manufactured goods (ibid.: 51). According to the Statistical, Economic and Social Research and Training Centre for Islamic Countries, by 2004 Malaysia's high-technology export figures ranked the highest amongst their member nations at $52,867.81 million, followed by Indonesia with $5,808.54 million (Science and Technology in the OIC Member Countries – Executive Summary, 2006: 13).

Through these accomplishments, the new Asian nations earned the attention of the rest of the world in search of a successful model for economic growth, giving rise to reports such as the World Bank's *East Asian Miracle* (*The East Asian Miracle: Economic Growth and Public Policy*, 1993). The following sums up the common view of their success well:

> [t]hey started at the simplest level of technology, by assembling devices such as television sets and simple computers for Western companies. The next stage was to manufacture simple components. Then local companies started to manufacture complete systems of increasing sophistication. (Gwynne, 1993: 12)

Within Southeast Asia, and in particular Singapore and Malaysia, much of the 'economic miracle' was attributed to what later became known as 'Asian values' based, as it were, on their cultural distinctions and emphasis on work ethic and discipline (Barr, 2000), and on a semi-authoritarian model of Asian style democracy (Neher, 1994). Broadly speaking, post-independence the attitudes Malaysia, Indonesia and Singapore held towards technology can be characterized as being of the view that '[t]echnology is inextricably linked to development' in that 'the successes and failures of both are bound together' (J. Smith, 2009: 1).

One way of understanding the interweaving of technology and national development in Malaysia, Indonesia and Singapore is to regard them as manifestations of techno-nationalism. This, as Segal and Naughton define it, is 'a policy orientation toward self-sustained autonomy and independence from other states' (Segal and Naughton, 2001: 2). Given the conditions from which these postcolonial nations emerged, the determination to gain technological autonomy was eminently sensible.

Edgerton argues that as an assumption, techno-nationalism is flawed because it mistakes 'the key unit of analysis for the study of technology' to be the nation (Edgerton, 2007: 1). Contrary to the innovation-centric view, Edgerton insists that 'national economic and technological performance' are not 'determined by *national* rates of innovation (ibid.: 5). Citing the example of the motor car, whose major site of use was the United States even though it was invented in Germany, Edgerton also maintains that the assumption that nations derive advantage from the technologies they innovate is a misperception (Edgerton, 2007: 8).

More important and indeed, according to Edgerton, more prevalent than the idea of technology transfer, is the practice of technology sharing in a global pool (Edgerton, 2007: 8). Hence, he reasons, we may conclude that 'global innovation may be the main determinant of global economic growth' but 'it does not follow that this is the case for particular nation-states' (ibid.). Nonetheless, techno-nationalism prevails because there are other reasons for technology's deep imbrication with the nation as a signification. Of these, one of the more important factors for the nations of Malaysia, Indonesia and Singapore is the link between technology and nation-building. What follows next is a brief discussion on this relationship between technology and nation-building in these contexts.

Technology and nation-building

It is commonly accepted that a society's understandings of time and space influence how the nation is imagined and experienced. This is because many nations cite historical antecedents as the foundation for their claim to nationhood. Israel, China and Japan, for example, continue to look to history and myths of origin from antiquity to anchor their claims to nationhood. However, many others have professed no more profound grounds than the will towards a common destiny born of a shared spatio-temporality (examples include the United States of America, Singapore and Papua New Guinea).

As explained in Chapter 2, in the case of Malaysia, Indonesia and Singapore, claims to nationhood are based on a mixture of claims to shared history and destiny. Whilst there is little dispute that the nation is an imported concept of European origin, following independence both the governments and the people of these lands contributed to the construction of the nation as a shared territory lived in by a human population who have in common historical memories, culture, purpose and destiny.

A number of technologies have been associated with the envisioning of the nation as a unified territory. The visualization of territorial boundaries that takes place in cartography is in itself an enforcement of the idea of rigid bounded borders that govern and delimit the nation. The conquest of distance (and vast tracts of land) is closely associated with the development of transport and communication technologies from telescopes, hot-air balloons (Calhoun, 1997: 15–16) and railways (Schivelbusch, 1980; Verstraete, 2002) to the telegraph (Morus, 2000). Notably, most of these theorists were referring to the influence of technology on the early formation of Western nations.

Anderson's work is amongst the more well known of those that link technology to nation-building. In *Imagined Communities* (1991), Anderson writes of map-making, censuses and museums as being instrumental to the formation of Indonesia. However, the connection Anderson makes between technology's influence on spatio-temporality and its revolutionary effect on politics (and the nation) is not unique and is, in fact, an established trope in socio-technological discourse. For example, Mumford's extensive work, *Technics and Civilization*, published in 1963, details extensively the continuing interplay between human society and technology through the centuries. Still others, such as Eisenstein (1979) have written of this link between socio-political change and technologies of the printing press.

For contemporary liberal democracies, an independent media system fulfils the traditional watchdog function within the adversarial system of checks and balances necessary to the processes of healthy democracies. More often than not, then, it is taken for granted today that the place of media technologies is to create discursive spaces that allow information to be provided, opinions to be expressed, and questions to be asked by an informed citizenry of its government on all manner of issues concerning their society (J. B. Thompson, 1999). At least this is what the Westernized world understands of the relationship between mass media and nations.

In the modern states of Southeast Asia, media technologies took on a different mien because of the sense of urgency surrounding the construction of a consensus within newly independent nations. The learnt sensibility towards racial distinctions, and common experiences of racial riots and the Communist threat meant that post-independence Malaysia as well as Singapore and Indonesia had an amplified awareness of the precarious state of their newly won nationhood and national unity. There was, thus, a heightened appreciation amongst these states of the need to consciously mould popular opinion to ensure support for the project of building a modern nation.

To begin with, the media in Malaysia and Singapore started off with set-ups that remain remarkably similar even today due to the common colonial systems. In both countries the media structure was modelled on the British tradition of state-owned public service broadcasting, which held the role of broadcast media to be 'for social betterment and cultural ideals'. In fact, to this day the Malaysian public service broadcaster, Radio Television Malaysia (RTM), holds the 'promotion of national unity, stimulation of public interest, development of civic consciousness and the provision of information and education' to be its core objectives (Leong and Yap, 2007: 157).

The perceived fragility of consensus has continued to produce a need to manage the instruments of disseminating information to the public so that even today, media in Malaysia, Indonesia and Singapore are subordinated to the task of nation-building. Media control is formally exerted and maintained through a potent mix of media structures, licensing regimes, repressive laws and ownership structures (Nain, 2007; Tsun, 2008; Birch, 1993; Kakiailatu, 2007; Ida, 2011).

Overall, the regime of licences and permits means the ever-present threat of withholding is held over media corporations who rely on their renewal to continue operations. To ensure issue and renewal of these permits and licences, a degree of self-censorship is enforced, aided by the insistence, for example, that the press in Singapore takes up a 'responsible', 'constrained yet constructive' role in nation-building (Tsun, 2008: 882–3; Leong and Yap, 2007: 164). As the struggles that online news portal, Malaysiakini, has undergone to secure a publishing permit under Malaysia's Printing Presses and Publications Act 1984 (PPPA) go to show, publishing information for public readership is regarded as a privilege rather than a right (*Malaysia news portal wins right to start newspaper*, 2012; *Publishing permit a 'privilege', not a right*, 2011).

The Press Publication Enterprise Permit (SIUPP) and its predecessors, the Printing Permit (SIC) and the Publishing Permit (SIT), performed the same duties in Indonesia (Kakiailatu, 2007: 63). As Kakiailatu goes on to explain, despite their opposite positions in reference to Communism during the eras of both President Sukarno and President Suharto, the press in Indonesia was expected to be similarly responsible, 'obeying rules, following instructions' (ibid.: 62) and generally 'complying with the ideology and interests of those in power' (ibid.: 65). With the forced resignation of Suharto in May 1998, President Habibe repealed the SIUPP and the Indonesian press was freed of its restrictions (ibid.: 66).

A suite of laws that are legacies of the colonial administration exert additional layers of media governance in Malaysia and Singapore. These include the Internal Security Act (ISA), the Sedition Act, and the Official Secrets Act, which originated as critical tools of governance during the periods of Communist insurgency of the late 1940s and the racial tensions in the early history of these nations (Tsun, 2008: 883). The threat of incarceration – without trial in the case of the ISA – means that producers of media content take great care that what is published, broadcast and printed cannot be interpreted as seditious or in any way undermining of current government agendas.

The last measure commonly employed in Malaysia, Indonesia and Singapore as an additional means of controlling the effects of media technologies in relation to the nation is media ownership. In Indonesia, traditional and/or broadcast media outlets are owned by major businesses whose interests are aligned with the ruling government (Ida, 2011: 15–16). In Malaysia, traditional media is either directly owned or indirectly controlled by the ruling coalition, Barisan Nasional (BN) (Leong and Yap, 2007: 164). Amongst the most blatant illustrations of how effective media ownership is as a means of managing media content and coverage is the disparity between the access to media enjoyed by the dominant party of the ruling coalition, UMNO, vis-à-vis opposition parties (ibid.: 165).

In Singapore, the 1974 Newspaper and Printing Presses Act (NPPA) was amended so that in addition to ownership by a 'government-linked print media monopoly' (T. Lee, 2010: 130), the state could also 'intervene and impose exacting constraints on the management affairs of newspaper corporations, as well as determine the composition of their boards of directors' (Tsun, 2008: 888). The changes to the media landscape in Indonesia since 1998 are a large part of the reason why while Indonesia rates a two as a country with free political rights and civil liberties, Freedom House's *Freedom in the World*

2012 Report ranks freedom in Malaysia and Singapore at four (partly free) (*Freedom in the World 2012: Table of Independent Countries*, 2012).

Importantly, as will be discussed in Chapter 6, the governments of both Singapore and Malaysia have responded quite differently in recent times to criticisms regarding governmental control of media. For example, amidst criticisms that the changes serve to co-opt media content producers into further self-regulation rather than relax governmental control of media in Malaysia, the annually renewable PPPA was replaced with a one-off licence subject to cancellation and the ISA with the Security Offences Act in Malaysia (Pathmawathy and Zakaria, 2012; Rudra, 2012). In contrast, the Singapore government continues to insist that laws such as the ISA remain relevant to its society (Tengku, 2011).

Into these tightly controlled media environments, the Internet was introduced as a global medium of communication in the middle part of the 1990s. Initially imagined as an independent, anarchic space of expression outside the bounds of the state (Barlow, 1996), the Internet's place in social imaginaries has certainly upset the status quo in these nations and asked questions of the close relationship between media technologies and nation-building even as it raised hopes for national development. What follows in the final section of this chapter is a discussion of the Internet as a signification, which explains the origins of the paradoxical reception the Internet receives in Malaysia, Indonesia and Singapore.

The Internet as a signification

To hear the public speak of the Internet nowadays, it would be easy to believe that its sole purpose is socialization. Yet, as the generations of terms cycled through social imaginaries in the forty years since the Internet's inception demonstrate, the Internet facilitates a lot more than socialization. Of course, in themselves the terms most heavily associated with the Internet at various points – ranging from information super highway, information and communication technologies (ICTs), the World Wide Web, cyberspace, virtual community, e-everything, Web 2.0, social media and new media – are an indication of the functions uppermost in various social imaginaries amongst the suite of technologies that constitute the Internet.

In the idiom of social imaginaries developed here, each term is a potentiality of the Internet as a signification. How these different potentialities emerged is of course an outcome of technological developments. However, rather than highlight the various technical characteristics of the Internet (interactivity, hypertextuality, decentralization, amongst others), I have elected to sketch the socio-cultural influences that led to the dominant ways by which the Internet is understood and experienced.[1] I make no claim to presenting an all-encompassing history of the multiple narratives that are linked to the Internet, its origins or its many technological manifestations. In this book, the Internet is selectively traced through its beginnings as part of socio-technological discourse. For the same reason, the roles of individual inventors, particular innovations and technological advances are also downplayed.

There is some dispute over the original intentions for the Internet and though largely understood as the consequence of the US policy to create a nuclear-proof system of communication during the Cold War era (Abbate, 1999: 21), the Internet owes its beginnings to a more prosaic and familiar objective: that of enabling the sharing of information (Flichy, 2002). This is a task at which it excels, but equally important to the reasons for which the Internet was created is the environment and users for which it was created.

The design of the early Internet was funded by the US government to interlink the information systems of university departments that were engaged in work for the Department of Defense (Abbate, 1999; Naughton, 2000). Founded on public money and created for use in military-scientific environments then gradually adopted into the academic sphere, the Internet was developed with two underlying principles in mind: decentralization, and free as well as shared access to knowledge. These two characteristics of the Internet's earliest manifestations remain influential today and continue to underpin major debates surrounding the Internet, such as that of net neutrality (Nunziato, 2009), copyright (Lessig, 2001) and the Free and Open Source Software (FOSS) movement.

Technology and its implications for societies have long been a matter of speculation, doubt and discussion (Ellul, 1980; Heidegger, 1977; Postman, 1993). The idea that technology affects society is, therefore, a well-established trope and one evinced in both popular media and academic circles. It is quite common in these accounts to associate technological change with new eras in society. Mumford's *Technics and Civilization*, for example, divides sociotechnological development into three distinct phases – the eotechnic, paleotechnic and the neotechnic – each characterized by and associated with the use of certain raw materials or resources, inventions and methods of production (Mumford, 1963: 108).

The classic example of this way of thinking about the relationship between technology and society is Kuhn's *The Structure of Scientific Revolution* (1996, originally published in 1962). Others include volumes such as *Turning Points in Western Technology* (Cardwell, 1972), *Technology in World Civilization* (Pacey, 1990), *A History of Science in History* (Ede and Cormack, 2004) and *Shift! The Unfolding Internet* (Burman, 2003). Like many other technologies before it, the main characteristic imparted to the Internet in these accounts of socio-technological discourse is its consistent casting as a catalyst for change in societies.

Nowhere is the purported capacity of technology to bring about change more highly exaggerated than in science fiction. In this genre, the characteristic understanding of technology has been utilized most often to depict extreme (and outlandish) possibilities of technology. There is, however, a serious side to the entertaining art of writing science fiction and that is the task of dramatizing 'social inquiry' (Amis, 1975: 63). Indeed, the possible effects of technology have been the subject of literary exploration for a long time. One early seventeenth-century example is *New Atlantis* by Francis Bacon (1974, originally published in 1627) in which the advancement of science and/or technology was imagined to be the universal panacea and enabler of utopia.

However, the purposes to which technological knowledge might be lent and the paths down which its pursuit might lead have also been questioned with much unease. Change has not always been associated with progress. Mary Shelley's *Frankenstein* (1973, originally published in 1818) is a classic example. Much serious inquiry into the possible dire consequences of technologically enabled change for societies has also been provoked by writings such as Orwell's *1984* (1954), Huxley's *Brave New World* (1977) and Lessing's *The Sirian Experiments* (1980).

In more recent years, cinematic texts have performed a similar task, albeit in more spectacular fashion. Examples include the *Matrix* trilogy of films produced by the Wachowski brothers (Wachowski and Wachowski, 1999, 2003a, 2003b) and the *Terminator* series directed by Cameron (J. Cameron et al., 2003, 2004). In many instances, the tradition of social inquiry in science fiction is achieved through the employment of the 'novum' (Suvin, cited in Kitchin and Kneale, 2002: 4), a neologism that combines novelty with innovation that is, in turn, validated by cognitive logic. In science fiction works the novum acts to produce cognitive estrangement. In doing so, science fiction forces readers, viewers and listeners to traverse the (intellectual and imaginative) distance between the real and the fantastic through its extension and extrapolation of possibilities, which, over time, renders even the unbelievable believable (Suvin, cited in Kitchin and Kneale, 2002: 5–7).

It is in part this self-appointed mission of science fiction to dramatize social inquiry that lends it and its sub-genre, cyberpunk, a seductive quasi-legitimacy to depict outlandish scenarios as future possibilities. Stationed between that which is known and unknown, cyberpunk literature has led the way and some would argue, given birth to discourses surrounding the Internet through its articulation of new ideas, sensations and words. It was cyberpunk authors who coined terms like 'cyberspace' (Bethke, 1995) and phrases like 'consensual hallucination' (Gibson, 1984: 51).

They were also instrumental to the creation of a counter and/or sub-culture that found expression not only in dress, music and film-making but also attitudes and ways of thinking about technology and authority (Cavallaro, 2000). The work of cyberpunk authors as well as those, like film directors and animation artists, who reproduce their ideas in their films, cartoons and animations, are a major conduit through which ideas about the Internet and cyberspace are disseminated into wider society.

Aside from this particular legacy, socio-technological discourse lends another characteristic to understandings of the Internet: that of an aura of power and mystery. This aura stems in part from technology's roots in the awe and secrecy surrounding the arts of alchemy and magic (Davis, 2002; Ede and Cormack, 2004). The discovery of unknowns and the image of power and prestige attached to the expert as the authority with the answers is an intrinsic component that has been retained in general socio-technological discourse (Marvin, 1988: 61).

The aura of mystery and power was employed, for example, to great effect by latter-day 'magicians' like the electricians of the late nineteenth century who sought to distinguish their profession from that of 'mechanics and tinkerers' (Marvin, 1988: 61) and set themselves up as 'an informed priesthood' (ibid.: 56). In pursuit of social status, acknowledgement, legitimation, and reward, the electricians 'elevat[ed] the theoretical over the practical, the textual over the manual, and science over craft' (ibid.: 61). Today, the elements of power, mystery and romanticism still suffuse the socio-technological discourse and have found their way, firstly, into the understanding and expectations of computers and later into those of the Internet (Coyne, 1999; Mosco, 2004). As Coyne notes:

> The IT [information technologies] world, from computer games to supposed anarchy on the net, similarly celebrates romantic medievalism, its tangled aesthetic, its sense of carnival, and the chaos of the marketplace. The dominant IT culture looks back to a golden age but is always projecting forward. (Coyne, 1999: 10)

Some of this privileging of elites appeared in the titles, systems of hierarchy and governance that prevailed in the earlier forms of Internet games, chat rooms and electronic bulletin boards (Wertheim, 2002: 222). When things go awry in virtual environments, for example, 'wizards' and 'sysops' (system operators), the resident expert and sometimes the creator of the virtual world, are invariably appealed to for rescue. And very often, with a keystroke or two these programmers are able to restyle and reshape online social worlds (Dibbell, 1998: 319).

To a certain extent, the aura of power ascribed to individual expertise is also evinced in accounts of the Internet's development that push the role of visionary individuals such as Vannevar Bush, J. C. R. Licklider and Ted Nelson to the fore (Rheingold, 2000). While there is no doubt as to the importance of their contributions, such emphasis can sometimes have the effect of obscuring the various other forces (ideological, cultural and historical) that are instrumental in the visions themselves (Kitzmann, 2001). The sense of awe for the expert combines with the belief that technology can bring about paradigmatic change, to give the Internet an aura of agency. McLuhan's *Understanding Media: Extensions of Man* (1964) is an early example of this discourse at work. The writings of techno-evangelists like Gilder (1989, 1996) and Negroponte (1995) are later manifestations of the same discourse at work.

Such an understanding is technologically deterministic and has at times been referred to as media determinism, but the purported power of technology to change society remains one of the biggest drawcards of technology and the Internet is no exception. It is easy to understand how such a cause-and-effect understanding of the Internet appeals to nations where social change is urgent but difficult to effect. It is to this overly sanguine understanding of technology as the creator of change that governments and corporations often appeal when launching a new policy, product or service. Visions of the overwhelmingly positive changes that will arrive once a new technology, technological policy or system is implemented are used, for example, to placate disgruntled voters and taxpayers fatigued and outraged by ineffectual state systems.

Together, the potency of its agency and a seductive quasi-legitimacy are two dominant understandings of the Internet that hail from its beginnings within socio-technological discourse and cyberpunk literature. However, as a set of technologies, the Internet hails from a mix of traditions and technologies; the present shape of the Internet was not inevitable as neither the invention nor the routes by which it developed were ever as straightforward as the linear accounts above suggest (Abbate, 1999: 3, 6; Thomas and Wyatt, 1999; Flichy, 2002). There were many developments, social and institutional actors who could at various points have taken different directions and possibly changed the course of what we now know as the Internet. There remain still many future actions that could alter the course of the Internet. The development of the Internet entailed the involvement of multiple layers of players and agencies, and their choices were not always consistent in purpose or vision.

Hence, that the Internet is today a global technology is probably more an incidental than intended consequence of its spread from the confines of the military and experimental scientific communities to the freewheeling ambience of university campuses (Naughton, 2000). Abbate suggests the Internet to be very much the result of an 'unusual (and sometimes uneasy) alliance between civilian and military interests' (1999: 2). The mixed influences of these varied communities, from the scientific and academic to that of the hacker, have left their mark. Their influence is most evident in the Internet's reputation as a medium that promotes collegiality and the open exchange of information.

The examples set by software creators such as Tim Berners-Lee of the World Wide Web (Berners-Lee and Fischetti, 1999) and Linus Torvald of the Linux operating system in making both inventions freely accessible to users and programmers both illustrate and perpetuate this understanding of the Internet. Yet, in the early history of the Internet they were by no means the exception. Small groups and individuals put these attitudes into practice on a daily basis developing share and freeware and beta testing software.

One of the core influences that fed into the playful, experimental and sometimes subversive attitudes of these diverse groups of early adopters was cyberpunk literature. For these 'lead users' (Oudshoorn and Pinch, 2008) the Internet was both a space and a technology that could be used to imagine, create, build, test, change, adapt, exchange and erase all kinds of boundaries from the spatio-temporal and corporeal to the national. The identities they created for themselves were not always consistent with their day-to-day identities,[2] as different and multiple identities were created and explored (Turkle, 1995).

The communities and worlds these users created were based on commonalities seemingly as trivial as a love for Siamese cats and electric guitars. Many of these communities and virtual worlds aggregated members over days who literally built their world together over thousands of conversations and interactions. Others morphed and dissolved under surreal circumstances (Dibbell, 1998). In doing so, these pioneers not only underwent but also documented experiences wherein many of the constraints of the non-digital world were transcended. These included the constraints generally placed on individuals by their specific educational and income level, gender and identity as well as the constraints of time, space, distance, reach and nation-state borders.

The near-viral circulation of optimistic early accounts, such as *The Virtual Community* (Rheingold, 1993), *Cyberspace and the American Dream* (Dyson et al., 1994), *Being Digital* (Negroponte, 1995), and *A Declaration of the Independence of Cyberspace* (Barlow, 1996) were accompanied by academic research on the phenomenon of the Internet itself (Benedikt, 1991; Castells, 1996; Hayles, 1993; Heim, 1995; Poster, 1995a, 1995b). In combination, these narratives both fostered and questioned the belief that the '[i]nternet belongs to everyone and no one' but is rather 'an institution that resists institutionalization' (Sterling, 1993). It was the Internet's socio-political potential that most clearly caught and fired the imagination of its early adopters.

When the Internet was eventually commercialized in the mid-1990s, entrepreneurs who sought to capitalize on the Internet's reputed ability to defy spatio-temporal and nation-state boundaries were quick to appropriate this understanding for their purposes. It is to these overlapping influences, attitudes, exploits and their accounts that the Internet owes its enduring underlying understanding as an anarchic environment. The history of the Internet is peppered with claims that it is responsible for many revolutions. These range from the creation of a separate, anarchic realm outside of national jurisdiction and constraints (Barlow, 1996) and the empowerment of the oppressed (Cleaver, 1994) to the reinvigoration of the public sphere and democracy (Dahlberg, 2001). Many of these claims have at least some part of their origins in the dominant understandings of the Internet as an environment conducive to anarchy, possessed of an aura of agency and a quasi-legitimacy to effect change.

Alongside its growth from novel and exclusive to emerging, then down to commonplace and ubiquitous, the Internet has been endowed with a multitude of labels. In earlier versions, these comprised mostly metaphors that sought to focus attention on the future potentialities of the technologies and user experiences. Current terminologies such as 'Web 2.0 [3.0 too]', 'semantic Web', and 'mobile or wireless Internet' tend towards 'the logic of linking, categorizing and accessing information through different platforms' and as such are 'decidedly technical and descriptive in nature' (Paasonen, 2008: 28).

Paasonen notes that Anglophonic conceptualizations dominate this habit but goes on to reason that this is due to 'the US influence in the development of the Internet technology and content, as well as the real dominance of English in academia' (Paasonen, 2008: 27). Flichy suggests that '[w]ithout the myths produced by the American counter-culture in the early seventies, the microcomputer would probably have remained a mere curiosity' (Flichy, 2002: 139), which suggests the Internet might have followed suit. The fact of this dominance is important because how technologies are imagined, what Thomas and Wyatt term the 'technological imagination', is an intrinsic part of how technologies eventually develop (Thomas and Wyatt, 1999: 695).

For example, the contemporary term 'social media' clearly favours the place of the Internet in everyday socialization but it does so at the expense of downplaying the other capacities the Internet enables in our world. Though social media such as the microblogging platform Twitter and social networking sites like Facebook, MySpace, Bebo and Friendster represent but a fraction of the Internet, their current pre-eminence in many societies serves to obscure other potentialities of the Internet. Somewhat alarmingly, for many it also associates socialization so tightly with Internet technologies that increasingly to socialize in the twenty-first century is to do so via social media.

All this is not to indulge in the futile sport of social media bashing. Rather, it is to make the point that how technologies are used is often a consequence of what is assumed and expected of them. If these assumptions and expectations are biased towards one aspect and negligent of others, our usage of these technologies will be similarly directed. Though it is now common sense and a 'linguistic habit' to name an age after the technologies that most dominate that period and society (Wyatt, 2008: 168), it is folly to think it a natural matter of course. Metaphors, labels or hyperbole, the ascent of some and the obsolescence of others capture the various social, economic, political and cultural forces that tug at each other in the background even as they inflect the course of future technological development.

In more recent times, such understandings of the Internet have also been tempered in developed nations like the United States, Japan and South Korea by an alternative view of the Internet as a ubiquitous technology. This understanding argues the Internet has become so commonplace and such a blasé part of human society that it has blended into the background of daily life. Like the telephone and the microwave, the Internet is no longer novel, unusual or remarkable but merely yet another integrated technology to be utilized as per one's needs (Mosco, 2004; Wellman and Haythornthwaite, 2002).

In fact, Wellman and Haythornthwaite suggest that we have moved 'from a world of Internet wizards to a world of ordinary people routinely using the Internet as an embedded part of their life' (Wellman and Haythornthwaite, 2002: 6). It needs to be said that such a statement is generally applicable only in parts of the world where Internet accessibility is readily available and affordable to the majority. In nations where the advent of the Internet is linked to broader state agendas of modernization, socio-economic development and redistribution of wealth, such ubiquity appears to be the objective rather than the context of Internet development.

For better or worse, taken together, the various histories, origins and myths surrounding the Internet as a suite of technologies has provided it with a range of potentialities within social imaginaries. These range from its banal function as a medium of communication and a space where commercial profit may be spun out of little and an instrument of change, by virtue of the connectivity it enables amongst people. Decentralized, anarchic and transcendentally global, the Internet in all its forms has been associated in social imaginaries around the world with the good – such as the 2011 Arab Spring movement that saw the topple of governments across North Africa and the Middle East (K. K. Taylor, 2011) – the bad, like the London riots (D. Cameron, 2011), and depending on one's perspective, the obscene or the ridiculous like the US$38 price of Facebook shares at its initial public offering (*Facebook share price halves since IPO*, 2012).

These potentialities feed into the possibilities that governments envision when they introduce, expand and invest in the Internet. In Malaysia the Internet first became available in 1990 when its first Internet service provider, JARING (Joint Advanced Research Integrated Networking) was established (Bahfen, 2008: 166). A year later in 1991 then Prime Minister Mahathir launched the *Vision 2020* concept (Mahathir, 1991). It was another five years before the Multimedia Super Corridor (MSC) mega project was launched in 1996 (*Malaysia's Multimedia Super Corridor Proposal*, 1996).

Conclusion

There is enormous promise in technology for development, which is why governments continue to turn to science and technology to generate economic growth, create jobs and spur innovations. At the same time, there is also great potential in media technologies for the creation of commonalities, influencing of public opinion and nation-building. In the first two sections of this chapter I have shown how Malaysia, like Indonesia and Singapore, has enlisted technology in its economic development and, in particular, managed the characteristics of media technologies to aid in its national agendas.

The shape of the relationships between technology and nations such as Malaysia, Indonesia and Singapore emerges as much out of the conditions within which they were formed as the futures these nations aspired to. As Smith asserts, 'science and technology do not exist as some abstraction of a process of modernization. They are absolutely contingent on the contours of inequality and social, political and economic problems that shape our world. In other words, like science, technologies such as the Internet are "absolutely enmeshed in society"' (J. Smith, 2009: 126).

In the last section I have argued that while it is possible to reduce a technology to its bare-boned hardware components, technologies are far from neutral elements. From electricity and telegraph to the automobile the introduction of technologies into societies brings not just new practices and ways of doing things that were previously more onerous, but also embedded within technologies like the Internet are ways of understanding and assumptions about the world that can have profound consequences when newly introduced into social imaginaries.

In the next chapter I will focus on the Multimedia Super Corridor as a specific manifestation of the relationship between the nation of Malaysia and the Internet as a suite of technologies. Although primarily advanced as a strategy for developing certain technological and economic objectives, the possibilities that informed its conception by the Malaysian government were almost certainly derived from the discourses that surrounded the early days of the Internet such as those described above. It is worth noting that in the MSC, the zoning technology, the need to set Malaysia apart from its Asian neighbours and the potential of leapfrogging to the status of developed nation, and the practices and ideas discussed in the various sections above, were brought together to considerable effect (Tidd and Brocklehurst, 1999: 251).

The MSC was always nested within Prime Minister Mahathir's grand plan to lift Malaysia from developing to developed nation status by the year 2020, Vision 2020. It also formed the basis of many of Mahathir's most ambitious schemes in the last decade or so of his regime. Within that plan, 'information [was] singled out as the "factor of change" that would allow Malaysia to pass both "industrial society" and "developed society" and become a "post-industrial/advanced industrial society"' (National IT Council, cited in Uimonen, 2003: 301). In itself that is not highly unusual, as many smaller nations look on 'ICT [information and communication technology] as "a sign of things to come, a tool for the future as well as a means of national self-promotion"' (Paasonen, 2008: 24). Some of the factors that fed into the formation of the MSC have been explored here; the next chapter discusses how the project was envisioned and the implications its ongoing realization has created within the Malaysian social imaginary thus far.

Notes

1 A detailed account of the technical challenges that had to be faced and the solutions that various parties arrived at in order to make the Internet a reality can be found in Leiner et al., 2000.
2 As the literature shows, the Internet's earliest adopters were predominantly white, affluent and male in their 20s to 40s (Clemente, 1998: 53; Brown et al., 1995).

4 Malaysia and new media
The Multimedia Super Corridor

In previous chapters I have discussed the nation and the Internet as significations. The nation, I argue, is lived and experienced in Malaysia as inextricably interwoven with understandings of race and religion. As a signification the Internet emerges from a multiplicity of histories and assumptions about technology that accompanied its introduction into the Malaysian social imaginary in the middle of the 1990s. These same implicit understandings are also the foundation from which the Multimedia Super Corridor (MSC) mega project was envisioned. This chapter discusses the MSC project as a uniquely Malaysian manifestation of the imbrication between the nation and the Internet.

I argue this manifestation to be particular to Malaysia because of its colonial history and the place that technology occupies in the nation's early development. It is also specific to this nation because of the manner in which technology, in the form of media and communication, is applied to the task of nation-building in Malaysia. In this chapter I bring together all of the four significations discussed in previous chapters – nation, Internet, race and religion – and use the MSC to explain how the dynamics between them come to create expectations and experiences of the Internet as a signification that are unique to Malaysia.

It is my argument that there is an irreconcilable conflict between the MSC mega project's ideation and execution. This conflict arises from the incompatibility between the liberal technological space from which the MSC's ideation emerges and the national society within which the project is executed. In other words, the signification of nation enacted as Malaysia does not match the signification of the Internet that is depicted, as it is with the MSC, as the engine of socio-technological and economic progress. Further, I contend that, being cognizant of the potential conflict between ideation and execution, those who envisioned the mega project took measures to reconcile and contain the incongruities.

The first of these measures is the construction of a distinctly Malaysian approach towards technology and an associated knowledge-based economy that is imbued with specific Islamic qualities, and is thus values-based rather than values-neutral (Shariffadeen, 2009). The values in question are drawn from the discourse of an Islamic modernity of which Mohamad Mahathir, the nation's Prime Minister from 1981 to 2003, is a long-time and key proponent. Though Mahathir's advancement of such an understanding pre-dates the MSC, it gains added import from the advocacy and credentials of the project's other founder-visionary, Tengku Mohd Azzman Shariffadeen (hereafter Shariffadeen). Notably, the discourse of a values-based knowledge society is one that Shariffadeen (2012) continues to expound today.

The overriding intention for the construction of such an approach is to convince the Muslim majority in Malaysia that technological advancement with a view to material progress is compatible with the teachings of Islam, and is hence worthwhile and desirable. The second set of measures rests primarily on the notion of zoning technologies (Aihwa Ong, 2004) and is combined with existing stringent laws regarding the expression of public dissent. Its main purpose is to confine the techno-liberalism introduced alongside the unfettered Internet demanded by multinational (if mostly Western) corporations as a condition of their initial participation in the MSC (Furlow, 2009: 206).

From the perspective of the general population of Malaysia, the obvious and immediate impact of the MSC derives from two developments: the physical and legal infrastructures the mega project has enabled, such as the high-speed broadband networks and capital works financed by the state, and the flagship applications designed to provide content and reason for accessing said networks. However, up to this point, despite the above-mentioned measures to contain and restrain them, the greater impact of the MSC seems to be coming from the shifts in the levels of participation in political expression and action that have accompanied the enlargement of civil society inadvertently facilitated by the project's implementation.

To analyse the MSC mega project's ideation, I focus on two of its highest profile shapers: Malaysia's fourth Prime Minister, Mohamad Mahathir, and Tengku Mohd Azzman Shariffadeen. They are, of course, not the only ones to have had a hand in envisioning the project. Others working within committees have clearly been vital to the process (Huff, 2002: 240). However, as the public faces of the political and techno-scientific aspects of the MSC project respectively, their influence has been crucial to understanding how the MSC was formed and experienced on the national and global fronts. The account of their influence is followed by a brief review of the MSC as enacted to-date. Finally, I conclude that despite its inherent internal conflicts and uncertain progress as a plan for national development, the responses and reactions to the mega project may still produce unintended changes in how Malaysia is imagined and experienced as a nation.

Ideation

In the interest of brevity, I begin the narrative of the MSC with the launch of the Vision 2020 statement. This is not to negate that fact that Malaysia has an established nation-building framework of five-year plans (currently in its tenth incarnation) that outline and align its emphases and future directions. Among other things, successive Malaysia Plans map the population's changing needs, expectations and demands of technology. The Malaysia Plans are complemented by a series of overlapping national policy frameworks that shape Malaysia's economic direction (The Ninth Malaysia Plan: 2006–2010, 2006: 3).

These include the New Economic Policy (NEP) introduced in 1971, which was succeeded by the New Development Policy (NDP) in 1990 to 2000, and then itself replaced by the National Vision Policy (NVP) in 2001. The current policy in place is the New Economic Model (NEM), initiated by Malaysia's sixth and incumbent Prime Minister, Najib Razak.[1] These intersecting plans and initiatives both pre- and post-date the MSC and constituted many of the socio-political and material conditions of its ideation, development, execution and operation. The MSC must, therefore, be proportionately viewed within the overall nation-building efforts of the Malaysian government.

Prime Minister Mohamad Mahathir first broached the notion that developed nation status was within Malaysia's grasp in 1991 with the public announcement of the Vision 2020 Statement (Mahathir, 1991). The turn of phrase 'Vision 2020', as has been pointed out by Uimonen (2003: 300), is both a play on the twentieth spot on the list of developed nations that Malaysia aspires to, and is rich with utopian, temporal and visual associations (perfect vision being commonly referred to as '20–20' vision). Mahathir confirms as much in his latest memoirs where he describes Vision 2020 as an effort to provide a 'clear idea of where we wanted to go and what we wanted to be by the year 2020' (Mahathir, 2011: 596). In Mahathir's vision of Malaysia's future direction, the attainment of developed nation status was proclaimed a long-term objective for Malaysia (Mahathir, 1991).

Technology was not a prominent feature of Vision 2020 until the Multimedia Super Corridor mega project's launch, five years later, in 1996. According to Mahathir, it was Kenichi Ohmae, a Japanese business consultant then working with McKinsey & Co, who helped him understand the technologies involved. It was also Ohmae who first mooted the 'unique approach' of creating 'an identified area within which certain concessions and advantages would be made available to people working in the IT field' (Mahathir, 2011: 634). From the moment the MSC was launched, Mahathir's zealous efforts to persuade Malaysians of the virtues of investing in a custom-designed technological zone in his country[2] meant that within the nation the MSC is regarded primarily as Mahathir's brain-child (Huff, 2002).

The MSC was an essential part of Mahathir's plan to move the country away from its heavy reliance on mass manufacturing that had until then typified industrialization in Malaysia. The Prime Minister was convinced that information technology (IT) would 'speed up national development' (Harun, 1995). Once launched, both Mahathir and his ministers worked hard at home to convince Malaysians that the Internet was 'key to economic growth', as well as abroad to announce their ambitious blueprint to the world, tie it to the then fascination with the East Asian miracle, and encourage investors from all over the world to be part of it (*In a quest to upgrade the industries*, 1996). It is fair to say, then, that the MSC is a further exemplification of Malaysian techno-nationalism discussed in the previous chapter.

When Prime Minister Mahathir launched the MSC mega project in 1996, he described it as a 'test-bed' where there would be: 'the new roles of Government, new cyber laws and guarantees, collaborations between Government and companies, companies and companies, new broadcasting and new types of entertainment, education, delivery of healthcare, and applications of new technologies' (Mahathir, 1997).

Mahathir's words have been interpreted to mean that the MSC was also an experiment to test whether race could replace class as a primary category of social organization in Malaysia (Lepawsky, 2005b: 718; Bunnell and Coe, 2005: 843). Given that spatially the MSC began as a land corridor of specific proportions (15 × 50 km), it seems eminently suitable to consider it as an effort to conduct an experiment under controlled conditions.

Such tentative readings should, of course, be performed alongside Mahathir's tendency to leave some of his ideas open to surmise rather than spell out exactly what he means to convey. For example, in the speech announcing Vision 2020, *The Way Forward*, Mahathir urged all Malaysians to eschew the deep and old resentments against the pro-*Bumiputera* affirmative action in order to achieve 'a mental revolution' and a 'cultural transformation' and unite as one 'Bangsa Malaysia' (Mahathir, 1991). The term 'Bangsa Malaysia' itself is variously translatable as Malaysian race or nation. Given how deeply ingrained racial differences remain in how Malaysia is organized as a nation and how much race structures the lives of Malaysians, the possibility that Mahathir meant that all three clear and separate races (Chinese, Malay, Indian and Others, CMIO) may be collapsed into one broad unifying category remains a controversial and optimistic reading.[3]

However one interprets the multifarious intentions that prompted the ideation of the MSC, the underlying link between its two prime movers, Mahathir and Shariffadeen, is a version of Islam that some have called 'pragmatic Islam' (Wain, 2009). Pragmatic Islam, as it was and still is asserted by Mahathir, is a religion that finds it 'incumbent upon Muslims to embrace modernity and economic progress to overcome their backwardness and recover Islam's past glory' (Wain, 2009: 217).

According to Wain, Mahathir's main objective in espousing such an interpretation of Islam is to contrast it against 'Malay-style' Islam, which Mahathir criticized as 'a cause of Malay failure and a barrier to national development' (Wain, 2009: 221). In Mahathir's books, the passivity encouraged by 'fatalistic tendencies', 'disinclination' to competition and 'preference for spiritual over material pursuits' of such a style of Islam is the cause of the Malay community's backwardness. Seen in the light of Mahathir's authorship of *The Malay Dilemma* (1970), where such views were first voiced, and his subsequent political rise as the champion of Malays in the 1980s, Mahathir's determination and exhortations towards Muslims[4] to abandon the old ways in favour of progress was understandable.

The authority Mahathir claims for advancing such an interpretation comes from the argument that 'individual Muslims had the right to engage in rationalistic re-readings of the sources of Islamic law' (Schottmann, 2011: 356). Rather than rely on the mediation of Islam scholars and their interpretations of the Koran, Mahathir pushed for ordinary Muslims to take up the direct study and practice of Islam personally. Schottmann argues that it is appropriate to dub this rationalized interpretation of Islam as 'Mahathir's Islam' because it was consistently articulated and elaborated on by Mahathir both before, during and after his tenure as Prime Minister of Malaysia (Schottmann, 2011).

Additionally, Schottmann believes it is possible to divide the public discourse of 'Mahathir's Islam' into four broad areas:

> (1) the teachings of the prophet Muhammad as a this-worldly manual encouraging material success; (2) the inapplicability of the secular principle to Islam; (3) the range of virtues and behaviours Muslims should adopt; and (4) a depiction of a suitably contemporary practice and observance of Islam. (Schottmann, 2011: 357)

All four aspects have played a part in what Noor describes as the battle for reformist Islam in Malaysia. Notably, this is a struggle that also occurs in Indonesia (Laffan, 2003).

Within the framework of social imaginaries developed in this book, we could consider 'Mahathir's Islam' a potentiality of Islam as a signification. Whilst Schottmann speaks of 'Mahathir's Islam', both Noor (2008) and Wain (2009) aver that much of what developed into this discourse had its genesis in political objectives. In their view it was more the need to assert UMNO's place as the party representative of the majority Muslim population vis-à-vis the conservative Pan-Malaysian Islamic Party's (PAS) that motivated the increasingly assertive advocacy of moderate Islam by UMNO and Mahathir.

Additionally, Noor suggests that 'contests over the form, meaning, and content of Islam have been raging since long before the country gained independence' (Noor, 2008: 208). As such, the reinvention of Islam is not particular to Mahathir's administration but rather part of the 'close interaction between Islam and politics in Malaysia [that] dates from the late nineteenth century' (ibid.: 209). I have argued as much in the discussion on the imbrications between race, religion and nation in Chapter 2.

Nonetheless, however far back we reach for its antecedents and whatever labels we ascribe to it – Mahathir's Islam, pragmatic Islam, moderate Islam – what is important in the context of this chapter is that the 'core message, that there is no conflict between Islamic values and Malaysian-style capitalism, development and prosperity' (Wain, 2009: 223), is one of the foundations on which the Multimedia Super Corridor was formed and the platform from which Shariffadeen's ideas about a 'values-based knowledge economy' were launched (2012).

Shariffadeen is the other person instrumental to the envisioning of the MSC project. An academic and technologist, Shariffadeen is part of Malaysia's 'technological elite' (Huff, 2001: 450; Huff, 2002: 263). He founded the Islamic Academy of Science (ASAS) in 1978, an institute that 'plays the role of advocating Islamic science' (Lotfalian, 2004: 64) and is as such a bona fide technocrat. Made Director-General of the Malaysian Institute of Microelectronic Systems (MIMOS) in 1984, Shariffadeen was appointed Chief Executive of MIMOS on its corporatization in 1996 (*Azzman appointed chief executive of Mimos Berhad*, 1996) and became the chief spokesperson for the MSC, a role he continues to fulfil up to the present moment (Shariffadeen, 2012). For these reasons it is possible to say Shariffadeen's role in the MSC is to provide the project with techno-scientific credentials, much as B. J. Habibe did for the aircraft industry in Indonesia during an earlier decade (see Chapter 3).

During the ideation phase of the MSC, Mahathir and Shariffadeen shared the task of promoting the vision of technology as an integral part of Malaysia's plans to leapfrog from an industrialized to a post-industrial economy; Shariffadeen acknowledges as much in a 1997 interview with a local newspaper (Ang, 1997b). From the views Shariffadeen expressed through media reports, conference presentations and papers, it is evident that he has always been aware of the implications that the MSC – as a developmental strategy built around globally networked technologies – might have for Malaysia.

For example, in a 1995 paper entitled 'New Communications Era: Economic, Social, and Cultural Consequences for Developing Nations', Shariffadeen advocates an Open Strategy with regard to national development based on seven principles, including political openness in the form of access to information and knowledge regardless of 'a nation's political stance, the religion of its people, or its racial make-up' (Shariffadeen, 1995: 82). However, he concludes that: '[t]he new communications era should not be perceived as a purely technological phenomenon. *Its ultimate impact is social and cultural*' (ibid., my emphasis). Not surprisingly, in 1997 Shariffadeen described the MSC as a 'multimedia utopia' (Shariffadeen, 1997: 3) consisting of 'globally free flowing content' within an 'orderly anarchy' with the potential to be 'democratic and open, participative and consensus-building' (Ang, 1997b).

At the same time, Shariffadeen also advocates that the challenges presented to 'traditional values and indigenous cultures' by said utopia be met by a values-based civil society (*Country has long way to go in information technology*, 1996). The notion of a values-based knowledge society was first raised in the National IT Agenda (NITA). Its tacit critique of Western societies as secular and value-neutral is Shariffadeen's basis for the constructions of an alternative world-view wherein knowledge is regarded as 'the true basis of faith and belief' (Shariffadeen, 1996).

Accordingly, for Shariffadeen, the best defence against the threat of encroachment is the formation of a Malaysian civil society based on some form of non-Western communitarian model wherein '[s]hared values and attitudes, common cultural norms, the sense of belonging and loyalty to a particular group and an implied social contract are all present in such communities in one form or another' (Shariffadeen, 1996).

Shariffadeen clarifies exactly whose values and which community he alludes to in later papers and presentations (2006, 2009). In these, he invokes the *Maqasid al Shari'ah* (the Objectives of Islamic Law) as the basis for a 'soft approach' towards enabling the knowledge-based economy. Faith (*din*), self (*nafs*), intellect (*'aql*), posterity (*nasl*) and wealth (*mal*) are all named as that which the Law safeguards.

They are, in turn, interlinked with notions of 'knowledge-driven individuals' who possess and create '[k]nowledge for human development' in order to build and participate in an 'Equitable Knowledge Economy' that ultimately brings about '[f]amily solidarity and [e]cological balance' (Shariffadeen, 2009). Shariffadeen's description of these intelligent knowledge workers certainly seems to echo Mahathir's vision of the 'Melayu Baru' (new Malay) (Furlow, 2009: 205).

It is important to note that the erection of such a binary opposition was par for the course in the context of Southeast Asia, where the notion of a corporatist Asian democracy wherein 'economic development must precede liberal democracy' had been building up through the 1980s (Neher, 1994: 959). Indeed, whereas the 'Singapore school' of Asian values had through the strenuous efforts of its elder statesman, Lee Kuan Yew, ascribed the nation's part in the East Asian Miracle to Confucian values (Barr, 2000: 309), the corresponding 'Malaysian school' can be said to have been attempting to explain Malaysia's success as an outcome of Islamic values.

What is clear from the above is that Shariffadeen understands Islamic values to be the ideal foundation of a Malaysian civil society. Going by his reference to the 'implied social contract' in the passage cited above, Shariffadeen also appears to subscribe to the notion of *Ketuanan Melayu* or Malay supremacy/ paramountcy, introduced by the colonial administration and still widely held by some today to be a sacrosanct principle of the Malaysian political system (Chin, 2009: 1).

True to his techno-scientific sensibilities, Shariffadeen has always acknowledged the possibility of failure (Amry, 1997), so much so that more than a dozen years into the project in 2009, he continued to refer to the MSC and its ultimate objective of creating a knowledge-based economy in Malaysia as an experiment (Shariffadeen, 2006). As a developmental strategy, the MSC is a hybrid of many different technologies of governance and administration (Indergaard, 2003: 397). Felker argues that such a strategy might be more appropriately known as techno-glocalism, where techniques are adopted that 'seek to harness global dynamics and partner with global actors, in order to build capabilities that are localized' (Felker, 2009: 478).

In the words of Mahathir, the MSC is 'a carefully constructed mechanism to enable mutual enrichment of companies and countries using leading technologies and the borderless world' by employing a 'singled-minded approach to developing the country' (Mahathir, 1996). Shariffadeen phrases it differently as an invitation to both foreign and local investors to 'tak[e] advantage of the state-of-the-art IT infrastructure to develop multimedia and other related products and services' (C. Nelson, 1995).

The MDeC (Multimedia Development Corporation), the company formed to manage the MSC, states that the project is deliberately modelled on Silicon Valley in the United States (*What is the MSC Malaysia?*, 2011). According to Castells (2000), Silicon Valley is an instance of 'the network society'[5] 'where the key social structures and activities are organized around electronically processed information networks' (Kreisler, 2001). I suggest that despite the MDeC's claim, some parts of the MSC blueprint borrow from another instance of the network society – the Finnish model as typified by the networks surrounding mobile telephone firm Nokia. This difference is important because it speaks to the conflict that exists between the ideation and execution of the MSC. Let me explain.

The bulk of the capital investment and demand that led to the start up of Silicon Valley in the United States came from the US Defense Department during the 1950s and 1960s. As part of the US strategy to shore up its own military capabilities and maintain its place as a leading superpower against the Soviet Union, the US was motivated to fund technological development in corporations and universities in the San Francisco Bay Area (Himanen and Castells, 2004: 56–7). Both the Internet and the subsequent development of Silicon Valley itself are a result of the state's patronage, though private capital is now their largest source of funding.

In Finland, the role of the state was much more dispersed both temporally and spatially. In the first instance, the Finnish state encourages innovation through policies biased towards an open regulatory environment (Himanen and Castells, 2004: 69). State support is also apparent in the long-term establishment of a free, public and world-class university system, which is heavily geared towards technological disciplines and the training of top calibre science, engineering and mathematics graduates (Himanen and Castells, 2004: 70). In 56 institutions spread across the nation, Finland's highly inclusive university system educates no less than 70 per cent of the young generation (ibid.). However, this is not the only way that the Finnish state intervenes to create the right conditions for a 'milieu of innovation' (Castells, 2000).

The welfare state system works in tandem with the education system to provide a level of security and comfort for Finns that is highly conducive to intellectual and technological innovation. The lack of financial pressure on students, for example, allows Finns to spend considerable lengths of time at tertiary level researching, experimenting and developing ideas while working with others. This culture of innovation is well established and there are many, like Linus Torvalds of Linux fame, who owe their innovations and inventions to the intellectual and physical environment fostered by these conditions (Himanen and Castells, 2004: 74–7).

Conversely, the universities in the San Francisco Bay Area where Silicon Valley is situated are elite tertiary institutions. Students pay exorbitant fees to study there and competition is fierce both within and between universities. While the culture of innovation is now established and responsible for attracting inter-state and overseas talent to work there, the universities in the Bay Area provided the main pool of talent from which Silicon Valley was started (Himanen and Castells, 2004: 56, 60).

According to Himanen and Castells, what distinguishes Silicon Valley from other models is 'a strong entrepreneurial culture' (2004: 61). In fact, small specialist firms started up at astonishing rates by techno-visionaries with a pioneering mindset, financed by venture capitalists and advisers experienced in the financial risks involved, are typical in Silicon Valley (ibid.: 61–3). Both Silicon Valley and the Finnish model are similar in that they are communities built around technological innovation in which the major social structures and activities are organized around electronic networks that developed at around the same period of the twentieth century. Yet, aside from having been created by social, cultural and economic conditions and ways of thinking that are markedly different, they are also sustained in very different ways.

For example, while the American model is largely sustained nowadays by individual and corporate entrepreneurialism in the form of technological advances and venture capital, the Finnish model is fuelled by the continuing flow of technologically inclined talent from universities and the corporate 'sharing of signals about future expectations' with both internal and external parties, spearheaded by mobile telephone firm Nokia (Himanen and Castells, 2004: 76). It seems remarkable that two such similar techno-inspired economic developments emerged from such deeply contrasting styles of governance as American liberalism and Finnish socialism, and their infrastructural and institutional contexts. As Himanen and Castells (2004) illustrate, either the state or commercial interests or a combination of both can provide physical framework and infrastructure.

The acquisition of land for the purposes of setting up these ventures, for example, can be accomplished by state allocation or paid for by corporations. It could equally be facilitated by the state making land available to corporations under favourable conditions. The same is true of infrastructure like bandwidth, fibre links, investment capital and policy frameworks. In almost all cases, because these high-tech developments are seen to be beneficial to national progress, states work with corporations to ensure the optimal conditions for operations to exist. The one exception is the supply of human capital, which in most cases is primarily the task of the state. This is usually part of a long-term education strategy and is probably amongst the most crucial of the institutional factors.

Entrepreneurial factors include a culture that encourages innovation; for example, a predisposition towards experimentation, and openness towards sharing of knowledge with others. Importantly, they also include qualities like resourcefulness and adaptability, a robust work ethic, and resilience in the face of risks and failure (B. Ramasamy et al., 2003: 880–1). Clearly, these attributes cannot be cultivated over the short term as they are a result of social, cultural and institutional influences that individuals experience. Interestingly, entrepreneurial factors are not, as the Finnish model illustrates, solely the characteristics of those who thrive in a market-driven system but can also be fostered by a benevolent state.

Both the state and the prevailing socio-political climate within the nation can and do play vital roles in creating the combination of institutional and entrepreneurial factors crucial to the success of these 'intelligent corridors' (Corey, 2000: 1). Certainly, they play no less a role when it comes to the facilitation of tangible arrangements of land, buildings, cables and the abstract framework of policies and regulations, than the ephemeral qualities of a pioneering spirit and attitude towards risk or failure.

The material conditions necessary to the cultivation of institutional and entrepreneurial factors include an environment and infrastructure conducive to technological and entrepreneurial innovation, universities strategically located to provide a steady stream of university-educated science and engineering graduates, a variety of sources happy to fund multiple speculative ventures, and a vibrant network providing legal and marketing support services (Himanen and Castells, 2004).

In itself, the expectation that a local version of these 'milieux of innovation' (Castells, 2000: 419) can be created in Malaysia once the right mechanisms, incentives and resources are in place is reasonable. After all, as has been argued, there appears to be 'no single path to the achievement of a successful technopole' (Castells and Hall, 1994: 250). This seems evident too from the vastly differing socio-political situations within which the successes of Silicon Valley and Finland have emerged. While the former is a product of America's liberal democracy, the latter is that of a welfare state.

Despite being 'contrasting models' (Himanen and Castells, 2004: 81) and hailing from such divergent conditions, both of these cases managed to create outstanding cultures of innovation, and logic dictates that the Malaysian nation-state should be more than equal to the task. Still, there are those who insist 'particular growth experience ... cannot be generalised to the rest of the world. Precisely because they took place where and when they did, by definition they prevented the rest of the world from doing the same' (Saravanamuttu, 1988: 10).

Corey suggests that another way to understand how the success of these 'intelligent corridors' (2000: 1) has been achieved is through the factors that have contributed to the realization of these 'digital districts', which he argues are quite easily grouped into one of two categories: institutional and entrepreneurial. Ramasamy, Chakrabarty and Cheah further explain that institutional factors include the physical framework, infrastructure and human capital, whilst entrepreneurial factors are much less tangible and refer to the culture and socio-institutional conditions that encourage the spirit of innovation and entrepreneurialism (B. Ramasamy et al., 2003: 873).

One might say that the MSC's current enactment of the innovation milieu, given the Malaysian state's prominent institutional role as prime mover in the developmental strategy, owes more to the Finnish model than that of Silicon Valley. After all, despite the exhortations to excellence under one's own entrepreneurial steam within the MSC, the decades-long expectation that the government would aid the *Bumiputeras* in all matters socio-economic remains on all fronts (Chin, 2009).

Yet it remains the case that, rather than the Finnish model, it is the Silicon Valley model that emerged from a full-blown, freewheeling liberalism of competitive enterprise. To paraphrase Shariffadeen, it is part accident and part plan that this is the model that the MSC aspires to eventually transition to (Nelson, 1995). It is in this ambition to evolve from the hybrid model to the Silicon Valley model that the first cracks between the MSC's ideation and execution show. Given this, why does MDeC persist in claiming Silicon Valley as ideational seed, when the perceived need to define the MSC in deep contradistinction to Western versions of the knowledge society is equally urgent?

To be sure, refusal to import Western ideas wholesale is not a spur-of-the-moment invention of either Shariffadeen or Mahathir. The latter, in particular, has a well-known and trenchant dislike of 'big countries' (Wain, 2009: 242) and a history of preferring to look to the East rather than the West (Furuoka, 2007). Such is evidenced right from the start of the MSC by the Japanese Corporation NTT's role in drawing up the MSC proposal (Huff, 2002). Mahathir was also later to halt the decline of the Malaysian economy during the currency crisis affecting Asian economies between 1997 and 1998 through the maverick decision to impose strict capital controls (Jasin et al., 1998). Indeed, given Mahathir's anti-Western posture Wain is not wrong to call Mahathir a 'strident voice for the Third World' (2009: 242).

Shariffadeen expresses a similar though less adamant stance through his frequent references to the differences between Asian and Western ways, arguing, for example, that collectivism comes more naturally to Eastern peoples than it does to Westerners (Ang, 1997b). As with the discourses of Asian-style democracy and values (Barr, 2000), steadfast avowal of a different way of understanding and doing things is present in both Vision 2020 and the MSC mega project. In his articulation of Vision 2020, for example, Mahathir was adamant that rather than following in the footsteps of the other nineteen developed nations, Malaysia would be 'a developed country in our mould' (Mahathir, 1991: 1). Such sentiment did not, however, deter him from observing that 'it can be no accident that there is today no wealthy developed country that is information-poor and no information-rich country that is poor and undeveloped' (Mahathir, 1991: 3).

Consideration of the zoning technologies deployed in the ideation of the MSC offers further insight into the insistence on a Malaysian version of the knowledge society. In the first instance, the mega project exists physically as a specially zoned 15 × 50 km corridor of interrelated and networked technological developments. With the Kuala Lumpur city centre and the Kuala Lumpur International Airport at opposite ends, the MSC also houses both the federal administration centre of Putrajaya and the intelligent city of Cyberjaya (Mahathir, 1996). This kind of configuration is fairly *de rigueur* as technology corridors go even if more commonly built on a more modest scale. However, as Ong argues in her analysis of China's use of zoning technologies, zoning practices are a means of 'safely accommodat[ing] pockets' to allow experiments not tolerated outside the designated areas (Aihwa Ong, 2004: 85).

Nonetheless, to allow the chaotic, free-flowing aspects of the Silicon Valley model to germinate and thrive, the MSC has since its inception caused a number of exceptions to be made to how life, work and nation are experienced in Malaysia. All of these are encapsulated in a 10 Point Bill of Guarantees and a set of Cyberlaws (*MSC Malaysia 10 Point: Bill of Guarantees*, 2008). Although unsought and unexpected these developments were some of the first unintended consequences arising from the MSC project. At the time, Shariffadeen explained candidly that: 'Malaysia could not impose some of its laws on companies that would be operating in the MSC as this would go against the original objective of making it attractive to foreign companies and investors' (Rahman, 1996). Mahathir reasoned pragmatically that it was 'a choice between having nothing or giving some and receive something in return' (*Bill to ensure best deal for investors*, 1996).

The first concession introduced courtesy of the MSC is the lifting of restrictions on employment and business ownership, which are conditional on 30 per cent *Bumiputera* participation by law (Mahathir, 1996). This freed 'MSC-status' companies to structure ownership in configurations that are very different to all other businesses in Malaysia and invite direct foreign investment. It also left them free to hire local and foreign knowledge workers as they saw fit. The other concession is the undertaking to keep the Internet in Malaysia free of censorship.

Aihwa Ong argues that the MSC could be understood as the deliberate creation of 'a space in which a certain kind of governmentality seeks to break the association between race privilege and citizenship' (Aihwa Ong, 2005: 348). Mahathir's later exhortation to the Malays to free themselves of their reliance on the 'crutches of Malay privileges' seems to lend credence to these views (Mahathir, 2002). In other words, the MSC might well have been the beginning of an alternative positioning of the Malays that attempts to wean them off reliance on the state's economic assistance. It is equally plausible to consider the MSC as a strategy conceived to bring socio-economic progress without allowing socio-political concerns and political dissent to enter much into the equation.

Indeed, it is my contention that the MSC mega project's visionaries and planners foresaw its inherent conflict and took great care to craft a plan that would bring nation and technology together in a fashion that would allow the coexistence of the tacit social contract mentioned earlier with the experiment of socio-cultural change. Their strategy consists of two main devices: zoning technologies and the discourse of alternative modernity enacted as a Malaysian version of a civil society. The notion of the corridor as a zone of exception is an idea that has its origins in the colonial period when special ports and customs areas were created within colonized territories by treaties (Aihwa Ong, 2004: 75).

There is ample evidence to suggest that Malaysian leaders of the time were well aware of the potentialities of the Internet for deviance, dissent and democracy. It is illuminating in view of the new configurations we discuss in Chapter 6 to see, for example, then Deputy Prime Minister Anwar Ibrahim, who after the 2008 General Elections became the de facto Leader of the Opposition, opine that Malaysia must:

> not forget that an informed citizenry is also a responsible citizenry. We should, therefore, utilize the Internet to reinforce social responsibility among citizens.... information is a significant factor in a functioning democracy, its spread and accessibility is important for the survival of democratic institutions in any society. (Menon, 1996)

Equally illuminating is Mahathir's assertion even then that 'there should be some international agreement on what can go or cannot go on this free media' because 'with the Internet, just about anything can be spread' and 'freedom could not be absolute'. This is despite the belief that 'the benefits of the new technology promise to outweigh these misapplications' (*Wanted – Pact to Check Internet Smut*, 1996).

For the most part within these spaces, specific laws either varying from, or opposite to, those prevailing elsewhere are not only applicable but incentivized by the state. It is clear that exceptional freedom from certain aspects of governance is an intrinsic component of the MSC Status' constructed appeal to business, as an outstanding example of 'sites of transformation where market-driven calculations are introduced into the management of populations and administration of special spaces' (Aihwa Ong, 2006: 3–4).

There is a double twist with the MSC because it facilitates exemption from the affirmative action requirements introduced with the New Economic Policy (NEP) to uplift the socio-economic prospects of *Bumiputeras* (Heng, 1997: 268) and applied nationwide since 1971.[6] Such twists, I would add, are a legacy of the administrative mentality inculcated by 'colonial capitalism', wherein the socio-political concerns of the native population were neglected by the colonizers in favour of prioritizing the turnover of trading profits (Alatas, 1977: 2). Given that contemporary Malaysia brands itself a multicultural nation with a population made up of three main races, it remains problematic at best to insist on singling out one ethnic group – the slightly over 53 per cent of Malaysia's 28.3 million population that make up the *Bumiputeras* (US Department of State, 2011) – for preference.

From the care taken to construct a values-based knowledge society as distinctly Malaysian and alternative to the liberal Western model, it would seem some level of socio-political dissent was anticipated with the mass introduction of ICTs. However, there is also likely to have been an expectation that any burgeoning socio-political empowerment that emerged could be quickly quashed and contained by (1) the alternative modernity discourse with its emphasis on collectivism over individuality; and (2) the deployment of the laws enacted during and closely after the end of the colonial era of governance. With very few exceptions, since the establishment of the Malaysian nation and up to 1996, the Internal Security Act (ISA), the Sedition Act, the Printing Presses and Publishing Act and the Universities and University Colleges Act (Laws of Malaysia: Act 15, Sedition Act 1948; Laws of Malaysia: Act 301, Printing Presses and Publications Act 1984, 2006; *Repressive Laws*, 2000) have been more than equal to the task of deterring and suppressing public dissent.

Since the 2008 General Elections where the ruling coalition, Barisan Nasional (BN, National Front), lost its two-thirds majority in parliament, the government of Prime Minister Najib Razak has been developing new laws and modifying existing ones to mollify a populace emboldened by the results of their resistance to the established political hegemony of BN. These shifts are another of the unintended consequences of introducing the Internet into the Malaysian social imaginary and I discuss them in greater detail in Chapter 6.

Overall, the ideation of the MSC was meticulously constructed to justify what are extraordinary conditions in Malaysia in the name of socio-economic development. At the same time, it was also carefully hedged with a discourse of alternative modernity to guard against the intrusion of liberal values and way of life in Malaysia. Containment, in this sense, serves to keep disruptive elements neatly boxed in with geographical, discursive and legal limits at the same time as it restricts concessions made to enable the MSC within the specially created zone. In the next section, I discuss the extent to which the ideation has been realized and the conflicts that have arisen in the process.

The execution of a mega project: the MSC as realized so far

The 2009 Annual Industry Report published by the MDeC (Multimedia Development Corporation), the company formed to manage MSC Malaysia, reveals that at that point 2,520 companies had been awarded MSC Malaysia Status (MSC Annual Industry Report, 2009: 10). Compared to just 94 in 1997, the increase has been impressive. Of these companies, 77 per cent were Malaysian owned, 20 per cent foreign-owned and 3 per cent joint partnerships (MSC Annual Industry Report, 2009: 12).

Total combined sales by MSC status companies reached RM (Ringgit Malaysia) 24,826 million in 2009, out of which RM7,174 million were from export sales. Given that Gross Domestic Product (GDP) and export growth were both negative (1.7 per cent and 21.1 per cent respectively) in 2009 after slowing down over the previous four years, the MSC's results the same year are important if modest successes (*Asian Development Bank and Malaysia: Fact Sheet*, 2011: 1). Additionally, to-date MSC Malaysia companies have created 99,590 jobs, registered 5,721 IPs (intellectual properties) (MSC Annual Industry Report, 2009: 30, 36) and generated RM24 billion (*What is the MSC Malaysia?* 2011). More broadly, the mean income of Malaysians reached RM3,828 in 2008 up from RM3,011 in 2002 (K. N. Karim, 2010: 31) and the incidence of poverty in Malaysia has also steadily declined from 60 per cent of the rural population in 1957 to around 10 per cent in 2002, and from 51.2 to 5.1 per cent for the urban population (*Poverty in Malaysia 1957–2002*).

Eight flagship applications (paperless and electronic government, national multipurpose smart cards, borderless marketing, manufacturing web, research and development clusters, smart schools, multimedia financial haven and telemedicine) were proposed when the MSC mega project was launched (*'People-oriented' IT agenda required*, 1996). The flagship applications were to provide content to 'induce' the broader Malaysian population to use the Internet infrastructure developed as part and parcel of the MSC (Huff, 2002: 257). The manufacturing web flagship application was eventually dropped. The two flagship applications that appear to have advanced furthest are MyKad and Smart Schools.

A multi-purpose smart card with the capacity to store personal information in its chip, MyKad operates as a single platform from which Malaysians are able to access services ranging from transport and education to e-government.[7] It is also gradually replacing the identity card, the primary document of identification issued to all Malaysian citizens and permanent residents over the age of 12. According to reports, Smart Schools completed a massive computerization phase for all 10,000 schools in Malaysia in 2009 (Razali, 2009: 23). The other two flagship applications that have achieved significant progress are Telehealth[8] (previously Telemedicine) and e-government, with the set up of a new electronic procurement system known as e-procurement. In a sense, then, Internet technologies are an inevitable part of everyday life in Malaysia.

Outside of MDeC-produced reports and the intermittent release of government data, there are few independent means of reviewing the MSC. One rare exception is the report commissioned by the Malaysian government 4.5 years into the MSC mega project and prepared by McKinsey and Associates in 2001. Delivered in confidence to the Malaysian government in March 2001, its draft findings were leaked to the press and caused what Huff calls a 'crisis of confidence' (Huff, 2002). In his paper, Huff lists ten criticisms contained in the report that were gleaned from press reports. These ranged from the overabundance of red tape surrounding the approval of MSC status and the lack of intellectual capital to the insufficient impact on economic development (Huff, 2002: 253).

Of the others listed, the 'need to allow MSC companies to locate anywhere they desire' (Huff, 2002: 253) indicates that early attempts to contain the MSC experiment by geo-physical and other means met with resistance. The same theme of resistance to (spatial) containment persists in a paper by Lepawsky in 2005. In it, he suggests that with approximately 60 per cent of MSC-status companies located outside the MSC's spatial boundaries, 'the state's attempt to manage the MSC as a spatially isolated zone' is 'equivocal' at best (Lepawsky, 2005a: 18).

One of Lepawsky's interviewees (Michael) speaks of the incentives on offer to MSC-status companies as a 'radical departure' from the norm in Malaysia (Lepawsky, 2005a: 13–14) – the norm in question being the employment and ownership restrictions that apply to all other non-MSC-status companies in Malaysia. From this remark, it is possible to infer that the idea that the MSC is intended to be a contained test-bed for a 'non-bumi' way of life (Lepawsky, 2005a: 18) has filtered into the Malaysian social imaginary.

Excerpts of interviews contained in Lepawsky's study provide some idea of how ordinary Malaysians perceive the MSC (Lepawsky, 2005a: 16–17). For example, all three interviewees cited were sufficiently aware of the potential positive and negative effects to express a need for caution and balance in approaching the Internet. Additionally, there also exists a general sense of disconnection of both conceptual and material distance between everyday Malaysians and the MSC mega project (Lepawsky, 2005a: 16–17).

A rare account by a foreign businessman running an MSC-status business provides further insight into the reasons behind the 'disconnect between the MSC and the rest of Malaysia' (W. L. Lee, 2007). His complaint of a lack of wider support for MSC-status businesses outside the realm governed by the MSC is illustrative of the gap and conflict between the ideation and execution of the MSC. For example, despite its MSC-status, his company's application for additional funding to aid overseas expansion was rejected because his company did not meet the *Bumiputera* ownership requirement.

This not only contradicts the exemption from ownership requirement that comes with MSC-status; it also highlights the incompatibility between the free, open and liberal context of the MSC's ideation and the constrained business environment existing outside the specially created zone. The prospect of any vibrancy generated via the MSC jumping across the boundaries of the zone to ignite broader growth cannot be good when MSC-status businesses are hemmed in on all sides by the intractability of pro-*Bumiputera* business restrictions.

Only a handful of studies have managed to collate sufficient government data to properly assess the MSC's relevance to the broader Malaysian public. Indeed, shifting categories in released government data confound and obstruct the possibility of conducting meaningful longitudinal reviews of the project's effectiveness. Due to this, analysis of the clusters under which MSC-status businesses are grouped show that while Shared Services and Outsourcing and Content development (after being renamed Creative Multimedia) have been fairly constant categories for data collation, the Information Technology category has gradually morphed into the largest cluster of MSC-status companies as it absorbed increasing types of technological activities, from 'Vertical Applications' (*Multimedia Super Corridor: Impact Survey 2004*, 2004) and 'Mobility, Embedded Software and Hardware' to 'Application Software' (*MSC Malaysia Impact Survey 2008*, 2008).

Nonetheless, in their paper on the knowledge economy in Malaysia, Jarman and Chopra argue that due to the emphasis in the ideation phase on multimedia content production – expressed by Shariffadeen's appraisal that 'what provides value is content' (Nelson, 1995; Jacobs, 1997) – there was an initial 'official defensiveness' about admitting to the existence of the SSO (Shared Service and Outsourcing) cluster in the MSC (Jarman and Chopra, 2007). However, with close to half of those employed in the MSC working in the Shared Services and Outsourcing (SSO) cluster in 2009 (MSC Annual Industry Report, 2009: 12), there seems to be little choice but to bow to the adjustment.

The original vision of a 'high-end artistic and creative multimedia hub' has been supplanted by 'the reality of a lower level industry focused much more heavily on business support activities and call centres' (Jarman and Chopra, 2007: 198). The two authors go on to contend that the issue lies with the failure of the literature on the knowledge economy to differentiate between the wide range of activities that should be included within its classification (ibid.: 200).

Perhaps, as Ramasamy, Chakrabaty and Cheah contend, there are certain less tangible factors arising from 'the attitude and culture of the society that makes up the essence of a technopole' not present in the MSC formula so meticulously crafted by the state (B. Ramasamy et al., 2003: 882). This lack speaks to the fact that while material conditions like infrastructure, laws and policies might be created given enough political will, less material factors arising from the social fabric of the nation are not as easily manufactured. Intellectual capital of the calibre that is able to participate in high-end technological activities such as content creation is a long-term investment.

Whether nurtured via the competitive cauldron of exclusive, private education *à la* Silicon Valley, or quality, state-funded systems of training, there seem to be no short cuts possible. Indergaard hints as much but nevertheless insists that the credibility of the MSC is 'on the rise' (Indergaard, 2003: 395–6). In his ideation of the MSC, Shariffadeen opined that it would be a 'natural transition' for Malaysia, '[h]aving evolved from a natural resources producing country to a manufacturing and export-import oriented country … to move on yet again, to producing information or content-based products and services' that would transform Malaysia's 'entire economical and social structure' (Nelson, 1995).

In the years since its inception, many special provisions have been made in order to attract international corporations and vital foreign direct investment to the MSC. These include the lifting of restrictions on foreign hire and ownership requirements (and by inference, the pro-*Bumiputera* affirmative action policy) to permit the smooth in-flow of global knowledge workers and capital essential to the plan's success. An array of cyberlaws such as the Computer Crimes Act (1997) and the E-Commerce Act (2006) have also been enacted to ensure the legal infrastructure was in place to protect the anticipated IPs that would emerge from the mega project (*Cyberlaws and Intellectual Property Laws*, 2007). Of these, perhaps the boldest is the promise of an uncensored Internet enshrined in the Bill of Guarantees (*MSC Malaysia 10 Point: Bill of Guarantees*, 2008). The project has also expanded to include residential spaces for the inhabitants of this brave new world (Lepawsky, 2005b). Overall, as Huff maintains, planning on the part of the technological elite has been meticulous (Huff, 2002: 268).

However, as I have argued elsewhere, the MSC is plagued by the incongruities that arise from the valorization of informational virtuosity as the identifying characteristic of social organization within the MSC, against the backdrop of state-sanctioned practices that privilege one section of the nation's population (Malays) solely on the basis of race; and the contrast between the undertaking to keep the Internet free of censorship and the punitive laws and regulations that control mainstream media (S. Leong, 2008). Broadly speaking, some of the core features granted privilege in Malaysian society as well as the general primacy of socio-political control over freedom, grate against those qualities that have proven necessary to a successful 'milieu of innovation' elsewhere (Castells, 2000: 419) that Malaysia seeks to replicate with the MSC.

When significations are imported, borrowed or extended from one social imaginary to another as the notion of a digital corridor has been, a certain level of adjustment to the local social imaginary is expected. However, whenever a schism exists between two social imaginaries the translation of significations can be highly problematic. In the case of the MSC, the values of the US and Finnish systems that individually harnessed the Internet for socio-economic development could not be made to align with the system in Malaysia where ethno-communalism still reigns.

In the face of this, immense effort and thought has gone into bridging that gulf through the years. The systematic construction of a discourse of a values-based Malaysian modernity and the attempt to contain values laced with Western liberalism to a narrow corridor of exception are ongoing; however, the attempt to restrict a way of life based on meritocratic capitalism and liberalism to the MSC is fraught with inconsistencies and flaws. Whether their foresight and measures have managed to secure a future knowledge society so that 2020 will actually see Malaysia attain the developed nation status is still too early to call but there is no doubt that significations like the Internet cannot simply be transplanted sans context and expected to operate like before. Each signification has multiple potentialities but all are outcomes of the societies within which they are deemed relevant and typical.

Conclusion

In a 1997 interview, Shariffadeen had cause to lament that Malaysians were not 'ready for the MSC yet' (Amry, 1997). Today, Malaysians are the leading users of social networking in Southeast Asia (*Malaysia is Top in Social Networking in Southeast Asia*, 2011) and the freedom of expression facilitated by a censorship-free Internet has spawned a vibrant civil society with a diversity of institutes and activists that are increasingly vocal with their questions on how the nation is imagined, lived and experienced.

Malaysiakini, the online-only news subscription which started in 1999, has also survived as a profitable business for over a decade to become one of the most trusted and widely read news sources in Malaysia. This is despite a recent Nielsen study which reveals that only 41 per cent of Malaysians access the Internet, up from 26 per cent in 2009. The top three activities carried out online are social networking, instant messaging and reading local news (*Malaysian Internet Usage Takes Off in 2010*, 2011). Additionally, broadband Internet penetration in urban Malaysia is at 57.4 per cent – just shy of the 60 per cent target (*Three Per Cent More Broadband Penetration To Reach Target – Rais*, 2011).

Although the notion of an (Islamic) values-based knowledge society as masterminded by Mahathir and Shariffadeen seems to have made little headway into the Malaysian social imaginary, the Internet as a signification enabling socio-political expression on a level not experienced before is now widely accepted in Malaysia. Indeed, in Malaysia the Internet has been widely credited with the electoral result of a reduced majority that Prime Minister Najib Razak's administration now holds in government after the 2008 General Elections. The ruling coalition's loss of several key states is attributed to the dominant political alliance of the Barisan Nasional's failure to employ the Internet to any successful degree, banking instead on its enormous presence in mainstream broadcasting media (Gong, 2010).

Space constraints have precluded much mention of Singapore's success at creating an 'intelligent island' discourse (A. Lim, 2001) and implementing its ambitious series of technology plans of which the Science, Technology and Enterprise Plan 2015 is the latest (Science, Technology and Enterprise Plan 2015, 2011). Nonetheless, it is obvious that to make sense of the above claims with regard to the effects of the Internet in Malaysia and the dismay of the ruling coalition over the unintended consequences, Malaysia's situation has to be read alongside the experiences of neighbouring Singapore and Indonesia.

For example, despite generally higher rates of technological literacy and the highest Internet penetration rate of 67 per cent in Southeast Asia (*Singaporeans Can't Get Enough of Digital Media: Nielsen*, 2011), Singapore has a much tamer and more acquiescent civil society whose growth remains stymied (T. Lee, 2001; Mathi, 2008; Ho, 2009). For better or worse, what the Singapore experience illustrates is that Internet technologies-inspired developmental strategies can be successfully rolled out without upsetting the status quo. The extent of control over the nation's citizenry necessary to 'negate' the political implications of said technologies is another matter, as is the question of what further consequences such neutralization might have for the nation down the road. On the surface Indonesia's *reformasi* experience since 1998 appears, by contrast, to give fair warning of the increased opportunity for socio-political activism and disruption that follows on from the introduction of the Internet into a nation's social imaginary (M. Lim, 2011).

Ultimately, whether comprehended as such or not, it seems appropriate to remember that projects like the MSC:

> are not simply calls for new technologies to be transferred.... They are calls for the creation of new technological spaces: new ways of thinking about science and technology, new places where technologies can be created, new policies to support science for development, and new societal configurations which can assimilate, adapt and absorb new technologies. (J. Smith, 2009, 20)

In this chapter I have outlined the trouble that the key visionaries and the government of Malaysia have taken to create the new places, spaces and policies in support of the of the MSC project. Despite their efforts at preventing their diffusion, though, the concerted push to promote the Internet as an engine of national economic growth has also resulted in the embedded liberal values infiltrating the broader social imaginary in Malaysia to generate new societal configurations. I detail some of these still unfolding configurations in Chapter 6. In the next chapter I explore the processes that allowed the sharing of these Westernized ideals between Internet users and non-users in order to better understand the relationship between the nation and the Internet in Malaysia.

Notes

1 Copies and details of these various plans can be accessed at: http://www.pmo.gov.my
2 It is important to bear in mind that by the time he launched the MSC mega project in 1996, Mahathir had been Prime Minister of Malaysia for about 15 years. He was arguably at or near the zenith of his power in Malaysia. Nor did he relinquish the post until 2003 when he stepped down to make way for his successor, Abdullah Badawi.
3 See, for example, The Making of Bangsa Malaysia, http://www.icassecretariat.org/node/398 (accessed 1 August 2011).
4 According to Malaysia's Constitution, all Malays are automatically registered as Muslims although not all Muslims are Malay as there are also ethnic Chinese and Indian Muslims.
5 The inclusion of the network society as an example here is not an indication that the notion, as proposed by Castells, is unproblematic. If anything, I am inclined to agree with van Dijk, who considers Castells' magnum opus to provide 'concise, deep and well-documented analyses' of 'many of the large-scale trends in current affairs';

but still finds the understanding of technology underlying the theory of the network society to be 'deterministic and one-dimensional' (van Dijk, 1999: 136).
6 The current Prime Minister, Najib Razak, has gradually eased some of these restrictions. See *Malaysia's Racial-Preference Policy: Son versus Sons* (2009).
7 See http://www.mscmalaysia.my/topic/More+with+MyKad, accessed 31 July 2011.
8 See http://www.mscmalaysia.my/topic/IHE+Connectathon, accessed 31 July 2011.

5 Users and non-users in the Malaysian social imaginary

This chapter continues the previous discussion of the Multimedia Super Corridor and the efforts expended therein to manage and anticipate the effects of the Internet in Malaysian society. Here, I bring the various threads of arguments made in previous chapters together to contend firstly, that the values and ideas embedded within the Internet cannot be isolated from the social imaginary from which the technologies emerged. Secondly, that as such, the Internet's intrinsic qualities cannot be separated, let alone wholly substituted, with a different set of values, however packaged. Thirdly, that even if successfully geographically contained, the Internet's influence and consequences cannot be limited to the circle of its users but will inevitably seep into the wider, non-user community within which it is experienced.

To explain the processes whereby ideas, values and understandings embedded within the Internet are transmitted beyond their intended boundaries of use, I turn in this chapter to look at the exchange of information obtained online between users and non-users of the Internet. It is my hypothesis that non-users of the Internet have as great a role to play as users whenever national policies that aim to promote the use of a technology are implemented.

This is the case even if, as in the case of the MSC, the basic premise of the national technology policy seems either to discount non-users by virtue of their non-participation or cast them as techno-laggards compelled to catch up with inevitable technological advancement. My objective is to understand how, as a project designed ultimately to bring about socio-economic change the MSC has facilitated and introduced broader, unsought for socio-political transformations in the Malaysian social imaginary.

In part, what I aim to make plain is what it means when, despite an Internet penetration rate in Malaysia of 63.7 per cent per 100 households and 19.8 per cent per 100 inhabitants (Communications & Multimedia: Pocket Book of Statistics, Q2 2012: 3), over half of Malaysia's population (53 per cent) profess to look to online newspapers for their information needs while 47 per cent visit Internet portals for the same purpose (Mandel, 2011). Given that Internet penetration rates are a measure of the proportion of a population that uses the Internet, there is evidence of a mismatch, and hence stories untold which require explication here.

The lack of correspondence between Internet penetration rates and online readership in Malaysia is a classic example of a situation where the number of people who access the Internet is not representative of the size of the public that engages with the content. It is clear that further sharing and exchange of information takes place between those who use the Internet to obtain information and those who do not.

Some part of the discrepancy between Internet use and its circle of influence can be explained by the fact that compared to broadcast media, online content has the advantage of being producible at great speed and relatively low costs. This allows online spaces to disseminate information at a rate that broadcast media, with its rigid structures and high-end production values and systems, cannot match.

While the statistics on Internet penetration rate in Malaysia tell one story about new media in the nation, other types of evidence tell us different stories. For one thing, the number of people who receive information is often a lot higher than those who first obtain it online. Secondly, there are intersecting circuits between many forms of media – old, new, formal and informal – that allow the effect of information obtained online to travel beyond users of the Internet.

For example, in an account of how the dismissal and arrest of the 1998 Deputy Prime Minister, Anwar Ibrahim, set off online activism in Malaysia, Bahfen argues that the 'readership of alternative news sites' was grossly underrated because it was thought to be limited to those with Internet access (Bahfen, 2008: 168). According to Bahfen, 'printing, photocopying, faxing and snail mail' were some of the other means of communication employed by Malaysians to extend and share information gathered online.

For our purposes, the crucial point in Bahfen's account is the reference made to the further exchange and circulation of information between those who use the Internet and those who passed it on via informal, digital and non-digital means. This is an important point that goes beyond the ongoing concern with the digital divide, access and digital exclusion. Although research surrounding the Internet has moved on from the simple binary of use and non-use, few have actually addressed proxy or secondary use in any detail. Yet, as Dutton and Blank remind us:

> [p]roxy use remains a very important link to the Internet for over two-thirds of people who do not use the Internet themselves (Dutton and Blank, 2011). This is a point that is often lost in public discussions over Internet use: non-users often have access if they need it, but the access is via another, proxy user.

An indication of how widespread proxy use is in Malaysia can be obtained when we consider the fact that mobile phone (hand phone) penetration in Malaysia is 133.3 per cent (Communications & Multimedia: Pocket Book of Statistics, Q2 2012: 3), and that of these numbers, 74.4 per cent use their mobile phones for social networking purposes (Hand Phone Users Survey 2011, 2011: 18). Additionally, while slightly more than a quarter (25.2 per cent) of those who have mobile phones own at least two (Communications & Multimedia: Pocket Book of Statistics, Q2 2012: 3), only 8 per cent of those who use the Internet do so from the office. The majority of Internet usage (88.3 per cent) takes place at home (Household Use of the Internet Survey, 2011: 18). This set of figures tells us yet another story about the value that Malaysians place on the informal and mobile sharing of information within their social networks. At the same time it also hints at the many undocumented routes down which information travels in Malaysian society.

The point is that explanations like Bahfen's only go halfway towards explaining how concepts novel to a social imaginary make their way from being subjects of discussion among a few to becoming accepted ideas and norms. In this chapter I start with a brief overview of studies on the non-use of technologies and apply Schutz's (1972, 1974) work to explain how within a chosen social imaginary, ideas and discussions are passed from person to person, leading them to be introduced indirectly to users and non-users alike as well as to individuals who occupy positions along the continuum between the two poles. Schutz's theories on the four groups of others (contemporaries, consociates, successors and predecessors) that contribute to an individual's social reality are considered alongside anecdotal evidence of the circuits of information between users and non-users that operated during some of the major socio-political events that have taken place in Malaysia between 2007 and 2012. These events are the Bersih rallies from the first held in 2007 through to the one in 2012, the Hindraf (Hindu Rights Action Force) rally and the 2008 General Elections of Malaysia.

Discourses of non-use

Research on the Internet has traditionally classified non-use as a problem in need of analysis and solution. A large part of this attitude comes from early work on the group of issues gathered under the notion of the digital divide between the digital haves and have-nots. Basically this idea is driven by the assumption that digital inclusion is aligned with social inclusion and Internet use leads to greater access to life opportunities and vice versa (Chia et al., 2006). This logic valorizes the use of the Internet and indeed, digital virtuosity, as a highly desirable characteristic for individuals and the twenty-first century societies they inhabit.

Whilst studies have rightly noted a 'spectrum of Internet access' (Lenhart et al., 2003), non-use of Internet technologies remains associated with socio-economic lack and lag. The view of non-use as undesirable continues to inform the basis of recent research even in the face of other work which (1) argues that non-users or non-adopters contribute to and are vital to the co-construction of technologies because the outright rejection of any technology says as much about it as its modification, adoption and acceptance (Kline,

2003; Wyatt et al., 2002; Wyatt, 2003); and (2) has begun to discuss the notion of media refusal as a voluntary choice made in the interest of aesthetics and/or asceticism (Portwood-Stacer, 2012a, 2012b, 2012c).

According to Selwyn, there are four main discourses of technological non-use: diffusion, material and cognitive deficiency, technophobia and ideological refusal (Selwyn, 2003). The first discourse – of diffusion – holds that non-use will inevitably be overcome as technology filters downwards from its usage by early adopters to broad acceptance by the wider, less innovative majority (ibid.). The second discourse – of material and cognitive deficiency – attributes non-use to a lack of resources, either financial and/or intellectual. This discourse informs notions such as the digital divide and argues that the disparity between the haves and have-nots would begin to dissolve once suitable training and facilities are provided (ibid.).

The third discourse of non-use – technophobia – explains non-use as avoidance of technology due to anxiety. This is where individuals are inhibited from engaging with technologies through their perceived lack of facility or familiarity with them. The fourth discourse of non-use centres on ideological refusal, wherein individuals reject technology on the basis of ideology. While individuals who subscribe to such views are often labelled modern-day luddites, there are also communities like the Amish who reject technologies they consider damaging to their communitarian ethos.

In all of the four main discourses of non-use, technological usage is regarded as a virtue because it is perceived to represent an advancement of civilization. Such a view is consistent with the dominant foregone conclusion that technology confers sophistication and improvements to the lifestyles of humans. There is little to no consideration of the possibility that human-plus technology may sometimes result in a negative outcome.

This is despite popular culture's familiarity with the counter-discourse of technological dystopianism today. Through science fiction works such as the *Terminator* film franchise (J. Cameron et al., 2003, 2004), the costs of humanity's over-dependence on technologies are dramatized for entertainment value, often to such an extent that they seem too outlandish to have any relevance to mundane existence. That these same dramatizations frequently return to the reassuring triumph of humanity over technology might also explain why their cautionary notes are overlooked.

Whatever the reasons for the lack of discussion, the perception of non-usage of technologies as undesirable and backward, almost recalcitrant in certain cases, remains dominant even today. Overall, the four discourses and variations therein have been variously criticized as being technologically deterministic to different degrees and lacking nuance in how they discern the issues concerning technology use and adoption. Such nuances and critiques are, however, only very gradually filtering through into studies of Internet and new media use.

For example, some argue that while Internet access and lessons on browsing the World Wide Web and email, etc. can be arranged, there is no guarantee that users will continue on from there to build the Internet into their daily lives. Instead they contend that other factors, such as opportunity and relevance, outweigh factors like access and equipment in influencing how and to what extent individuals integrate technologies into everyday routines (Selwyn et al., 2005). Other researchers have looked further into the issue of non-use and suggest there is a continuum rather than polar relationship between use and non-use.

Zhao's (2006) study of Internet use, for example, suggests researchers should investigate a range of users, differentiating between those who are light and heavy users of various types of platform. Livingstone and Helsper argue that 'the simple assertion of a binary divide between haves and have-nots, or users and non-users, [is] no longer applicable to young people' (Livingstone and Helsper, 2007: 690). Instead, they suggest that there should be a 'gradation' in how users are categorized, from basic and moderate users to broad and all-round users (ibid.: 696). I contend the same level of nuance is applicable across the demographic of all users.

Moreover, intended user-groups do not always take to a technology, even if, as Clarke argues, all technologies are designed with an 'implicated user' in mind (Oudshoorn and Pinch, 2008: 546–7). The category of the implicated user can be further divided into 'those who are not physically present but who are discursively constructed and targeted by others', and 'those who are physically present but who are generally silenced/ignored/made invisible by those in power'. The fact that the majority of scissors manufactured today are designed for right- rather than left-handed people speaks to the fact that the default users of scissors are right-handed and left-handed people are largely ignored as users. As Dyer (1997) argues through the example of film manufacture, the politics of power and dominance inhere in technologies through the intentions of designers and manufacturers in the standards they adhere to as well as the users they build for.

Cowan's (1985) account, for example, of how gas refrigerators were rejected in favour of electric ones demonstrates that such decisions are seldom made from within a vacuum or without consequence. Far from a purely technological design decision, the adoption of any technology is a matter of prevailing social, cultural, economic and political conditions and contexts. The same might be said of SMS (Short Message Services), which, when introduced in the early 1990s as a feature of mobile phones, was not considered a major selling point for its predominantly business-oriented user base. Its subsequent mass appeal only came about after its adoption as a medium for social interaction and co-ordination (Ling, 2004: 5).

Non-use can thus sometimes be deliberately built into the objective of a technology's design. In the past, technologies such as bridge construction and design were subtly skewed to intentionally exclude those groups considered unsuitable for access to certain spaces (Winner, 1986). Generally, it is accepted that technologies can be tailored to direct how they may be utilized as resources. A contemporary example that comes to mind are the 'bum bars' that have been substituted for benches in bus stops across many Australian cities to deter what is regarded as deviant use of the technology of seating, i.e. the use of bench seats for repose by the homeless and the drunken in the small hours of the night. Certain technologies, like the safety locks on fencing surrounding suburban swimming pools and the press-and-turn caps on medicine bottles, are designed to preclude a specific group of users, i.e. young children.

Non-use is a design benefit in such instances but such an understanding is not readily translatable, or so it seems, to Internet and new media technologies. In fact, notwithstanding the value of non-use in the mediation between societies and technologies, with the Internet and new media the tendency is to emphasize non-use as an undesirable condition. This is because universal usage of the Internet is regarded as the foundation for the full and free formation of knowledge societies, and the issue of access continues to be a concern for many nation-states.

In Malaysia, where ICTs have been consistently and prominently constructed as an enabler of nationwide change, from developing to developed nation status as well as from an agriculture and manufacturing-based economy to a knowledge-based one, it is no surprise to find non-use of the Internet to be similarly problematized. Against the exhortations to decouple race from economic backwardness in his 1991 speech, *Vision 2020: The Way Forward*, Mahathir upheld a vision of a 'diversified and balanced economy' that was 'technologically proficient, fully able to adapt, innovate and invest, that is increasingly technology-intensive, moving in the direction of higher and higher levels of technology' (Mahathir, 1991). The MSC, ideated and implemented as the foundation from which a values-based knowledge society might spring in Malaysia, is a classic example of an innate bias against non-use.

Though the representation of non-use as an unwanted condition is tacit, the connection Mahathir makes between the sloughing off of backwardness and the uptake of technologies is clear enough. Shariffadeen, the other main visionary of the Multimedia Super Corridor mentioned in Chapter 4, has a similar though more nuanced understanding of use, distinguishing between four different levels of IT literacy: operational, informational, knowledge and social and cultural literacy (Ang, 1997a).

Given that creating a knowledge society is the avowed objective of Vision 2020 and the discourse of the knowledge society emerged from that of the information society, the ability of citizens to become virtuoso users of technology is deeply, almost inextricably intertwined with that of national progress within the Malaysian social imaginary. Non-users are, thus, by inference failing in their duty as citizens. Yet, despite the pathologizing of non-users, they are very much a part of the broader society and the socio-political changes in Malaysia brought about by online activism. In the next section, I discuss the social structures that facilitate the formation of these circuits of information based on the work of social phenomenologist, Alfred Schutz.

I want to clarify here that I am aware that Malaysian civil society has had many long-term campaigners who have fought hard, with and without the aid of new media, to voice their dissent and dissatisfaction with the status quo. Organizations such as *Suaram* (*Suara Rakyat Malaysia*, Voice of the Malaysian People), for example, have been working since 1989 to raise Malaysian consciousness of human rights abuses on a range of national and international issues – from the injustices of Malaysia's Internal Security Act (ISA) and the displacement of indigenous peoples in Sarawak to make way for the Bakun Dam, to the plight of the Burmese people under Junta rule (*About Us*, 2009; *Suaram 20 Years*, 2010). *Suaram* has also continuously published an annual *Human Rights Report* since 1998 that holds authorities to account (*SUARAM 2011 Human Rights Report Launched*, 2011).

Another veteran organization is *Aliran* (short for *Aliran Kesedaran Negara*, National Consciousness Movement). Started in 1977 and still based in Penang *Aliran* understands its main role as a 'social educator', 'upholding human dignity and promoting social justice' (*About Us*, 2012). Towards that end, the organization has persistently utilized its resources to publish the *Aliran Monthly*, one of the oldest non-partisan publications in Malaysia. Multi-ethnic and multi-focus in the causes it advocates, *Aliran Monthly* has been a steadfast critic of the government and opposition, consistently lending space to independent views that challenge the mainstream media's overly sanguine coverage of Malaysian affairs. Tellingly, for a large part of the time the government refused the organization licence to publish in Malay in order to curtail its reach to a wider audience (Crane et al., 1998, 210).

There are many other organizations that have played equally pivotal roles that are not mentioned here because this book is not so much about the civil society in Malaysia as it is about the interactions between new media and the nation. As such, it is my intention to chart the implications that the Internet has had for Malaysian society through a focus on three events, namely the Hindraf and Bersih rallies and the 2008 General Elections.

Many of the same activists who took part in and organized the events I describe below are part of groups like *Suaram* and still others received training from these organizations or cut their teeth on movements like the Article 11 Coalition, addressing controversial issues such as apostasy in Islam and freedom of religion (Tan, 2006). Theirs is important work that both emerges from and feeds into the relationship between new media and nation that I discuss here, but they are not the main focus.

Circuits of information: users, non-users and everyone in between

According to Schutz, human social worlds consist of two realms of social reality: the directly experienced and the indirectly experienced. Individuals partake of directly experienced social reality face-to-face with those who exist in the same time and space, the 'Here and Now' (Schutz, 1972: 142–3).

These individuals are known to each other as consociates and they share 'a community of space and a community of time' (ibid.: 163).

Take, for example, the 2,000 members of the Bar Council and other citizens who turned up to protest in September 2007, after a video clip was released in which prominent Malaysian lawyer V. K. Lingam was allegedly brokering Supreme Court appointments over the phone (*Malaysian Bar Council Walk for Justice Rally*, 2007). They were definitely consociates (Schutz, 1972: 163) because they occupied a shared spatio-temporality during the march. In a very obvious and direct fashion, they were consociated because they inhabited the same time zone and surroundings of Kuala Lumpur.

The same can be said of the 30,000 members and supporters of Hindraf (Hindu Rights Action Force) who were part of the 25 November rally in the same year (S. Leong, 2009). As consociates they shared a temporality and spatiality and their realities were directly and mutually constituted by each other. Directly experienced social reality, therefore, consists of experiences that are immediately present to the individual.

One informant who was a participant speaks of Hindraf's efforts as being cumulative, with consistent information regarding 'hall meetings' being disseminated via text (SMS) on mobile (hand) phones in both English and Tamil (Arumugam, 2012). Additionally, a video put together by Malaysiakini video journalist Indrani Kopalan (2006) was screened at every temple hall meeting and many copies were distributed free to low-income group Indians, Hindu and non-Hindu.

Interestingly, the same informant also notes that despite the existence of a Hindraf website, Police Watch, and all the above efforts, it was partly the government's crackdown on their communal actions that attracted the attention of online media and set off the spate of emails and Facebook posts regarding the issue. In other words, the overly aggressive reaction from the Badawi government had something to do with the flurry of video footage, news of meetings and mobilizations that were subsequently circulated between users and non-users of the Internet, aired over television and, no doubt, discussed in homes and workplaces.

The thousands of Malaysians who participated in these collective acts of protest were mobilized through many different avenues but the Internet and new media played crucial roles due in part to the low cost and speed of production, replication and response of online information. According to another informant (D. Lim, 2012), what caught many by surprise was how quickly these disparate actions coalesced into joint action despite decentralized and less than co-ordinated efforts. Hindraf did not succeed in its expressed objective of taking its historical grievances to the British (*30,000 Hindraf protesters rally in KL streets*, 2007) and has suffered several internally inflicted and state-sanctioned setbacks since (*Malaysia: Continued criminalisation of Hindu Rights Action Force (HINDRAF) and the Human Rights Party*, 2011). However, it has managed to bring the plight of the Malaysia Indian population to light and it continues to be a focus of political action today (Woon, 2012).

The example that best illustrates the growing understanding of how new media information circuits work can be found in the Bersih campaign. It began in 2006 as a trans-ethnic coalition of 69 NGO and activist groups. Bersih (Coalition for Clean and Fair Elections) endeavoured to 'push for a thorough reform of the electoral process in Malaysia' based on eight calls for change (*Bersih 2.0 – About*, 2011). The first rally for the cause of clean and fair elections in Malaysia took place on 10 November 2007 (*Bersih People's Gathering, 10 November 2007*, 2007), the second on 9 July 2011 (*Press statement: Launch of Perhimpunan BERSIH 2.0*, 2011) and the third in 2012 on 28 April (*Bersih 3.0*, 2012).

The 2007 rally was amongst the biggest held in Malaysia and as a member of its secretariat points out, made more use of political forums held by opposition parties in its mobilization towards the cause than of new media (Abdullah, 2012). Yet, as Lim (2012) recalls, much of the progressive information relayed via SMS on the Bersih as well as Hindraf rallies, which took place slightly more than two weeks apart, was also uploaded onto blogs for further dissemination. It is worth remembering that this took place at a time when the Internet had been available in Malaysia for many years and the influential online subscription news portal, Malaysiakini, had been publishing since 1999 (*About Us*, 1999).

In 2011, an estimated 50,000 Malaysians gathered en masse once more for the Bersih 2.0 protest rally (S. Leong, 2009). Considerably more was made of new media in this follow-up campaign, and Bersih not only had its own social networking site on Facebook and multiple hashtags on microblogging site Twitter, it also had its own website. For example, a web page appropriately titled 'Spread Multimedia' (*Spread Multimedia: Bersih 2.0*, 2011) ensured a co-ordinated array of multimedia resources, which consisted of a rich mix of rousing, thought-provoking and promotional videos and interviews; Bersih 2.0 logos suitable for replication on banners and T-shirts; as well as two mobile phone ringtones. Finally, there is also an audio recording featuring Malaysia's National Laureate Samad Said's recitation of the moving poem *Unggun Bersih* (Cleansing Fire).

Throughout the planning, execution and aftermath of the 2011 event itself, details of the negotiations and entreaties exchanged with the government over the launch, and the organization and eventual denial of a permit for the march were documented as well as transparently and widely publicized and disseminated online (*Press statement: Launch of Perhimpunan BERSIH 2.0*, 2011; Pragalath, 2011; Othman et al., 2011). Not only were an official Facebook page and Twitter hashtags set up before and during the event, communication and information about the movement was conveyed, shared and circulated by the organization itself and its supporters and detractors. Video footage of the event was also posted online on the Bersih and other sites after the occasion.

Another page of the Bersih site had ready-designed leaflets containing details of the events obviously available for download and copying by various means. The availability of multimedia resources for download and replication is important for two reasons. Once downloaded, the resources can be passed from person to person, user to non-user and back again. The ringtone, for example, is now available on the World Wide Web at a multitude of online sites.[1] Consociates were thus able to share their resources and through doing so engage with the cause as well as mobilize others.

However, beyond the ability for multimedia resources to be accessed and shared by those who inhabit the same space and time, being housed online also meant that all the coverage, documents and multimedia resources were also accessible to those who were not consociates but rather contemporaries. According to Schutz, contemporaries are individuals who exist in the same time but dwell in different spaces. Information and resources available online are eminently suited for sharing with contemporaries because they can be accessed and shared by individuals who are not co-present as long as they can log on to the Internet.

Specifically, for Schutz, contemporaries comprise those whose lives fall 'in the same present span of world time' (Schutz and Luckmann, 1974: 69), but who do not share the same directly experienced temporality and spatiality (Schutz, 1972: 181), because these individuals are physically separated by geographic distance. In theory, it is always possible for one's contemporaries to become one's consociates and vice versa (ibid.).

Peer groups are the classic example of contemporaries. The weight of peer group pressure can dictate the choice of clothing and interests of many individuals, but it can also have a significant influence on individual issues like moral decisions, ethical behaviour and social allegiances. It is only necessary to witness the increasing number of young people around the world who consider environmental concerns to be an essential part of their social world and sign petitions as well as stage protests over ecological issues in other countries to understand the power of this influence. Although environmental issues are not new, their prominence and prevalence among younger people as an area of concern can be explained, at least in part, as a result of peer group pressures.

In the case of Bersih 2.0, for example, online content and resources kept contemporaries apprised of events in Malaysia, engaging and mobilizing them in turn. This led, amongst other things, to members of the Malaysian diaspora in the USA, Australia and UK spontaneously expressing their support through the staging of local versions of the Bersih 2.0 rally. Thus, more than 4,000 overseas Malaysians (*Global Bersih 2.0*, 2011) in Washington, Perth, Melbourne Sydney, Singapore, Auckland, Turkey, Canada, Hong Kong, New York, South Korea, Osaka and London acted in solidarity with their compatriots in Malaysia. Global Bersih, as the international version of the Bersih movement came to be named, was also an important part of the third Bersih rally, which took place on 28 April 2012 (*Global Bersih 3.0*, 2012a).

It would be impossible to measure the degree to which new media facilitated these events, and indeed counter-productive to even attempt to apportion the role new media play, given the social imaginary framework. However, the widespread and growing mobilization of Malaysians located overseas on both occasions – 38 locations for Bersih 2.0 with groups ranging from 11 to 1,000 (*Global Bersih 2.0*, 2011), and 85 locations for Bersih 3.0 (*Global Bersih 3.0*, 2012b) – as well as the many reports posted online after the events (*Bersih 2.0 in Washington D.C.*, 2011; *Bersih 2.0 Worldwide*, 2011), are an indication of healthy interest and connectivity to the issue.

The many protests organized and participated in by Malaysian students of international institutes (and others) located outside the Malaysian nation-state make for a good case in point about how new media inflect understandings and experiences of the nation. In order to understand why, it pays to bear in mind that all students of Malaysian higher tertiary institutes, whether located within the borders of the nation or elsewhere, are restrained from political action by law. Malaysia's Universities and University Colleges Act (UUCA) of 1971, denies students of Malaysian tertiary institutes the entire gamut of socio-political expression and action ranging from issuing a simple statement of support and joining an outlawed organization to instigating a protest movement (Hambali et al., 2009).

More recent developments in 2012 show that these conditions are now undergoing change and I discuss them in the next chapter. In the context of Global Bersih in 2011 and 2012, it is important to bear in mind that when both events took place the UUCA was still firmly in place. And in the past, the UUCA has managed to quell most impulses for revolution in Malaysia – a trait for which tertiary study populations are infamous elsewhere. Whilst threats were made to students sponsored by the Malaysian government for their overseas studies and veiled threats of not representing privately sponsored students should they 'get into trouble' for protesting overseas were also made, few were deterred. Not only were protests widespread, as the above list of cities shows, they were also immensely embarrassing for the floundering Najib administration.

It is clear that the accessibility and array of news, photographs,[2] reports and multimedia footage online affected these Malaysian contemporaries (students and others) differently but their effects were no less emphatic, and reactions were equally vocal. The low cost and speed of the production, replication and circulation of online information, combined with the breaching of the barrier of distance it facilitated allowed contemporaries to be reached, engaged and mobilized with a rapidity and intensity that broadcast media could not have achieved.

However, the flow of information is multi-directional and while located overseas many Malaysians enrolled in foreign institutes of learning have used the forum of new media to express their dissatisfaction with the state of affairs in their homeland. The example of Wee Meng Chee (more commonly known by his online alias, Namewee), a Chinese Malaysian graduate of a Taiwanese university, brings this into relief. In 2007, one of Wee's productions – a rap based on Malaysia's national anthem, *Negaraku* in which he expressed his unhappiness at the preferences allotted to *Bumiputeras* in various spheres of life in Malaysia – was uploaded online.

Retitled *Negarakuku* (Wee, 2007), the piece caused an uproar when brought to the attention of the wider Malaysian society because it was then still relatively unusual for Malaysians to so publicly risk a critique of the principle of *Ketuanan Melayu* (Malay paramountcy) on which Malaysia is arguably founded (Ting, 2009). Wee was accused of denigrating religious practices like the Azan (the Islamic call to prayer that takes place five times a day) and treading on racial and religious sensitivities.

Although based in Taiwan, Wee and his father were sufficiently cowed by thinly veiled threats aimed at him and his immediate family resident in Malaysia into offering separate apologies (*Student Says Sorry for Negarakuku Rap*, 2007). The video clip in question has now been officially withdrawn by Wee. Notwithstanding the musical merits of the piece, at its peak Wee's expression of grievance attracted upwards of 1 million hits and clearly struck a chord with many. Its rise and fall, as it were, amply demonstrates the multidirectional flow that is typical of the circuits of information between consociates who share a temporality without inhabiting the same spatiality.

Two other groups of people create one's indirectly experienced social reality: predecessors and successors (Schutz, 1972: 143). Predecessors include those who have existed but no longer do, with whom one may or may not have been personally acquainted. Such individuals may include, for example, visionaries, writers, artists, inventors, ancestors, politicians, neighbours and the ordinary citizen and layperson. In this respect, the vivid accounts of the subjugation and humiliation borne by earlier Malaysian Indians referred to in Hindraf's 2007 petition to the British government are a prime example.

Brought in by British colonizers to Malaya to work in rubber and other plantations as indentured labourers, the earliest arrivals from India tended to be Hindus from the Tamil-speaking parts of India and most hailed from low socio-economic backgrounds. Treated with little respect and care then, many of their descendants still endure unfortunate and precarious living conditions in present-day Malaysia. Despite the many successful professionals who count themselves part of the Indian community in modern Malaysia, for many of them the historical accounts of the hardships experienced by their predecessors still rankle and add to the overall sense of injustice inflicted on their community (S. Leong, 2009). Many thousands of their descendants remain stateless within Malaysia even today (Shankar, 2009).

Some activists amongst them have taken to placing versions of these tales online in the form of video collages from personal and public archives.[3] Perhaps among the best known and most widely circulated is the account compiled courtesy of the online subscription news site Malaysiakini, dubbed *The Malaysian Indian Dilemma* (truthbetoldSir, 29 November 2007, parts 1–6) in a play on Mahathir's seminal book, *The Malay Dilemma* (Mahathir, 1970). According to an informant these videos were released upon the first arrests of the Hindraf leadership group (Suryanarayana, 2007), known collectively as the Hindraf 5, not long after the 2007 rally to 'sustain support for their release' (Arumugam, 2012).

In the account circulated online, a tale of the indignities suffered by the Malaysian Indian community over the decades is related to the demolition of unofficial Hindu temples that have been erected as part of folk worship since the days of the first arrivals. The video clips were uploaded online but also replicated in many forms and distributed. The Hindraf Rally of 2007 was one manifestation of the accumulative ire created by the realities experienced by predecessors, recounted and reiterated with every telling and viewing, on and offline.

Successors are, by comparison, those who are yet to exist and to whom one may or may not be personally related (Schutz, 1972: 143). This group comprises the unborn and can include strangers such as fellow citizens or those to whom one is personally related such as one's descendants. Contemporaries, predecessors and successors can create an individual's indirectly experienced social reality through the influences they wield on that person's actions (knowingly or otherwise).

For example, should the issue of electoral fraud remain unresolved, successors – those who are latecomers to the cause of Bersih 2.0 and 3.0 – might turn to the archived online material and resources to revive the issue. Other successors might be sufficiently concerned over the consequences of electoral fraud for future generations to change their intention to abstain from voting in the next general election. Similarly, indignation and outrage at the references to an anonymous, long-dead group of predecessors like the Malaysian Indians in the proposed high school history textbook, *Interlok* (Navaratnam, 2011), might move an individual to engage in activism or sour their affection for the nation today.

The notion of one's own deeds and words influencing and shaping the lives of those who may follow, one's successors, is also key to how individuals experience their reality. Predecessors and successors are able to affect one's actions, decisions, behaviour and beliefs despite their lack of bodily presence. They are the 'absent partners' that individuals encounter within the 'webs of interlocution' (C. Taylor, 1989: 38). The multitude of hyperlinked and cross-platform resources,[4] textual, photographic, video and otherwise of myriad major and minor events over the years that now reside online constitute an important record. They are a source of both reference and witness and an important component in the ongoing narrative of dissent.

Schutz breaks down the types of relationships that individuals share with consociates and contemporaries into two different orientations. He uses the term '[t]hou-orientation' to describe the ways in which the experiences of one's consociates are apprehended. As one's consociates are known, one lives their experiences as the 'unique experiences of a particular person' (Schutz, 1972: 183), occurring within a specific context of meaning. It is possible to live with and through the experiences of consociates, sharing them in an immediate, face-to-face manner.

Conversely, the experiences of one's contemporaries are apprehended with the '[t]hey-orientation' (Schutz, 1972: 183). As one does not know one's contemporaries, their experiences are grasped as anonymous processes. The specific context of their experience is unknown to one and hence, one's knowledge of these contemporaries and their experiences is 'inferential and discursive' (Schutz, 1972: 183), derived from 'indirect evidence' (ibid., 143). Though one lives with the experiences of contemporaries, one does not live through them.

According to Schutz, the quality of the actions between one's contemporaries and one's consociates also differs. Whereas actions between contemporaries are 'mutually *related*', those between consociates are 'mutually *interlocked*' (Schutz, 1972, original emphasis). This is because whilst the engagement between consociates is immediate, the 'being related to each other of contemporaries occurs in imagination' as contemporaries do not share the same space, only time (Schutz, 1972). As such, they can be described as further removed.

If we accept Benedict Anderson's definition of the nation as an 'imagined political community' (Anderson, 1991: 1) this means that to a certain extent whether 40 or 60 or 80 per cent of Malaysians use and access the Internet and new media is immaterial. Matters in Malaysia have reached the point where information obtained online regarding the main socio-political issues of the day is routinely passed round via new and other media to sufficient users and non-users within and outside Malaysia to influence socio-political action. The readership of online information cannot be restricted to the Internet users only.

Arguably, the event that most vividly illustrates the futility of the use/non-use discourse is the 2008 General Elections of Malaysia, which took place on 8 March. In the weeks and months leading up to the general election itself, anecdotal evidence was already eloquent of the migration of information between users and non-users of the Internet. At the Ijok State Assembly by-election of April 2007, for example, Lim writes of the 'floating voters' of young people residing away from Ijok, Selangor, who are exposed to the Internet who then carry news from the world outside back home to inform others and influence matters (D. Lim, 2012).

Admittedly, during the general elections, opposition parties stymied by micro-budgets and fewer resources were forced to turn their collective attention to the Internet to find creative ways of reaching out to the electorate. So, having new media as an affordable means of disseminating news and information related to the minor parties and opposition was an important part of levelling what was a very uneven playing field. Not much attention was given to secondary use of the Internet by either side of politics but reports filed after the event were recounted, and information obtained online was replicated via other means, e.g. photocopied leaflets, videos and SMS (Yeoh, 2008; Mohamad, 2008).

Uploaded video footage of the Kota Bharu crowd's reactions on election night gives some indication as to how matters unfolded (D. Lim, 2008a). The film captures a predominantly Muslim crowd in Kota Bharu, Kelantan, that had assembled to view television coverage of election results projected onto a large outdoor screen. An informant climbs up on a table and yells out the latest update on election results, which he takes care to mention was obtained via online news portal Malaysiakini. The news was greeted with alacrity and much cheering. The footage offers a rare eyewitness account of how secondary use occurs, as well as how it complements rather than competes with mainstream media.

As such, whether better use and greater leverage of new media by BN would have made a substantial difference to the election results is a moot point. The futility of the use/non-use discourse is all the more telling because of the subsequent myth advanced as explanation after Barisan Nasional lost its two-thirds parliamentary majority. Chagrined admissions from the top as to their inattention to the Internet as the cause of shock election results were the first blocks on which the myth was built (Aw, 2011c; *Abdullah: Big mistake to ignore cyber-campaign*, 2008). Subsequent declarations that with the help of 'BN cybertroopers' the coalition would be better armed for the anticipated 'Internet war' preceding the next election added further blocks to the construction of the myth (Darwis, 2012; Teoh, 2011; Mokhtar, 2011).

The diagnosis that poor use of new media was the cause of the 2008 election results is, at best, a convenient myth. Not only is it politically expedient, reducing a plethora of shortcomings to one simply ameliorated, it is also typical of the technological deterministic attitude discussed in Chapter 3 that underlines how governments understand the relationship between nation and technology. Post-election, thoughtful analyses by some have sought to correct the overstatement by placing the neglect of new media amongst several other factors that tipped the scale (Welsh, 2008; Mohamad, 2008; Saravanamuttu, 2009). Nonetheless, the idea of new media's overriding importance appears to have gained sufficient foothold for every minor use of social media and new media by BN and Prime Minister Najib Razak to be hailed as an accomplishment (*BN a bigger hit on Twitter, says study*, 2012; Sim, 2012).

Over and above the level of sophistry with which either side utilizes new media is the shift in the temper of the people of Malaysia. After all, Malaysians are by and large well past the point where information from any form of media circulates only within the sphere of that medium's users. If nothing else, the rate and growth of social networking via mobile phones in Malaysia should have put the notion of such divided and clearly delineated media spaces to bed. Information is shared freely and widely, and the more indignant a people, the greater the speed at which they are motivated to disseminate information, mobilize and answer the calls to action.

George describes secondary use as a 'sort of two-step flow' and reasons that:

> it should not be surprising that even if the vast majority of people in a country have no computers or Internet access, the technology can have a significant impact if it is in the right hands ... What in fact matters is not

the overall or average level of Internet use in any quantifiable sense, but the qualitative success with which agents of change exploit specific aspects of the technology within a broader offline strategy. (George, 2005: 916)

What is important to remember, then, is that non-users and users of the Internet do not occupy two sides of a chasm which nothing can bridge. Instead, living within the same society, non-users and users are spread out, firstly, across a continuum within which their use of the Internet fluctuates. Beyond opportunity, access, education and socio-economic status, 'life-stage' (Sheldon, 2012: 1961) and 'life fit' (Selwyn, 2006: 284) also determine when Internet use is appropriate. In other words, non-users become users and vice versa at different times for different purposes. Individuals can and do dip in and out of Internet usage and adjust to different degrees of intensity and complexity according to the demands of the situations they find themselves in.

Secondly, non-use of the Internet does not completely cut individuals off from its influences or implications. Simply by existing within societies today where the Internet or knowledge of the Internet is rife, individuals cannot but see, hear and experience by proxy some part of the discourses, news and ideas that circulate within their social imaginaries. Via their coevality with consociates and contemporaries and their interactions, individuals learn of and act on this knowledge and in so doing also become predecessors who leave traces for unknown successors.

Thus, the social reality of our worlds is formed and shaped by those who share our time, sometimes our space and often those who come before and after us. What we know of the rules of the worlds we inhabit is drawn from the tacit knowledge of our social imaginaries, a collective repository of bits of knowledge added to, extracted from, built up and discarded over time by our predecessors, consociates and contemporaries, which our successors also become a part of in time. Because this repository is shared and cumulative, the knowledge it comprises need not come from personal experience. Non-use of a technology is thus as important and effective as its use.

To sum up, so far I have endeavoured to explain the same process from both ends of its operations. In Chapter 1, I used the theoretical framework of social imaginaries to broadly explain how multiple meanings of any signification enter into a society's common knowledge bank, where they often coexist with and contest each other. In the first instance, ideas enter into a social imaginary and remain if they are deemed to be relevant and typical.

A single signification such as a nation, for example, or the Internet, may take on different meanings and be enacted variously as they are interpreted. Significations eventually fall into disuse when they are no longer relevant to everyday life within said social imaginary. In this chapter, I have used Schutz's work to further delineate the social structures that facilitate the formation of the circuits of information that exist between users and non-users of the Internet and new media. In other words, I have explained how ideas are disseminated and transferred from person to person, whether individuals are primary, secondary or unintended recipients of the information.

It is a mistake to understand the users of the Internet and new media as the only ones to engage with the information communicated, because once received, the information is just as likely to circulate at a rate and fashion that surpasses that which is possible with broadcast media. Indeed, given the sheer multiplicity and increasing affordability of devices that can be used to create, relay, replicate, remix, store and access digitized information, and Malaysians' wont to transfer them onto other communication platforms such as print, banner, fabric and other digital forms (sound, video, text, animation, cartoon, etc.), it is almost foolhardy to assume that control over the transmission of information can be maintained.

The socio-political vigilance awakened and enabled in users and non-users of new media through the introduction of the Internet in Malaysia was anticipated but its magnitude and durability were probably grossly underestimated. Surely what remains is the burning issue of how to respond to the consequences of the unexpected level of prolonged scrutiny that is possible as all kinds of information are passed from predecessors to successors, between consociates and contemporaries, and then made available to successors.

Conclusion

Foster (2005: 225) writes in *The Souls of Cyberfolk* that the Internet poses a problem for the imagined community of the nation because it facilitates the creation of intimate circuits that prematurely foreclose the 'open speech terrain' (Price, 1995). According to Foster, because the Internet enables individuals to direct their attention to narrow interests and interactions with like-minded people, broader forms of social cohesion nurtured through wider and, in some cases, less explicit connections, are in danger. In other words, opportunities for incidental interaction are reduced.

Contra Foster I argue that knowledge of the possibilities and consequences the Internet brings, as well as what they mean, can be inferred from indirect evidence, observation and the telling and retelling of other people's experiences. It can also be distributed onwards to be shared by others just as the information on Hindu rights, electoral reform, alleged corruption and bias has been in Malaysia in the past few years.

Non-users of the Internet and new media can be and are affected by the technologies because of the others they exist alongside of. It is not necessary to know someone personally or even to meet them face-to-face to have their life intersect with, influence and inflect one's own understandings and expectations of the nation. This is because social worlds are made up of directly and indirectly experienced social realities and in the case of the latter, it is possible to infer much knowledge from the experiences and tales of those living contemporaneously with one. It is thus highly possible for those who live in the same temporal community to influence each other without sharing the same spatial community.

As far as the imagined community of the nation is concerned, even those located in distant lands such as transnationals, exiles, diaspora, migrants and other non-residents can continue to inform and feed off each other's experiences and knowledge of the originating nation, as well as feed back into the resident national's own understanding and experience of the nation. In doing so, the behaviour, actions, ideas and decisions of these distantly located individuals exert pressure on and influence societies far beyond the ones in which they reside and can produce social implications for the nation. Similarly, it is not necessary to personally experience the vast vistas of the cosmopolitan, post, trans- and supranational world via the Internet for these notions to intrude on how one might live the nation.

In their ideation of Vision 2020, Malaysia's knowledge-based economy and the Multimedia Super Corridor mega project, Mahathir and Shariffadeen both refer to Asian and Malaysian values as distinct from those of the West. They argue that it is because Malaysia's culture is different from Western liberal values that valorize individual freedom, that the knowledge society that will flower in Malaysia through these efforts will be different and better. For instead of a values-free civil society that places the individual above community, Malaysia's 'values-based knowledge society' will prize community over individual and be all the richer for that (Shariffadeen, 2006, 2009).

That Asians practise communitarianism is an established part of ideologues' rhetoric in Asia (Chua, 1995) and one of the main arguments for self-determination and nationhood. It is also an important marker of difference vis-à-vis Western liberal individualism and a key part of the Asian values discourse. In the last quarter of the twentieth century, the notion of Asian values was employed to explain the economic progress of the Asian 'tiger' economies of Taiwan, South Korea, Hong Kong, Malaysia and Singapore (M. R. Thompson, 2000). The virtues of diligence, a strong work ethic and a strong sense of community said to be cultivated by Asian values were advanced as the reason behind the tiger economies' success.

The distinctions drawn between Asian and Western, East and West, heavily shaped the rhetoric of Mahathir and, to a lesser extent, Shariffadeen during the ideation of Vision 2020 and the values-based knowledge society. However, the habits of cultural essentialism and their associated arguments have been part of the political doctrine of Malaysian nation formation since the earliest postcolonial days. Mahathir even had modest success with a 'Look East' policy during the late 1980s (Furuoka, 2007).

It is the insistence on cultural (read ethnic or racial) differences as intractable and incapable of accommodation that underlies the shaping of Malaysia as an ethnocracy, divided on ethno-religious communal lines. The view of culture as constant and fixed is now regarded as a flawed theory. Nonetheless, however problematic, bonds of kinship, blood and belonging are experienced as real by many in Asian and African nations (Geertz, 1963).

In Malaysia, where UMNO, as part of the Barisan Nasional coalition government, has historically relied on its place as the political party representing the majority Malays in order to stay in power, cultural and racial differences have a reality that is reinforced daily in multiple facets of life. Through instruments of governance such as preferences accorded to *Bumiputeras* in the nation's education and economic systems as part of affirmative action, these theoretically problematic assumptions take on an all too tangible and lived truth. It is no exaggeration then to say that cultural essentialism is at the heart of the legitimacy of Malaysia's present coalition government.

In the years since the launch of Vision 2020 in 1991 and the Multimedia Super Corridor mega project in 1996, Malaysians have repeatedly demonstrated that they can assemble peacefully in pursuit of common causes across racial lines. In doing so they have begun to exorcize the ghosts of the 13 May 1969 racial riots. In the decades since the disastrous turn that inter-ethnic relationships took that day, the spectre and the suspicions they aroused have been repeatedly revived to dissuade Malaysians from engaging with the sociopolitical issues, mobilizing others and organizing change.

Despite the constant refrains of 'we are different', the Malays and non-Malays, the Chinese and the Indians have moved fractionally and incrementally towards 'let us communicate, pool resources and take measured action to secure common objectives'. A genuine and viable opposition to the government, made up of a coalition of minor parties and led by ex-Deputy Prime Minister, Anwar Ibrahim, is one result of such adjustments after the twelfth General Elections of 2008.

It would be an overstatement to attribute these changes solely to the Internet and new media, and as I have argued here, even more so to ascribe them to the users of said technologies alone. At this point, it is still too early to tell whether the changes will generate lasting results. However, it is possible to consider some of the new configurations that have arisen as a result of a confluence of factors and conditions, of which new media and the Internet remain an integral part. I discuss these configurations in the next chapter.

Notes

1 As a brief aside, an online search for 'Bersih' performed approximately one month after the event in August 2011 produced 300,000 hits on the Google search engine, more than 83,000 on Yahoo and 100+ on YouTube.
2 See, for example, this collection at: http://picasaweb.google.com/1073982444501277 30928?gsessionid=4Xvae6mJHwviECZ193_TZA
3 See, for example, Malaysian Indian Ethnic Cleansing by UMNO led government, available online at: http://malaysianindian1.blogspot.com/ and Photos: Indians in Malaysia, available online at: http://www.sepiamutiny.com/sepia/archives/004949.html
4 See, for example, http://www.facebook.com/pages/Bersih-20-Sister-Rallies-Worldwide/162151757184140?sk=info

6 Malaysia and the Internet
New configurations?

This chapter will place the connections made between new media and the broader socio-political shifts that have taken place so far within the context of a confluence of conditions. In doing so, it also outlines three possible new configurations leading into Malaysia's thirteenth general election. They are: (1) the rise of what Keane calls 'monitory democracy' (Keane, 2009) in Malaysia alongside the notion of sousveillance, otherwise known as inverse surveillance (Mann et al., 2001: 332); (2) the introduction and/or modification of laws surrounding the new mediascape; and (3) the emergence of transethnic sodalities between Malaysians. It is my overarching argument that underlying the possibility of all these new configurations is the erosion of the Barisan Nasional (National Front) government's legitimacy to rule within Malaysia and the issue of where the legitimacy now lies.

These are by no means foregone conclusions as matters remain very much in flux in Malaysia. So time may prove these configurations to be no more than ephemeral possibilities. Yet above and beyond the unfolding (or not) of these configurations, I suggest that the shifts in the habits and expectations of Malaysians are of the foremost importance. For example, whether users or non-users, sometimes dabblers or online activists, Malaysians are now generally *au fait* with the idea that a multiplicity of information sources should be accessible. The other shift is in the readiness of Malaysians to engage with civil society's movements.

I suggest that such readiness is born of a perception of and growing intolerance towards the inequitable media hegemony enjoyed by the ruling coalition, which has built up most significantly over the course of events since 2007. Daily, intimidating attacks on Bersih at the time of the Bersih 2.0 and 3.0 rallies in 2011 and 2012 as well as personal attacks on leaders of the civil society movements (Khor, 2011; Pathmawathy, 2012b) have also, in the words of Abdullah, 'served to fuel public anger and provided the Bersih movement with all the publicity they could need' (Sheriff, 2011).

The heavy-handed use of water cannons, tear gas and riot police to quell peaceful rallies that have sprung up around civil society movements such as Hindraf and Bersih (Ng and Yoong, 2012; *30,000 Hindraf protesters rally in KL streets*, 2007); the arrests of those attending candlelight vigils (M. Y. Lee,

2009; Zahild, 2009); the law suits brought against activist leaders (J. Gomez, 2012); and the attempted intimidation of Bersih supporters by arresting them for donning yellow (Bersih's signature colour) T-shirts printed with campaign slogans (*Eight arrested for wearing yellow t-shirts with 'Bersih 2.0' written in Jawi*, 2011), have hardened the resolve of those seeking change. The level of resistance has been added to with each of the government's excessively authoritarian responses to the expression of dissent.

Amongst the most striking accumulative effects of the state's (over)reactions to the efforts of these disparate activist groups advocating causes has been the bringing together of these motley groups into unified action, thus creating what Weiss calls 'coalitional capital' (Weiss, 2005: 3). Akin to social capital, Weiss explains that coalitional capital 'facilitates collaboration across groups' and encourages them to 'subordinate their particularistic interests to a broader agenda shared among a range of groups' (ibid.). The most visible such synergy in recent years in Malaysia has been the formation of the opposition coalition, *Pakatan Rakyat* (People's Alliance), which upset the status quo with their election results.

Comprising three main parties, *Parti Keadilan Rakyat* (PKR or People's Justice Party), *Parti Islam Se Malaysia* (PAS or Pan-Malaysian Islamic Party) and Democratic Action Party (DAP), *Pakatan Rakyat* was returned triumphant with 82 seats after the 2008 General Elections and won office to rule over the affairs of five of Malaysia's 13 states (Moten, 2009: 31–2). However, the most troubling aspect of the elections was not so much the presence of a opposition but the loss of a two-thirds majority which forced the government to relinquish 'the legislative strength required for constitutional amendment' that the ruling BN coalition had enjoyed for decades (Jha, 2009: 117). Much significance was attached to the election's outcomes both immediately after the event and since (Weiss, 2009). Amongst the most relevant here are the connections made between the use of new media and the success various parties have achieved at the electoral polls.

Some years have now passed since Malaysia's twelfth general election in early 2008 and the next election looms large on the horizon. How have the portents that greeted Malaysia post GE08 fared? Did the 'political tsunami' that opposition politician, Lim Kit Siang, described in his blog (K. S. Lim, 2008) sweep through and overturn the established political order in Malaysia? On certain terms one might be forgiven for thinking not, for while the election results cost one Prime Minister (Abdullah Badawi) his office and introduced Malaysia to its sixth Prime Minister, Najib Razak, the federal government is still dominated by the same party. Yet, since then Prime Minister Razak has introduced a number of initiatives to broadly address the dissatisfactions expressed by Malaysians. These include the 1Malaysia project, the Government Transformation Plan (GTP), the Economic Transformation Plan, the New Economic Model (NEM) and the 10th Malaysian Plan (RMK-10).[1]

Electoral reform continues to be an unresolved issue as the Bersih 3.0 rally that took place in April 2012 illustrated. Hindraf also continues to be a thorn in the side of the government with its focus on Indian Malaysian issues such as the plight of students who cannot complete their education due to being deemed stateless, despite being born in Malaysia (Woon, 2012). At the same time, the opposition coalition, *Pakatan Rakyat* (PR), has been plagued with internal rifts (B. N. Kumar, 2012), the resignations of key personnel (Habibu, 2010; Mahmood, 2012) and major differences of opinion between coalition partners over core ideas like PAS's intent to implement Hudud laws for Muslims (Islamic penal code) (Sabri, 2012; Zurairi, 2012). All of these might give one pause to wonder whether a PR government would perform better than a BN one.

However, beyond the question of whether a PR government would be better than the incumbent government is the issue of how Malaysians understand the current situation that confronts their nation. It is important to note that growing sympathy with the little person's struggle against a dominant political machinery is evident in all of the three events – the Hindraf and Bersih rallies as well as the general elections – discussed in Chapter 5. This awareness of a David and Goliath battle being waged between the political establishment and a fledgling opposition coalition and civil society was reinforced during the 2008 General Elections (D. Lim, 2008b). It would be difficult even for Malaysians previously content with their lot to ignore the very public altercations between supporters of social movements and the government. Nor would it be easy to dismiss any unease raised by the domineering display of power put on by the government.

At this stage it remains too early to tell if empathy with the underdog will coalesce sufficiently to motivate even more Malaysians to join the ranks of civil society and express their dissent with the government's conduct. There is also no telling whether the PR coalition will be voted into federal office, or even if they might form a more effective and fair government. However, by continuously reacting injudiciously to the prodding of civil society, counteracting the demands for openness, political engagement, diversity, reform and accountability by tweaking and enacting laws to clamp down on freedom of expression on and offline, the Najib administration is certainly keeping the discontent provoked by these issues in the forefront of most citizens' minds.

In doing so, what it risks is the whipping up of resistance where none existed before. A concept closely allied with anarchy, resistance is fundamental to how the Internet is imagined and experienced (Coyne, 1999; Barlow, 1996). The Internet's anti-authoritarian and defiant attitude to governance, regulation and control is not just the stuff of fables but is rooted in how the suite of technologies and platforms such as the World Wide Web, Wikileaks and Open Source Software function up to today. Aside from being a means of communicating dissent, the Internet's roots are powerful narratives, and if sufficiently allied to collective action can have important consequences. As Prime Minister Najib clearly appreciates, the Arab Spring revolt that saw several heads of governments deposed in the Middle East is a case in point (Aw, 2011d).

Given the continuing restrictions on broadcast and mainstream media (Sani, 2005), the Internet has become amongst the foremost sources of information because stories told online, such as those produced by state news agency, Bernama, often offer alternative views that challenge the status quo and party line. Malaysians are also beginning to view citizenship as an act requiring participation rather than a right obtained by birth to be held in passivity. A good example is social activist Pete Teo's latest campaign urging Malaysians to exercise their right to vote ahead of impending elections in the near future, which is encapsulated in the exhortation, *undi lah* (vote lah). Even prior to the campaign's launch on 16 September 2011, it already had its own website, Facebook page, rap video trailer and Twitter hashtag.[2] In the sub-region of Southeast Asia where the citizens of Philippines, Indonesia and Thailand have led the way, Malaysia is a latecomer to this understanding of citizenship as active participation. Nonetheless, the political mobilization and engagement of the Malaysian citizenry is still ahead of fellow ASEAN (Association of Southeast Asian Nations) members, Singapore and Myanmar.

What, then, are the new socio-political configurations that have and are developing leading into the thirteenth general election and what do they suggest for the future of Malaysia as a nation? It is my argument that underlying the possibility of all these new configurations is the erosion of the Barisan Nasional government's legitimacy to rule within Malaysia and the issue of where the legitimacy now lies.

To make this argument, I return firstly to the discussion begun in Chapter 2 on the emphasis of race categories as a source of legitimation to the representation of the Malays by UMNO in the early days of postcolonial Malaysia, and the hardening of these ethnic-communal divisions when the NEP (New Economic Policy) left off. Then I examine the intra-Malay and inter-class tensions heightened by the arrest of Anwar Ibrahim and the gradual Islamization that has alarmed and alienated parts of the populace.

These strategies, events and ideologies are all intricately intertwined and near impossible to disentangle or make complete sense of in one brief chapter. However, by using the growing presence of the Internet in the Malaysian social imaginary as the other trajectory, the intersections that occur should allow us some insights into the new configurations that are emerging and likely to develop leading into the next election and the changes it may herald.

Barisan Nasional, legitimacy and the right to govern

Gilley writes that '[p]olitical legitimacy can be defined as the degree to which a state is viewed and treated by citizens as rightfully holding and exercising political power' (Gilley, 2005: 31). The above presumes a democratic government rather than an authoritarian one. By and large, citizens within democracies acquiesce to the imposition of certain restrictions and constraints by the state in order to enable the greater public good. Of course, these same citizens must perceive some individual return within the system set up as such. Although what constitutes the public good is increasingly argued to be a homogeneous, universal set of values closely aligned to the notion of basic human rights, Asian democracies have been quite successful in the latter part of the last century in arguing for an alternative version built around the notion of Asian values.

Marked by its pragmatist rationale, the discourse of Asian values began as an explanation for the successful economic transformations experienced by the five tiger economies (Taiwan, South Korea, Hong Kong, Malaysia and Singapore) over three decades (M. R. Thompson, 2000: 654). In a sense, as Sun points out, the discourse of Asian values is an act of self-orientalism, performed in response and in contrast to Western dominance but 'directed against Asian Occidentalism' (Sun, 2007: 10). The tiger economies' impressive progress was slowed with the 1997–8 financial crisis in the Asia-Pacific but the discourse of Asian values has not abated. If anything, the accompanying discourse of Asian democracies that emerged from it has since garnered the Asian compromise between democracy and development much favoured within the region (Jones, 2007). Additionally, China's attention to this instance of 'cultural expediency' (Yúdice, 2003) as a source of legitimation for authoritarian, single-party states has increased its prominence and may yet elevate Asian values to a system of governance accepted by a significant proportion of the world's people (M. R. Thompson, 2000: 654).

Historically, Southeast Asian states have fought to achieve prosperity after the devolution of colonial masters. Some states have been able to achieve greater economic success than others and claim such successes to be the result of their adoption of 'non-liberal' democracy; amongst them, Malaysia and Singapore top this list. Simply put, the Asian democracy argument is that 'until prosperity is achieved, democracy is an unaffordable luxury' (M. R. Thompson, 2000: 655). In fact, one of its chief proponents, Singapore's elder statesman, Lee Kuan Yew, has dismissed pleas for liberal democracy as 'highfalutin' and 'dangerous' (K. Y. Lee, 2009). The main qualities so vaunted in the Asian drive towards prosperity are hard work, frugality, discipline and teamwork (M. R. Thompson, 2000: 655). In the decades before the 2008 General Elections, the one-party government of Malaysia flirted with and presented its own versions of Asian values and democracy in attempts to shore up its legitimacy to rule.

From the 1980s through to the 1990s, for example, Prime Minister Mahathir advocated his countrymen 'Look East' (rather than West) for guidance in their aspiration towards greater economic progress (Furuoka, 2007). Admittedly, an anti-Western, pro-Asian, postcolonial stance had always been part of Mahathir's political posture and he excelled in pitting his nation and his people against the West.[3] As Malaysia's longest-serving Prime Minister, his characteristic pugnacity left its own legacy on Malaysian foreign relations and added to the weight of the Asian values discourse. Islamic values also gained their increased accent in UMNO most noticeably after Mahathir took office as Prime Minister in 1981 amidst growing demands for an Islamic state and system of law within Malaysia (Noor, 2005: 221). Until then, although UMNO drew its support mostly from the Malays and all Malays are by law followers of Islam in Malaysia, UMNO remained largely secular in orientation. However, the party sought to reclaim its place as the champion of the Malays and strengthen its ties with Islam in the 1980s with a brand of Islam that has been described as 'statist-developmentalist-modernist' (Noor, 2005: 221).

This last development, as mentioned in Chapter 5, has to be understood against the rise of opposition party PAS as the conservative Islam party that genuinely represents the interests of the majority Muslim population (Noor, 2005, 2008). The fact that PAS has consistently been returned to government in the state of Kelantan since 1990 and intermittently so in the state of Terengganu and performed relatively well has only meant that UMNO could not rely solely on race and/or religion for its claims to legitimacy. Instead, UMNO as self-proclaimed representative of the Malays in Malaysia had to position itself strategically as a moderate and modern Islamic party of Malaysia.

The background to these attempts at shoring up legitimacy with values lies in the history of UMNO's formation as a party. Formed in 1946, UMNO obtained its legitimacy primarily through its representation of the majority Malay population. Through co-optation of the two other ethnic-communal parties, the Malaysian Chinese Association (MCA) and the Malaysian Indian Congress (MIC), into coalition, the BN has been in power since gaining independence from the British in 1957. In the decades since then, two major episodes and/or issues have shaken the faith of UMNO's support base. They are the 1998 arrest of then Deputy Prime Minister and now Opposition leader, Anwar Ibrahim, on corruption and sodomy charges (*Anwar's injuries investigated* 1998; *Anwar in court again* 1998) and the *reformasi* movement that emerged from that period of protest in Malaysia (E. T. Gomez, 2007: 1) and the failure of UMNO to deliver on its promise to improve the socio-economic position of the poorer, rural Malays despite 40 years of the New Economic Policy and more than half a century of continuous self-rule by the same coalition.

In 1997, for example, the poorest 20 per cent of Malaysians still earned just 4 per cent of national income (Gilley, 2005: 53). The figures for 2008 are no better, when the poorest 10 per cent of Malaysians earned a measly 1.7 per cent even as the top slice of Malaysian society account for 38.4 per cent of total income (Jha, 2009: 122). In other words, socio-economic inequalities between the different classes have worsened.

At the same time, as a result of Anwar's spell in government during the Mahathir era (1981–1997/8), intra-Malay tensions were also heightened. Rocked by the currency crisis of 1997/8 and tired of Mahathir's multitude of mega projects – which always promised much but failed to deliver meaningful alleviation of poverty – the traditional support base of UMNO, the rural Malays, were ready for an alternative. Despite its deeply conservative pro-Islam agenda, when PAS softened its stance sufficiently to collaborate with the other non-Islamic minor parties during the 1999 election, the Malay voters in Kelantan and Terengganu voted them into power. PAS secured a respectable 27 of the 193 seats in parliament in 1999 (Khalid, 2007: 14).

This strategy of Islamization within the broader discourse of Asian-Islamic values took on a moderate mien when Abdullah Badawi succeeded Mahathir in 2003. During the campaign period of the 2004 general election (the eleventh), Badawi introduced the concept of *Islam Hadhari* (Civilizational Islam) into the party manifesto and emphasized its moderate, progressive and inclusive nature in contrast to PAS's more stringent brand of Islam. Instead of *Sharī'ah* laws and an Islamic state, Islam Hadhari proffered a softer vision of a moderate Islam that would sanction the pursuit of development through scientific and technical knowledge and accommodate the other ethnicities within Malaysia (Khalid, 2007: 138, 145–6; Hamayotsu, 2010: 168).

When the BN government won the 2004 elections in a landslide victory, it was taken by some to be an endorsement of UMNO's general reorientation towards Islam. It needs also to be mentioned that given the religious fanaticism that motivated the events of 2001, global powers such as the US were eager to welcome allies in the region who espouse moderate and progressive Islamic views. That the Malaysian government has sought and gained international validation for their adoption of moderate Islam through gestures like the Global Movement of Moderates (GMM) has also had the effect of further reinforcing the rightness of and international endorsement of their strategy (F. N. Karim, 2010).

Through a theory named 'pluralist neutrality' Gilley has devised a system that measures the legitimacy of governments within contexts based on attitudinal and behavioural data (Gilley, 2005: 39). According to him, there are four main components to legitimacy. These are distributional essentials, right essentials, executive selection and policy process (Gilley, 2005: 39–41). There is not the space to delve into these in detail here. However, using this system and data from selected sources, Gilley finds that in 2004/5, legitimacy, defined earlier as 'the degree to which a state is viewed and treated by citizens as rightfully holding and exercising political power' (Gilley, 2005: 31), is not as high in the case of Malaysia as the government would like to believe. According to Gilley, the moderate levels of legitimacy are an accurate reflection of where the Malaysian government stands on the regulatory and redistribution fronts (Gilley, 2005: 30). That is to say, though not a runaway success with voters, the BN-led government was deemed to have done moderately well by its people.

Case argues that in a single-party dominant system (such as Malaysia's) the task of understanding how citizens evaluate legitimacy is less complicated because of the 'relative simplicity in the institutions and policies' of such a system (W. Case, 2010: 500). He lists two dimensions to be considered in such an exercise. The first dimension consists of 'the institutions and procedures by which a government acquires and exercises state power'. The second centres on the outputs of a government's policies (W. Case, 2010: 500–1). According to Case, Malaysians 'profoundly revis[ed] their preferences' in the elections of 2008 because they perceived the government to lack legitimacy on both counts: how the government exercises power as well as policy outcomes. Clearly, at some point between the moderate levels of legitimacy deemed in 2004 and the surprise election results of 2008, Malaysians must have changed their minds about the BN-led government's performance. What did happen to alter their views?

There is no shortage of accounts of the various controversies that have featured large in the period between 2004 and 2008 (Weiss, 2009; S. Leong, 2009). In earlier chapters I have mentioned the 2007 march held by the Bar Council over allegations of corruption in judiciary appointments sparked by the leaked Lingam video, the rally organized by Hindraf in search of redress for historical wrongs, and Bersih's protest rallies for clean and fair elections. Other incidents such as Lina Joy's unsuccessful bid to have her apostasy from Islam and conversion to Christianity recognized by the state have exacerbated the frustration felt by ethnic minorities over the increasing Islamization of Malaysia (Hamid and Azman, 2007).

At the same time, broader interest in the affairs of Islam aroused after the events of September 2001 in the US mean that international observers have also been keeping a close eye on events in Malaysia. Despite its self-promotion as a moderate Muslim nation, for example, the state has passed the severe sentence of caning on a Muslim woman guilty of drinking beer in 2009 (*Model to be caned for drinking beer in Malaysian bar*, 2009). The sentence was subsequently commuted by the Sultan of Pahang to three weeks of community service in 2010 (*Malaysia beer drink woman's caning sentence commuted*, 2010) but matters might well have been different if not for international criticism levelled at the handing down of a sentence of six strokes of caning for the consumption of an alcoholic beverage.

It is my argument that rather than the incidents described above, what precipitated changes to perceptions regarding the BN government's legitimacy to rule is the habit of scrutiny. I explain why in the next section and discuss possible developments leading into the next elections, i.e. the rise of monitory democracy and sousveillance by Malaysian citizens.

Monitory democracy in Malaysia?

Political theorist John Keane points to an emergent style of democracy that he names 'monitory democracy' (Keane, 2009). According to him, this development is in part a result of the easy and convenient tools of communication that have seen the growth of many 'extra-parliamentary, power-scrutinising mechanisms' within and outside the nation-state. Though he considers it a 'post-representative democracy', Keane maintains it is not particularly American, Western or European in character but can and does take on different colours.

In the case of Malaysia, one might think of the non-governmental organization Human Rights Watch[4] as one international component of monitory democracy. Sites such as The Malaysia Insider[5] and The Nut Graph[6] can also, in varying degrees, be considered part of this new mechanisms of scrutiny, as can the blogs Rocky's Bru[7] and the Blog of Disquiet,[8] as well as those authored by Susan Loone[9] and Zorro Unmasked.[10] Additionally, the organizations mentioned in previous chapters, such as *Suaram* and *Aliran* and the pre-Internet and conventional institutes like the Merdeka Center for Opinion Research,[11] are also significant participants in the task of examining and explaining the play of power and the space for democracy in Malaysia. Others, such as Politweet,[12] represent the newer crop of more specialized platform-specific democracy monitors. In themselves, not all of these groups are explicitly pro-democracy, but every single one named above is monitory in intent.

Given the proliferation of these mechanisms, it seems that, flawed as it is, democracy in Malaysia is taking a turn towards Keane's 'monitory democracy'. The fact that many of these instruments of scrutiny were first seeded in the period surrounding Anwar's arrest in 1998 demonstrates that such a development did not occur overnight. It also means that they are less likely to melt away once stated objectives are met. This is the case even if their aims are not nearly as altruistic as those expressed by Malaysiakini's co-founder, Premesh Chandran, as being to: 'inform the Malaysian public of the latest news and critical issues in an independent and fair manner, and to facilitate discussion of current concerns, thereby challenging the views produced by the government-dominated mainstream media' (*Interview with Premesh Chandran of Malaysiakini (Malaysia) on Media Reform*, 2011).

By definition, the goal of providing alternative views exists in perpetuity. Homogeneity on any level is beyond all contemporary nations and hegemony is disintegrating in Malaysia. It is my suggestion that monitory democracy is set to become a part of everyday life in Malaysia as watchfulness becomes habitual, expected behaviour.

There is an allied concept to the notion of monitory democracy – that of 'sousveillance' (Mann et al., 2001: 332). Defined contra surveillance, which involves observation from above via devices such as closed circuit television (CCTV), sousveillance is inverse, visual monitoring that occurs from below rather than above. Simply put, it involves members of the public using portable visual technologies to document events as they occur. In so doing, it 'hold[s] a mirror up to the establishment' (Mann et al., 2001: 332) and attempts to turn the tables on the surveillers and neutralize the power of surveillance.

Mann's original conception of sousveillance involved the use of heftier, much more obvious visual recording cameras mounted on the bodies (forehead, chest, back) of individuals, as the confrontation of surveillers with inverse surveillance was as much a part of the notion as the cameras and footage (Mann et al., 2001: 332). The routine inclusion of high resolution video and still cameras as standard features on mobile phones today has altered the performance of sousveillance somewhat with inverse monitoring now made relatively affordable and less obtrusive. Nonetheless, the nature of reverse surveillance as a means of grassroots scrutiny remains the same.

In Malaysia, where Internet penetration via mobile phone sits at 123.5 per cent in the second quarter of 2011 (*Penetration rates at a glance*, 2011),[13] sousveillance is a distinct avenue for those who prefer passive resistance. A few incidents have already come to light that illustrate both the potential and dangers of reverse surveillance. In 2009 a resident group from the city of Shah Alam used a severed cow's head (the cow is considered a sacred animal in Hinduism) as a prop in their protest over the relocation of a Hindu temple to an area close to their housing estate. In the fall-out over their crude attempts to offend, the protesters tried to deny having planned the addition of the animal's head (Andrew Ong, 2009). However, when confronted with 10 minutes of detailed, continuous video footage of their protest as they led the procession through streets,[14] they were unable to sustain their plea of innocence.

Even then, when called to a public dialogue to resolve the issue the residents concerned were adamant they were right to do as they did (*Malaysia: Public Dialogue on Hindu Temple Relocation After Cow Head Protest Disrupted*, 2009). It was only the furore that broke out after the footage was viewed online by hundreds of thousands in Malaysia and made news overseas that the chief instigators were arrested. Though perhaps no more than a slap on the wrist, the main perpetrators were eventually called to answer for their deeds (Jong, 2010). To be clear, the footage was not shot by an amateur but by a crew from online news portal Malaysiakini, but it is also arguably only because it was uploaded by this staunchly independent media outlet that it remains online in defiance of the governmental pressures to take it down (*Human Rights Watch: Stop harassing Malaysiakini*, 2009).

Conversely, in March 2011 a video clip by the Datuk T trio (later disclosed to be former Malacca chief minister Rahim Tamby Chik, businessman Eskay Abdullah and former treasurer of Malay rights group, Perkasa, Shuaib Lazim) allegedly featuring de facto opposition leader, Anwar Ibrahim, having illicit sex was publicly disseminated (*Datuk T trio may face charges*, 2011). Though not illegal, adultery is heavily frowned upon in Malaysia and if sustained, the accusation would have brought intense social condemnation down on Anwar Ibrahim. What is revealing is Anwar's spouse's faith that 'the people can see through this' (Aw, 2011a). The individuals responsible have since been fined for distributing pornography; the truth of the footage remains undetermined (ibid.). The same concerns with privacy that adhere to surveillance apply here, but as with Anwar's sex video, it relies on and places added onus on ordinary citizens to weigh up the value of raw video footage.

How the revelatory mechanisms and results of monitoring are employed, participated in, viewed and evaluated by private citizens, state institutions, civil society and the international community observing developments is crucial to the success of monitory democracy and sousveillance in Malaysia. If shorn of critical evaluation, it can descend into voyeurism and/or titillation and defeat even the noblest of objectives. What is undeniable is that along with the circuits of information between users and non-users, Malaysians are also called upon to exercise judgement and restraint in how they act in public life as well as how they react to the results of public scrutiny as they are made online.

This is all the more so as social networking platforms incorporate audio-visual capabilities into their software and facilitate ever more rapid sharing of information across social circles. Ultimately, as Keane puts it, in media-saturated democracies '[c]itizens are tempted to think for themselves; to see the same world in different ways, from different angles; and to sharpen their overall sense that prevailing power relationships are not "natural", but contingent' (Keane, 2009). That, in a nutshell, is the root of the challenge to UMNO's legitimacy to rule I referred to at the end of the last section.

Disciplining dissent

There is another new configuration that is firmly on the horizon in Malaysia. That is the rise of a legal regime surrounding the expression of dissent on and offline. Now, it is important to note that as mentioned in previous chapters, a whole range of media laws and ownership arrangements in relation to traditional media (press, television and radio) already exist that ensure the ruling coalition has tight rein over media content and coverage (Nain, 2007; P. Leong and Yap, 2007).

As is the case in Singapore, this combination of ownership, censorship and licensing controls has proven very effective in ensuring that the aims of mainstream media are subordinated to the task of nation-building. However, as also explained in earlier chapters, whereas Singapore has had no hesitation in extending the same level of control online (T. Lee, 2010: 103–28), Malaysia's commitment to the Multimedia Super Corridor project has seen the nation commit to a Bill of Guarantees that promises, amongst other things, 'no censorship of the Internet' (*MSC Malaysia 10 Point: Bill of Guarantees*, 2008). In the aftermath of an electoral loss that BN attributes to its lack of attention to the Internet, the urge to similarly discipline the online dissent and disorder that the ruling coalition sees as its undoing is not surprising.

Beginning with the early part of 2011, a number of potential changes to the Printing Press and Publication Act (PPPA) were raised by the Najib administration, framed initially as a response to calls for reform (*Malaysia to Consider Reviewing Law on Print Media*, 2011; *Do away with obsolete PPPA*, 2011). However, nested amongst the suggestions advanced was the idea of a media monitoring mechanism and the enlargement of laws like the PPPA to include online media (Kamal, 2011a). After resounding rejection of the suggestion from all sides of civil society, the proposed amendments was temporarily shelved (Gan, 2011). Subsequently, when the BN government later censored a report carried in *The Economist* on the second Bersih protest in July even as online sources carried the unabridged versions, it was subjected to a barrage of criticism at home and overseas (Gooch, 2011; *Malaysia censors Economist article on protest* 2011). The furore indicates the increasing strength of feeling against measures to curb the ability of citizens to keep check on broadcast media by using new media as alternative sources of information.

A year later, in 2012, a compromise allowed the PPPA to be amended and passed into law in Malaysia (Pathmawathy and Zakaria, 2012; Pathmawathy, 2012a). The primary concessions made were in two parts. Firstly, instead of annually renewable printing licences and permits, a one-off licence is now in place. Secondly, whereas the grant and continuance of the annual licence used to be at the absolute discretion of the Home Minister, it is now subject to judicial oversight (Printing Presses and Publication (Amendment) Act 2012, 2012). Notably, the proposed widened definition of 'publication' to include online media was excluded from the amended Act.

However, in view of the amendments, a problematic, 10-year-old proposal to set up a media council (Nain, 2011) to encourage 'media stakeholders' (Kamal, 2011a) towards self-regulation was revived and seems imminent. Critics of the proposed council have not hesitated to point out that rather than increased media freedom, what Malaysia may well end up with is greater restrictions on media (Rudra, 2012; J. L. Koh, 2012; *Malaysia (2012): State aims to control cyberspace* 2012). The amendments to the PPPA, though, are but one of a slew of amendments and changes to law surrounding the policing of dissent in Malaysia that have occurred in recent years.

With the Prime Minister's pleas that 'street demonstrations are not part of Malaysian culture' falling on stony ground (*Street demo will bring more bad than good, says King*, 2011; Anis and Rahim, 2011), the Peaceful Assembly Act (Peaceful Assembly Act, 2012) was introduced to replace the Police Act. The new Act restricts the minimum age of demonstration organizers to 21 years and participants to 15 and requires advanced notice of any planned assembly. It also forbids public assemblies to be held within 50 metres of a 'prohibited place' (Peaceful Assembly Act, 2012: 18), which includes, amongst others, schools and kindergartens, airports, places of worship, railways and hospitals.

While defended by the government against fierce condemnation as necessary to prevent the reoccurrence of the racial riots that took place on 13 May 1969 (*Nazri uses May 13 riots to justify street protest ban*, 2011; *Peaceful Assembly Bill comes under UN fire*, 2011; *Peaceful Assembly Bill mala fide, says ex-top cop*, 2011), the overall effect of the Peaceful Assembly Act, as Whiting observes, is to grant 'police ... an almost unlimited discretion to impose conditions and restrictions' (2011).

I have already mentioned the Universities and University Colleges Act (UUCA), which, up until 2012 forbade Malaysian university students in or outside Malaysia to express any political opinion or participate in any political activity. The year 2012 also saw crucial amendments made to the UUCA to allow students to participate in lawful and suitable societies, organizations, groups or bodies, including political parties. Following the amendments, support or activity on behalf of political parties is still forbidden but students can now express their opinions or make statements regarding academic matters which they are engaged in studying, or on research at lawful and suitable gatherings (*Amendments to UUCA Testimony of Government's Confidence in Undergrads – Najib*, 2012: 6–7). The vaguely defined nature of what is deemed 'suitable' has not been lost on observers.

The amendments to the UUCA follow a successful High Court challenge brought by four students – Muhummad Hilman Idham, Woon King Chai, Muhammad Ismail Aminuddin and Azlin Shafina Mohamad Adza – in October 2011, wherein the relevant Section 15 of the UUCA was ruled unconstitutional and in violation of students' freedom of expression (Yatim, 2011). Now graduates of the *Universiti Kebangsaan Malaysia* (UKM, National University of Malaysia), the four were summoned by the university to attend disciplinary proceedings for their alleged participation in the Hulu Selangor by-election in April 2010 (C., 2011b). Subsequent appeals by the government, university and higher education ministry failed to overturn the High Court ruling (*Section 15 (5) (a) UUCA: Federal Court dismisses appeal*, 2011). Notwithstanding this string of events, Prime Minister Najib Razak was not abashed to claim the amendment a sign of the 'government's confidence in undergraduates' ability to be mature thinkers and responsible citizens (*Amendments to UUCA Testimony of Government's Confidence in Undergrads – Najib*, 2012).

It is no coincidence that these amendments to the laws of Malaysia surrounding media, dissent and political expression are about the fastest methods of counteracting the rise of scrutiny by the citizenry *à la* monitory democracy. Perhaps the greatest sleight of hand managed so far is the repeal of the notorious Internal Security Act (ISA) and the Sedition Act and their replacement with the Security Offences (Special Measures) Act 2012, as well as amendments to the Penal Code and Evidence Act, and the proposed National Harmony Act to be tabled in 2013 (I. Lim, 2012).

Renowned for legalizing the detention of individuals without trial or criminal charges, the oppressive ISA has long been vilified as an archaic relic of the British colonial era. Hence, its repeal is not a minor step and was greeted, at least initially, with cautious hope (*Najib announces repeal of ISA*, 2011) though it was subsequently dampened (*Malaysia Replaces Its Worst Law: Najib is barely keeping up with society's demands for change*, 2012). As Malaysian Bar President Lim Chee Wee points out, the new Security Offences (Special Measures) Act is riddled with overly wide definitions, a lack of judicial oversight and 'radical departures from the current rules of evidence [such as the] use of a summary of the evidence (as opposed to the evidence itself) and the lowering of the admissibility threshold' (C. W. Lim, 2012).

By contrast, in likely reaction to these developments Singapore's government has wasted no time reasserting that the ISA is 'still relevant' for the nation (Tengku, 2011), citing its extreme vulnerability as a small nation as the basis of the need. At the same time, the single-party government has also done an exemplary job of curbing online criticism. During the early part of

2011, for example, the Prime Minister's Office gazetted the opinion blog, The Online Citizen (TOC), stating that:

> [a]s a website that provides coverage and analysis of political issues, TOC has the potential to influence the opinions of their readership and shape political outcomes in Singapore. It has been gazetted to ensure that it is not funded by foreign elements or sources. (C., 2011a)

Additionally, Singapore's Media Development Authority has separately asked the site's editors to identify its owners, editorial team and administrators as well as appoint a president, treasurer and secretary as it was to be registered under the Broadcasting (Class Licence) Notification (*The Online Citizen to be listed as political association*, 2011). Very few of those involved and others observing failed to note that this move by the authorities occurred a few months before the general election in May 2011.

At the same time, Prime Minister Lee Hsien Loong introduced the notion of doing away with anonymity for bloggers in Singapore into the 'national conversation' (PeoplePower, 2012; *PM Lee meets bloggers, netizens for tea at Istana*, 2012). It is very unlikely that Singapore will see fit to allow the level of online freedom of expression and access that Malaysians still enjoy at present. Whether they will continue to do so remains to be seen.

I have contended all along that the guarantee of an Internet free of censorship is the lynchpin of many of the changes that have occurred since 1995 in Malaysia. This is not the same as saying all the events and transformations have been due to the empowerment experienced by Internet users. The socio-political changes are much deeper and cut too broadly across the Malaysian social imaginary to be explained by the usage of new media, however liberating and innovative.

However, it is fair to say that without the guarantee in the first place, it would have been difficult to find discursive space for wider socio-political dissent in Malaysia, whatever the numbers of 'mainstream media doubters' (Mohamad, 2008: 453). The gaps inherent in the tensions between a mainstream mediascape straitened by laws, licensing and ownership arrangements, and an online media ecology populated by journalists with ideals, as well as activists and observers who can comment and discuss all the social and political issues and more that occupy daily life in Malaysia, have been productive.

Perhaps the greatest achievement in this respect has been the overcoming of the fear of a repeat of the racial riots of 13 May 1969 that was the reason for much of the paralysis over socio-political issues for many decades. Such a triumph would have counted for less if it had been confined online. What made it a greater and more valuable transition has been its translation into action, mobilizing thousands to participate and express their dissatisfaction over electoral fraud, for example, at the 2007, 2011 and 2012 Bersih rallies; encouraging Malaysians to exercise their right to vote for a government that represents their interests in 2008; and, prior to that, urging citizens to devote thought and discussion to what these interests might be.

The online media environment has seen a rich diversity of Malaysian interest groups, independent bloggers, socio-political institutions and bodies come to life. These have, in turn, created an alert and responsive civil society that has helped to defuse situations that might in the past have caused violent damage. In the cow's head protest mentioned earlier, for example, matters could easily have flared into worse confrontations given the insensitive and provocative nature of its instigators' actions (S. Leong, 2012). As it is, despite further religiously barbed aggravation on both sides the incident eventually subsided after some of the provocateurs were apprehended and censured. Though the fairness of such an outcome can still be disputed, it is apparent that unthinking responses have benefited from the counsel of cooler heads. It is this opening of consultation between groups using a mix of new and older forms of media across a variety of interests that is the real prize for Malaysia.

Trans-ethnic sodalities

Malaysians have from the very establishment of their nation been accustomed to think of themselves as 'naturally' divided into three main ethnicities: Malay, Chinese and Indian. Their postcolonial history has dictated their political parties to be organized along these lines and the same divisions have been instilled into their structures of life through governmental policies that identify citizens as members of ethnic communities before all else. Ethnicity is, thus, a major signification within the Malaysian social imaginary, relevant and typical because it is intertwined with nearly all the other major shapers of life. Within Malaysia, ethnicity impacts on how educational and employment opportunities are apportioned, how religious beliefs and practices predicate lifestyle and behavioural expectations, and even how the fundamental human rituals of birth, marriage and death are performed. To imagine Malaysia as a nation is also, then, to think of the ethnicities that inhere within.

This is why I suggest that the third new configuration that lies ahead for Malaysia is the emergence of trans- rather than post-ethnic sodalities. Mandal writes of trans-ethnic sodalities as 'a variety of efforts whereby Malaysians actively participate in society without respect to ethnic background and by rejecting primordial notions of ethnicity' (Mandal, cited in Gabriel, 2011: 357). There are a number of reasons why I think the trans-ethnic configuration a more likely prospect than the post-ethnic.

Firstly, on an experiential level Malaysians regularly transcend the divisions of ethnicity in matters of cuisine, language and relationships. Rare are the Malaysians who have no acquaintances outside of their ethnicity or cannot utter a few phrases in languages other than their mother tongue. There already exist, therefore, promising foundations for a trans-ethnic understanding within the Malaysian social imaginary. Secondly, whilst it is one thing to usher in an era of post-ethnic politics (Mohamad, 2008), it is another altogether to dismantle an established system of identification. This is supported by the emergent trend among civil society to phrase their causes, views and arguments in a fashion that indicates that while Malaysians admit to the divisiveness of ethnicity, they also recognize its centrality in their worldview.

To appreciate the fine line between ethnic division and identification, one can look to the 2009 online music video *Here in My Home* (*Here in My Home – Malaysian Artistes for Unity*, 2009), where all the language and ethnic groups of Malaysia are carefully represented in the musical assertion of unity. These creative collaborations, such as *Here in My Home* and the video teaser to the *Undi lah* campaign mentioned earlier wherein Malaysians are urged to vote, express a wish to unite not despite but because of ethnic differences. The same might be said of the Bersih movement. Through the variety of its campaign resources and the multi-ethnic composition of its steering committee, Bersih demonstrates an awareness that whilst its demand for transparency, clean and fair elections is pitched at a level that transcends ethnic politics, it still has to appeal for support from a populace steeped in ethnic identification. The thousands who turned up in support of the Bersih protests in 2007, 2011 and 2012 comprised all kinds of ethnicities, but I contend they turned up with a determination to unite for a common cause because of the ethnic differences that have prevented them from working together for too long.

The configuration of trans-ethnic sodalities is a logical transitional stage as Malaysians search for, introduce and adopt new articulations of the nation as a signification into their social imaginary. The discourses opened up in part via new media are a vital component of this process. Though not all Malaysians use the Internet, the conversations, topics and critiques generated, amplified and circulating through and from new media galvanize more and reach further than one might imagine. The protests launched in cities as far afield as Turkey, China and Austria supporting Bersih's campaign attest to the reach of new media (*Bersih 2.0 Worldwide*, 2011), as do the Malaysians living overseas who are agitating to have their voices and votes count (Yoga, 2011).

In themselves, because of the ethno-communal lines round which political parties are still organized in Malaysia, the general elections may not serve the development of broader, trans-ethnic alliances. However, causes like the protests against the rare earth plant, Lynas, in the state of Kuantan, the self-styled, *Himpunan Hijau* (Green March) (*Malaysians protest Aussie refinery*, 2011; Wong, 2012), are more likely to bring Malaysians together regardless of race, income or educational levels. Any heavy-handed reactions from the ruling BN coalition to these peaceful assemblies are also going to have some coalescing effect for the population.

As to what lasting form such trans-ethnic sodalities might take, Gabriel's work on the notion of *Bangsa Malaysia* suggests it may be a likely candidate. For Gabriel, the notion of *Bangsa Malaysia* hints tantalizingly at the possibility of a more inclusive, trans-ethnic identity that is 'commensurate with the nation's heterogeneous social realities and experiences' (Gabriel, 2011: 350). Though first mooted over 20 years ago by Mahathir in the same speech in which he outlined his vision for Malaysia leading up to the year 2020 (Mahathir, 1991), the concept of *Bangsa Malaysia* has never been officially defined or outlined by the state. However, that the word *bangsa* could be translated to mean nation or race means its ambiguities have been heavily debated ever since.

Gabriel argues that interpreting *Bangsa Malaysia* as a race upsets the relation between race and nation made so matter of fact in that context, rendering it a much more complex 'ideological tool' (Gabriel, 2011: 370). As such, it is an ideal first step in 'undoing the racial norms and hierarchies associated with the old, hegemonizing idea of race and nation' (ibid.: 372). Gabriel's objective is to move the discussion in Malaysia on from its obsession with race by arguing for more inclusive forms of identity. For her, rather than being lost, something is to be gained in the translations between cultures, ethnicities and languages that routinely take place in everyday life in Malaysia (Gabriel, 2011: 353). Immigrant and indigenous, native and incomer have no need to fear being tainted by each other but should instead welcome the accretion of the other's influence to their own.

Conclusion

Amidst the reminders from Prime Minister Najib Razak that reforms can only continue if BN is re-elected into federal government (Kamal, 2011b; Sivanandam, 2011) and the generous handing out of pre-election goodies in the 2013 budget across many sectors of Malaysia's population (Welsh, 2012; *Najib: Measures will help real poor*, 2012), it is clear that the ruling coalition understands its tenure is at stake. At this point in time the three new configurations discussed in this chapter are no more than nascent possibilities. While monitory democracy appears well set to become a part of the sociopolitical scenery in Malaysia, the situation could change with the rewriting and/or implementation of amended and new laws surrounding media and freedom of expression as well as how national interests are guarded in relation to information.

If and when these laws, amended and new, are enacted, they could mean on the one hand, greater liberation for mainstream media along the same lines as that currently enjoyed by online media. That may neutralize some of the novelty of the anti-governmental stance that at present finds expression mostly online. However, it may not be all that simple for media organizations habituated to their place in nation-building through the creation of consensus to fulfil a new role as media watchdogs for the people. Even if these restraints were removed, Malaysians would be mindful that the major mainstream media corporations are owned or controlled through various arrangements by members of the political elite.

On the other hand, if the proposed Media Council's remit extends to include online media and discourse, it could effectively muzzle criticism and opposition online. This is especially the case if it can be managed without the government having to renege on its guarantee not to censor the Internet. However, even if the decision is made to subject the Internet to some form of censorship either by setting up a monitoring body or bringing major civil society and media organizations into a licensing scheme, I suggest it is too late to wean Malaysian civil society off its habits of critique, engagement and mobilization. Even if the current flow of online expression is stemmed, new voices and instruments will be found that incorporate traditional as well as more personal technologies like photocopying, billboards, mobile texting and word-of-mouth. And as long as these newly formed but long-awaited habits of querying and expectations of explanations persist, with or without new media, the viability of trans-ethnic sodalities developing remains strong.

Notes

1. See http://www.pmo.gov.my/#
2. See http://www.undilah.com, https://www.facebook.com/undilah.msia, http://www.youtube.com/watch?v=JhlyvlstcM8 and http://twitter.com/#!/undilah
3. For example, in 1970 Mahathir penned a volume titled *The Malay Dilemma* (1970), in which he blamed the plight of the Malays on the greed of the Chinese. During the 1997–8 Asian currency crisis Mahathir also famously installed capital controls and accused the American-Jewish financier George Soros of being the mastermind behind the problems of the region (S. Vines, 1997).
4. See http://www.hrw.org
5. See http://www.themalaysianinsider.com/
6. See http://www.thenutgraph.com/
7. See http://www.rockybru.com.my/
8. See http://disquietblog.wordpress.com/
9. See http://sloone.wordpress.com/
10. See http://zorro-zorro-unmasked.blogspot.com.au/
11. See http://www.merdeka.org/
12. See http://www.politweet.org
13. Over 100% penetration rate is explained by multiple subscriptions.
14. See http://www.malaysiakini.tv/video/17689/temple-residents-march-with-cows-head.html

In closing

Over two decades of 'developmentalism', in which mega-sized investments into infrastructure have been matched with forward-looking visions backed by bold policies, the Internet has become firmly established in the Malaysian social imaginary as an agent of change. Although the rhetoric surrounding these projects has not always been matched by their realization, there are few more concrete examples of the powerful pull a cyber-libertarian discourse can exert on the everyday than what has taken shape in Malaysia. Some part of the Internet's perceived place in Malaysia has been amplified by the seeming successes of civil society in recent years, such as those discussed in this volume.

Not surprisingly, then, whatever the vagaries of the MSC and the state's projections of the benefits of new media, the focus remains on how new media use creates change in Malaysia. The introduction of the Internet has been accompanied by changes in the Malaysian nation. This is not in dispute. However, that these changes are the consequence of new media alone is not an argument that holds water. Oftentimes, as I have argued in Chapters 4 and 5, people do not always utilize technologies in the intended manner. They change, adapt and appropriate as they see fit, and sometimes they do not use technologies.

Whether a matter of choice or circumstance, non-use and, more importantly, non-users cannot be excluded from how societies understand the implications of new media. This is because the circuits of knowledge and information exist between contemporaries and consociates, users and non-users, and also because the flow of significations, potentialities and enactments continues between predecessors and successors. The same might be said of any suite of information and communication technologies. It is imperative, then, that the intersections and collisions between societies and technologies are framed in terms that allow us to view and understand the full measure of their multi-faceted implications.

I have proposed the social imaginary framework here as one approach. It has the advantage of being able to accommodate the multiple potentialities of any signification, allowing for a plurality of modernities and interpretations beyond the dominant Anglophone world. Others will have different approaches. What is evident is that as accessibility to the Internet improves across the world, more people of non-Anglophone/European cultures will encounter this seemingly endlessly growing suite of technologies. To study what and how these peoples understand, imagine and expect of new media will call for robust theories that can withstand the complex multiplicities of everyday realties.

To be sure, alternative media are not a new phenomenon in Malaysia. Indeed, Brown writes of the *surat layang* (flying letters) that circulated in towns and villages 'carrying rumour and innuendo about prominent politicians', as well as taped recordings of breakaway politician Razaleigh's speech distributed via cassette tapes in the late 1980s as examples of 'unofficial broadcast' (Brown, 2004: 85). In the 2000s, the mix of alternative media forms has been supplemented by SMS texts, tweets and social networking sites. The same strategy of subverting officially sanctioned media communication through the provision of counter-information has been translated into digital formats for both formal and informal dissemination.

Nonetheless, this moment marks an important passage in Malaysia's social imaginary. According to Weiss, political reform in Malaysia has progressed in two directions: institutional and cultural (Weiss, 2005: 240). In this volume I have argued that the new media have played a pivotal role in socio-political change through the information, mobilization and engagement of Malaysia's populace. The most obvious illustrations are the enduring campaign being waged for reform in the political institution of the electoral system in Malaysia through Bersih; the heightened accountability many more Malaysians now expect of their government; and the shift in their understanding of their own ability to bring about change. Some of this can be explained by the practice of scrutiny, evaluation and discussion enabled and habituated for the average citizen by new media – monitory democracy. In a sense, this has always been the self-appointed task of Malaysian civil society but their objective is now shared by increasing numbers able to contribute via new media.

Steele lays the burden for the habit of scrutiny at the feet of the subscription news site Malaysiakini (Steele, 2009). Started in 1999, Malaysiakini has withstood police questioning and threats, office raids and the confiscation of equipment (*Malaysia: End Intimidation of News Website*, 2003). However, it has remained consistent in its bid to provide balance to reporting news in Malaysia and in the process, both introduced and habituated the notion of scrutiny by citizens (i.e. citizen journalism) to Malaysia's countrymen and women. This runs counter to how mainstream or broadcast media have understood their mission in Malaysia, excelling in their allotted task of 'nation-building' *à la* Barisan Nasional (*Media must work for a united Malaysia: PM*, 2010) rather than performing their role as watchdogs for the people.

This brings me to the next point: for as long as they continue to inhabit the same mediasphere (Appadurai, 1990: 9), new media must always be considered in relation to mainstream media. For it is against the backdrop of constrained mainstream media that new media are seen as alternative and liberatory. Of course, this contrast varies from nation to nation and is more marked in nations like Malaysia and Indonesia than in Australia. In other words, it is because of the restraints placed on mainstream media in the form of permits, punitive laws and ownership that new media play the renegade role in Malaysia. Through these mechanisms, mainstream media in Malaysia remain compliant to the ruling coalition directives, whilst the Bill of Guarantees' undertaking not to censor the Internet that is part and parcel of the MSC project allows new media organizations such as Malaysiakini much greater latitude.

Nonetheless, there is no gainsaying the importance of Malaysia's veteran civil society organizations like *Suaram* and *Aliran*. However advanced and sophisticated, new media do not create social movements, mobilize citizens or engage populations. The fact that technologically advanced and thoroughly wired neighbouring Singapore's civil society (Ho, 2009; Liu, 2011) is nowhere near as active as Malaysia's is evidence that wider use of and proficiency with new media do not lead inevitably to citizen engagement or social transformation. An active civil society remains pivotal to the advocacy and enactment of socio-political change. Equally important to the practice of citizen rights and responsibility is the example that civil society proponents provide of the notion of agency within the social imaginary.

Right now many hard questions are being asked of the BN government. The government's efforts to divert the flow of discussion into the same tired issues of ethno-religious rights and quarrels demonstrates a dearth of political imagination and courage in their organization. Events may overtake any diversions these strategies offer as the pressure from the poorly handled controversy over the usage of 'Allah' in Christian bibles lingers on, and unhappiness over native land titles in Sabah and Sarawak mounts in the period leading up to the thirteenth general election (*Cops halt Orang Asli advance in Putrajaya*, 2011). At this stage, it is thanks to the two states in Borneo Malaysia that BN holds the majority to govern federally. The impasse on such matters bodes ill for the ruling coalition. I have not been able to explore the implications of new media for Borneo Malaysia here. Separated by the South China Sea, East Malaysia is geographically, demographically and historically distinct from West Malaysia. The broader implications of the Internet for East Malaysia, if different from that for West Malaysia, remain an area yet to be explored, and an area that I must leave to others, such as John Postill (2006).

In Chapter 6 I suggested that one of the new configurations that awaits further development in Malaysia is the formation of *Bangsa Malaysia*. According to Gabriel, this is a more inclusive trans-ethnic, Malaysian identity that is 'commensurate with the nation's heterogeneous social realities and experience' (Gabriel, 2011: 350). What form might that identity take and how might it be articulated? In Khoo's (2009) analysis of the late Malaysian filmmaker Yasmin Ahmad's oeuvre, the author eschews pluralism for its concern with maintaining existent, separate cultures and advocates instead the understanding of cosmopolitanism best suited to Malaysia as one that is 'willing to put the future of every culture at risk through the sympathetic but critical scrutiny of other cultures' (David Hollinger, quoted in Khoo, 2009). I find myself in sympathy with this view and, like Khoo, understand such a process to be part of the path towards the creation of *Bangsa Malaysia*.

In the meantime, in lieu of this transformation I look to Ahmad's work itself for a vision of what this Malaysian identity might be, and find great resonance in the characters of the film *Sepet* (Chinese Eyes) (2005). The film revolves around the story of two young lovers, Jason and Orked, who, on first examination, are opposites in socio-economic as well as racial terms. It opens with the seemingly Chinese male protagonist, Jason, reading a poem to his Malay-speaking mother in Mandarin and bantering with her in Cantonese. The opening scene then segues to the background music of a Cantonese song performed by Hong Kong singer-songwriter, Sam Hui. Middle-class and Muslim, Orked makes her first appearance in the film garbed for prayer and reading the Koran. She speaks Cantonese and impeccable English, is a fan of Hong Kong film director John Woo's films and admires Japanese actors. Orked's familiarity with Cantonese is explained later in the narrative by her mother's avid following of Hong Kong soap operas, accessed through subtitles.

No doubt there will be those who will inform me that Malays in Malaysia rarely speak Cantonese, let alone remark openly on the aroma of roast pork like Orked does in the film. Or that few Chinese jobless men recite Sufi poetry and give away the odd pirated compact discs they sell for profit as Jason does to Orked. In pointing out these anomalies they miss the point. Films, like science fiction, allow us all to envision what might be. And in Ahmad's film, at least two Malaysian families and their families from different cultures, religions and socio-economic backgrounds are able to converse, love and grieve together. The realities of class, religious and racial differences are not elided in *Sepet* but a vision of how they might coexist is gently articulated.

As I have shown in this volume, the formation of new significations within social imaginaries begins with the conception of ideas and their enactment by individuals within that society where the idea takes root. Social realities begin with these new significations and their interpretations. Such a translation of *Bangsa Malaysia* is not yet reality for the majority of Malaysians but the diffusion of such views via new media and other means are part of the progressive shift in this nation's social imaginary that may bring this vision to life. This is a vision wherein the people of the nation begin to regard themselves as Malaysians rather than Malays, Chinese or Indian. Popular sentiments found in narratives like the Bersih stories profess such to already be the case and condemn politics for the divisions within Malaysia (Hwa, 2012).

Attendant to this changed vision is the possibility that they will ask that their government sheds its reliance on ethno-religious communalism and instead of being the government that looks after the interests of the Malays, Chinese and Indians, that it be the government for all Malaysians. Governments are only as strong as they are deemed to be legitimate. As such, they should invite scrutiny and offer accountability if they wish to have the support of their people.

Rather than fear the damage that may be wrought if civil society is let loose in new media along with mainstream media, the Malaysia polity should welcome these developments. Their emergence and vibrancy are better signs of Malaysia's progress as a nation than any of the grandiloquent buildings erected in Putrajaya. The empty streets of Putrajaya after office hours make that point well. The Internet was identified and introduced as a major factor in helping Malaysia achieve developed nation status by 2020. Even if not achieved precisely as anticipated, the vision of a socially, politically, culturally as well as economically developed Malaysia is tantalizingly within reach.

Is the case of new media in Malaysia an unusual exception or can broader insights be derived from this example? Within the Southeast Asian context, the different trajectories that new media have taken in Malaysia, Indonesia and Singapore are already fertile grounds for comparative studies (Liu, 2011), but what further insights might be had of the interactions and relationship between nation and technology, users and non-users?

Writing of the study of the Internet as a field of research, Canadian sociologist Barry Wellman (2004) identifies three ages of Internet studies. Wellman's survey begins with the 'rampant punditry' of the early 1990s that led, according to him, to the second age where 'the systematic documentation of uses and users' began some time around 1998. Within this scheme, the third age began in the early 2000s when documentation gave way to analysis (presumably of uses and users) (Wellman, 2004: 124–7).

I am not about to declare the onset of a fourth age but I do want to suggest that alongside the various ages that Wellman identifies there has always been an accompanying discourse of non-use and non-users. For most of Internet studies' progress from the first to third age, apart from the noted exception of the digital divide, the study of non-use and non-users has been relegated to the margins of the stories we tell ourselves about the Internet. It is my suggestion that rather than problematized, non-use and non-users be regarded as an opportunity for the development of a contrapuntal attitude (Said, 1978) towards new media's implications for nations. The notion of contrapuntal reading is pivotal to postcolonial studies' insistence on the revelation of voices and narratives that are suppressed. Here, it serves to highlight the complexities of non-use and non-users that are far too often ignored as more nations forge ahead with the envisioning, formation and implementation of new media technology policies.

Finally, as increasing numbers of technologically deterministic accounts valorizing the role of new media as a catalyst for social change continue to build media participation into a fetish, the discourses of non-use and non-users can only become more important as a counterpoint. Within social imaginaries, the links made in these accounts between new media, participation, power and democracy are at risk of hardening. Yet, as Carpentier reminds us, participation should not 'be celebrated as the ultimate solution to all societal problems' (Carpentier, 2011: 358). Rather than an obligation, 'participation should remain an invitation – permanently on offer and embedded in balanced power relations – to those who want to have their voices heard' (ibid.: 389). Just as not every idea becomes a signification for every social imaginary, not all raised voices are heard nor does every person want to speak on every issue. For democracy to thrive and nations to move onwards, space must also be found to listen and time put aside to observe and consider those who speak and those who do not, those who use new media and those who do not.

Glossary

Bangsa Malaysia: the term refers to Prime Minister Mohamed Mahathir's suggestion that all three separate races within Malaysia (Chinese, Indian and Malay) may be unified as one under this term. 'Bangsa Malaysia' broadly translates as Malaysian race or nation. Thus, 'Bangsa Malaysia' may be understood as a 'trans-ethnic Malaysian identity'.

Bumiputeras: 'sons of the soil'. Malaysia identifies itself as a 'multicultural nation' and has a population comprised of three main races. The term 'bumiputeras', however, is used to refer specifically to native Malaysians, as opposed to the other races that occupy Malaysia.

Janji Ditepati: 'Promises Fulfilled' – the theme the Barisan Nasional chose to celebrate Merdeka Day in 2012.

Ketuanan Melayu: Malay paramountcy.

Vision 2020: Prime Minister Mohamed Mahathir announced the Vision 2020 Statement in 1991, in which he outlined his government's visions for the future development of the nation of Malaysia. He later described Vision 2020 as an effort to provide a 'clear idea of where [Malaysia] wanted to go and what we wanted to be by the year 2020' (Mahathir, 2011: 596). Obtaining developed nation status was a long-term vision for Malaysia within Vision 2020.

References

30,000 Hindraf protesters rally in KL streets (2007). Kuala Lumpur: *Malaysiakini*. Online. Available at: http://www.malaysiakini.com/news/75250, 25 November (accessed 19 October 2012).

Abbate, J. (1999). *Inventing the Internet,* Cambridge, MA: MIT Press.

Abdullah: Big mistake to ignore cyber-campaign (2008). Kuala Lumpur: *Malaysiakini*. Online. Available at: http://www.malaysiakini.com/news/80354, 25 March (accessed 18 October 2012).

Abdullah, M. C. (11 September 2012). *RE: Users and Non-Users of New Media in Malaysia.*

About Us (1999). *Malaysiakini*. Online. Available at: http://weblog.malaysiakini.com/?page_id=2 n/w (accessed 9 January 2009).

About Us (2009). Suara Rakyat Malaysia. Online. Available at: http://www.suaram.net/about (accessed 2 September 2009).

About Us (2012). *Aliran*. Online. Available at: http://aliran.com/about-us (accessed 9 December 2012).

Abshire, J. (2011). *The History of Singapore,* Santa Barbara: Greenwood.

Ahmad, S. K. (2012).'*One country, one soul' – Pakatan's Merdeka theme. Malaysiakini*. Online. Available at: http://www.malaysiakini.com/news/205177, 2 August (accessed 2 August 2012).

Ahmad, Y. (dir.) (2005). *Sepet*. Malaysia: Columbia Tristar.

Alatas, S. H. (1977). *The Myth of the Lazy Native,* London: Frank Cass.

Amendments to UUCA Testimony of Government's Confidence in Undergrads – Najib (2012). Shah Alam. Online. Available at: http://1malaysia.com.my/news_archive/amendments-to-uuca-testimony-of-governments-confidence-in-undergrads-najib/, 21 March (accessed 12 December 2012).

Aminullah, E. (2007). Long-Term Forecasting of Technology and Economic Growth in Indonesia. *Asia Journal of Technology Innovation,* 15: 1–20.

Amir, S. (2004). The Regime and the Airplane: High Technology and Nationalism in Indonesia. *Bulletin of Science, Technology & Society,* 24: 107–14.

Amis, K. (1975). *New Maps of Hell: A Survey of Science Fiction,* New York: Arno Press.

Amry, S. (1997). *Our level of IT-literacy needs work, says Mimos chief. New Sunday Times.* Online. Available at: http://news.google.com/newspapers?nid=1309&dat=19970810&id=pJxOAAAAIBAJ&sjid=HBUEAAAAIBAJ&pg=4397,1179980,10 August (accessed 20 July 2011).

Andaya, B. W. and Andaya, L. Y. (2001). *A History of Malaysia,* Basingstoke: Palgrave Macmillan.

Anderson, B. (1991). *Imagined Communities: Reflections on the Origins and Spread of Nationalism,* London: Verso.

Ang, B. L. (1997a). *Definition of an IT-literate society. New Straits Times.* Online. http://www.nst.com.my/, 28 October (accessed 23 July 2011).

Ang, B. L. (1997b). Moving ahead with an IT visionary. *Management Times,* 4 November.

Anis, M. N. and Rahim, R. (2011). *Street demonstrations not part of Malaysian culture, says PM.* Kuala Lumpur: *The Star Online.* Online. Available at: http://thestar.com.my/news/story.asp?file=/2011/7/11/nation/9077307&sec=nation July 11 (accessed 11 July 2011).

Anonymous (18 September 2012). *RE: SMSes from BN.* Type to S. Leong.

Anwar in court again (1998). BBC News. Online. Available at: http://news.bbc.co.uk/2/hi/asia-pacific/185943.stm, 5 October (accessed 9 September 2009).

Anwar's injuries investigated (1998). BBC News. Online. Available at: http://news.bbc.co.uk/2/hi/asia-pacific/185035.stm, 2 October (accessed 9 September 2009).

Appadurai, A. (1990). Disjuncture and Difference in the Global Cultural Economy. *Public Culture,* 2: 1–24.

Arthurs, A. (2003). Social Imaginaries and Global Realities. *Public Culture,* 15: 579–86.

Arumugam, J. (24 August 2012). *RE: Users and Non-Users of New Media in Malaysia.* Type to S. Leong.

Asian Development Bank and Malaysia: Fact Sheet (2011). Asian Development Bank. Online. Available at: http://www.adb.org/Documents/Fact_Sheets/MAL.pdf, April (accessed 31 July 2011).

Aw, N. (2011a). *Azizah thankful public can see through sex video. Malaysiakini.* Online. Available at: http://www.malaysiakini.com/news/171934 – Malaysia, 4 August (accessed 13 August 2011).

Aw, N. (2011b). *Dr M confident Arab Spring won't reach M'sia. Malaysiakini.* Online. Available at: http://www.malaysiakini.com/news/182626, 28 November (accessed 29 November 2011).

Aw, N. (2011c). *Minister: We lost the Internet war on rally. Malaysiakini.* Online. Available at: http://www.malaysiakini.com/news/170581, 21 July (accessed 21 July 2011).

Aw, N. (2011d). *Najib to Umno: Reform or face an Arab Spring. Malaysiakini.* Online. Available at: http://www.malaysiakini.com/news/182610, 28 November (accessed 29 November 2011).

Aziz, A. and Shamsul, A. B. (2006). The Religious, the Plural, the Secular and the Modern: A Brief Critical Survey on Islam in Malaysia. *Inter-Asia Cultural Studies,* 5: 341–56.

Azzman appointed chief executive of Mimos Berhad (1996). Kuala Lumpur: *New Straits Times.* Online. http://www.nst.com.my/, 6 November (accessed 29 November 2012).

Bacon, F. (1974). *The Advancement of Learning and New Atlantis,* Oxford: Clarendon Press.

Bahfen, N. (2008). Modems, Malaysia and Modernity: Characteristics and Policy Challenges in Internet-Led Development. In: G. Goggin and M. McLelland (eds.),

Internationalizing Internet Studies: Beyond Anglophone Paradigms, New York: Routledge.

Barlow, J. P. (1996). *A Declaration of the Independence of Cyberspace.* Electronic Frontier Foundation. Online. Available at: http://www.eff.org/~barlow/Declaration-Final.html (accessed 20 April 2002).

Barr, M. D. (2000). Lee Kuan Yew and the 'Asian Values' Debate. *Asian Studies Review,* 24: 309–34.

Bell, D. (2001). Storying Cyberspace 1: Material and Symbolic Stories. In: *An Introduction to Cybercultures,* London: Routledge.

Benedikt, M. (ed.) (1991). *Cyberspace: First Steps,* Cambridge, MA: MIT Press.

Berners-Lee, T. and Fischetti, M. (1999). *Weaving the Web,* London: Orion Business.

Bersih 2.0 – About (2011). Bersih. Online. Available at: http://www.bersih.org/?page_id=4109 (accessed 9 December 2012).

Bersih 2.0 in Washington D.C. (2011). Washington: *Malaysiakini.* Online. Available at: http://www.youtube.com/watch?v=KkI9hwhYBz0, 10 July (accessed 11 July 2011).

Bersih 2.0 Worldwide (2011). ukchannelsss. Online. Available at: http://www.youtube.com/watch?v=JZyLYFXobk0&feature=related, 9 July (accessed 11 July 2011).

Bersih 2.0's 8 Demands (2011). Kuala Lumpur: Bersih Steering Committee. Online. Available at: http://www.bersih.org/?page_id=4111, 26 June (accessed 23 October 2012).

Bersih 3.0 (2012). Bersih.org. Online. Available at: http://www.bersih.org/?p=4696, 14 April (accessed 24 April 2012).

Bersih People's Gathering, 10 November 2007 (2007). Bersih 2.0. Online. Available at: http://bersih.org/?p=335, 23 October (accessed 2 March 2011).

Bethke, B. (1995). *Headcrash,* New York: Warner-Aspect.

Bill to ensure best deal for investors (1996). *Business Times. Factiva.* Online. 2 August (accessed 29 November 2012).

Billig, M. (1995). *Banal Nationalism,* London: Sage.

Birch, D. (1993). *Singapore Media: Communication Strategies & Practices,* Melbourne: Longman Cheshire.

BN a bigger hit on Twitter, says study (2012). *Malaysiakini.* Online. Available at: http://www.malaysiakini.com/news/206980, 24 August (accessed 24 August 2012).

Bolt, C. (1971). *Victorian Attitudes to Race,* London: Routledge & Kegan Paul.

Brown, G. K. (2004). Between Games and Graffiti: Opposition Politics and the Impact of the Internet in Malaysia. In: J. P. Abbott (ed.), *The Political Economy of the Internet in Asia and the Pacific: Digital Divides, Economic Competitiveness, and Security Challenges,* Santa Barbara: Praeger.

Brown, R. H., Barram, D. J. and Irving, L. (1995). *A Survey of the 'Have Nots' in Rural and Urban America.* Washington, DC: National Telecommunications and Information Administration.

Bunnell, T. and Coe, N. N. (2005). Re-fragmenting the 'Political': Globalization, Governmentality and Malaysia's Multimedia Super Corridor. *Political Geography,* 24: 831–49.

Burman, E. (2003). *Shift! The Unfolding Internet: Hype, Hope and History,* Chichester: Wiley.

C., R. (2011a). *A chill in the blogosphere.* Singapore: *The Economist.* Online. Available at: http://www.economist.com/blogs/banyan/2011/01/singapores_media, 19 January (accessed 12 September 2011).

C., R. (2011b). *Students in Malaysia: Up with the UKM4!* Kuala Lumpur. Online. Available at: http://www.economist.com/blogs/banyan/2011/01/students_malaysia, 20 January (accessed 13 December 2012).

Calhoun, C. J. (1997). *Nationalism,* Buckingham: Open University Press.

Cameron, D. (2011). *PM Statement on Social Disorder in England.* London: Prime Minister's Office. Online. Available at: http://www.number10.gov.uk/news/pm-statement-on-disorder-in-england/, 11 August (accessed 26 November 2012).

Cameron, J., Wisher, W., Schwarzenegger, A., Patrick, R., Hamilton, L., Fiedel, B., Buff, C., Greenberg, A. and Carolco Pictures Inc. (dirs.) (2003). *Terminator 2: Judgment Day.* Videorecording. Australia: Universal Pictures (Australasia).

Cameron, J., Schwarzenegger, A., Hamilton, L. and Bieln, M. (dirs.) (2004). *The Terminator* Film. Sydney, NSW: MGM Home Entertainment Australia [distributor].

Cardwell, D. S. L. (1972). *Turning Points in Western Technology: A Study of Technology, Science and History,* New York: Science History Publications.

Carpentier, N. (2011). *Media and Participation: A Site of Ideological-Democratic Struggle,* Bristol: Intellect.

Case, W. (2010). Political Legitimacy in Malaysia: Historical Roots and Contemporary Deficits. *Politics & Policy,* 38: 497–522.

Case, W. F. (2000). The New Malaysian Nationalism: Infirm Beginnings, Crashing Finale. *Asian Ethnicity,* 1: 131–47.

Castells, M. (1996). The Culture of Real Virtuality: The Integration of Electronic Communication, the End of the Mass Audience, and the Rise of Interactive Networks. In: *The Rise of the Network Society,* Malden, MA: Blackwell.

Castells, M. (2000). *The Rise of the Network Society,* 2nd edn., Malden, MA: Blackwell.

Castells, M. and Hall, P. (1994). *Technopoles of the World: The Making of 21st Century Industrial Complexes,* London: Routledge.

Castoriadis, C. (1987). *The Imaginary Institution of Society,* Cambridge: Polity Press.

Castoriadis, C. (1997).The Social Imaginary and the Institution. In: D. A. Curtis (ed.), *The Castoriadis Reader,* Cambridge, MA: Blackwell.

Cavallaro, D. (2000). *Cyberpunk and Cyberculture: Science Fiction and the Work of William Gibson,* London & New Brunswick, NJ: Athlone Press.

Chia, S. C., Li, H., Detenber, B. and Lee, W. (2006). Mining the Internet Plateau: An Exploration of the Adoption Intention of Non-Users in Singapore. *New Media and Society,* 8: 589–609.

Chin, J. (2009). The Malaysian Chinese Dilemma: The Never Ending Policy (NEP). *Chinese Southern Diaspora Studies,* 2: 167–82.

Chua, B.-H. (1995). *Communitarian Ideology and Democracy in Singapore,* London: Routledge.

Cleaver, H. (1994). *The Zapatistas and the Electronic Fabric of Struggle.* University of Texas. Online. Available at: http://www.eco.utexas.edu/Homepages/Faculty/Cleaver/ (accessed August 22 2000).

Clemente, P. C. (1998). *State of the Net: The New Frontier,* New York: McGraw Hill.

Communications & Multimedia: Pocket Book of Statistics, Q2 2012 (2012). Cyberjaya: Malaysian Communications and Multimedia Commission.

Cops halt Orang Asli advance in Putrajaya (2011). Putrajaya: *Malaysiakini.* Online. Available at: http://www.malaysiakini.com/news/126760, 17 March (accessed 18 March 2010).

Corey, K. (2000). Intelligent Corridors: Outcomes of Electronic Space Policies. *Journal of Urban Technology,* 7: 1–22.

Country has long way to go in information technology (1996). Kuala Lumpur: *New Straits Times.* Online. http://www.nst.com.my/, 21 November (accessed 20 July 2011).

Cowan, R. S. (1985). How the Refrigerator got its Hum. In: D. Mackenzie and J. Wajcman (eds.), *The Social Shaping of Technology,* Milton Keynes: Open University Press.

Coyne, R. (1999). *Technoromanticism: Digital Narrative, Holism, and the Romance of the Real,* Cambridge, MA: MIT Press.

Crane, C., Gillen, M. and McDorman, T. L. (1998). Parliamentary Supremacy in Canada, Malaysia and Singapore. In: *Asia-Pacific Legal Development.* Vancouver: University of British Columbia Press.

Cyberlaws and Intellectual Property Laws (2007). Putrajaya: Multimedia Development Corporation Sdn Bhd. Online. Available at: http://www.msc.com.my/cyberlaws/ (accessed 11 April 2007).

Dahlberg, L. (2001). *Extending the Public Sphere through Cyberspace: The Case of Minnesota E-Democracy.* University of Illinois at Chicago University Library. Online. Available at: http://firstmonday/org/issues/issue6_3/Dahlberg, 2–5 March (accessed 28 August 2005).

Darwis, M. F. (2012). *Saifuddin: Cybertroopers, social media key to BN's GE13 success.* Kuala Lumpur: *The Malaysian Insider.* Online. Available at: http://www.themalaysianinsider.com/malaysia/article/saifuddin-cybertroopers-social-media-key-to-bns-ge13-success, 14 October (accessed 18 October 2012).

Datuk T trio may face charges (2011). Petaling Jaya: The Star/Asia News Network. Online. Available at: http://www.asiaone.com/News/AsiaOne%2BNews/Malaysia/Story/A1Story20110419-274347.html, 19 April (accessed 12 December 2012).

Davis, E. (2002). Synthetic Meditations: Cogito in the Matrix. In: D. Tofts, A. Jonson and A. Cavallaro (eds.), *Prefiguring Cyberculture: An Intellectual History,* London: MIT Press.

Descola, P. (2005). No Politics Please. In: B. Latour and P. Weibel (eds.), *Making Things Public: Atmospheres of Democracy,* Cambridge, MA: MIT Press.

Devadas, V. (2009). Makkal Sakthi: The Hindraf Effect, Race and Postcolonial Democracy in Malaysia. In: D. P. S. Goh, M. Gabrielpillai, P. Holden and G. C. Khoo (eds.), *Race and Multiculturalism in Malaysia and Singapore,* Abingdon: Routledge.

Dibbell, J. (1998). *My Tiny Life: Crime and Passion in a Virtual World,* New York: Henry Holt.

Do away with obsolete PPPA (2011). *The Sun Daily.* Online. Available at: http://www.thesundaily.my/news/151058, 21 September (accessed 28 September 2011).

Dutton, W. H. and Blank, G. (2011). *Next Generation Users: The Internet in Britain. Oxford Internet Survey 2011 Report,* Oxford: Oxford Internet Institute.

Dyer, R. (1997). *White: Essays on Race and Culture,* London: Routledge.

Dyson, E., Gilder, G., Keyworth, G. and Toffler, A. (1994). *Cyberspace and the American Dream: A Magna Carta for the Knowledge Age.* Progress & Freedom Foundation. Online. Available at: http://www.pff.org/issues-pubs/futureinsights/fi1.2magnacarta.html, August (accessed 14 April 2004).

The East Asian Miracle: Economic Growth and Public Policy (1993). New York: The World Bank.

Ede, A. and Cormack, L. B. (2004). *A History of Science in Society: From Philosophy to Utility,* Peterborough, ON: Broadview Press.
Edgerton, D. (2006). *The Shock of the Old: Technology and Global History since 1900,* Oxford: Oxford University Press.
Edgerton, D. (2007). The Contradictions of Techno-Nationalism and Techno-Globalism: A Historical Perspective. *New Global Studies,* 1: 1–32.
Eight arrested for wearing yellow t-shirts with 'Bersih 2.0' written in Jawi (2011). Kuala Lumpur: NST Online. Online. Available at: http://www.nst.com.my/articles/ Eightarrestedforwearingyellowt-shirtswith_Bersih2_0_writteninJawi/Article/, 26 June (accessed 27 June 2011).
Eisenstein, E. L. (1979). *The Printing Press as an Agent of Change: Communications and Cultural Transformations in Early Modern Europe,* Cambridge: Cambridge University Press.
Elections (Registration of Electors) Regulations (2002). Prime Minister's Department. The Elections Commission, Malaysia.
Elliott, A. (2002). The Social Imaginary: A Critical Assessment of Castoriadis' Psychoanalytic Social Theory. *American Imago,* 59: 141–70.
Ellul, J. (1980). *The Technological System,* New York: Continuum.
Facebook share price halves since IPO (2012). Sydney: Sydney Morning Herald. Online. Available at: http://www.smh.com.au/business/world-business/facebook-share-price-halves-since-ipo-20120821–24j5t.html, 2 August (accessed 26 November 2012).
Felker, G. (2009). The Political Economy of Southeast Asia's Techno-Glocalism. *Cambridge Review of International Affairs,* 22: 469–91.
Fichte, J. G. (2001). Addresses to the German Nation. In: V. P. Pecora (ed.), *Nations and Identities: Classic Readings,* Oxford: Blackwell.
Flichy, P. (2002). New Media History. In: L. A. Lievrouw and S. Livingstone (eds.), *Handbook of New Media: Social Shaping and Consequences of ICTs,* London: Sage.
Foster, T. (2005). *The Souls of Cyberfolk: Posthumanism as Vernacular Theory,* Minneapolis: University of Minnesota Press.
Foucault, M. (1982). The Subject and Power. *Critical Inquiry,* 8: 777–95.
Freedom in the World 2012: Table of Independent Countries (2012). Freedom House. Online. Available at: http://www.freedomhouse.org/sites/default/files/inline_images/ Table of Independent Countries%2C FIW 2012 draft.pdf (accessed 26 November 2012).
Furlow, C. (2009). Malaysian Modernities: Cultural Politics and the Construction of Muslim Technoscientific Identities. *Anthropological Quarterly,* 82: 197–228.
Furuoka, F. (2007). Malaysia–Japan Relations Under the Mahathir Administration: Case Studies of the 'Look East' Policy and Japanese Investment in Malaysia. *Asian Survey,* 47: 505–19.
Gabriel, S. P. (2011). Translating Bangsa Malaysia. *Critical Asian Studies,* 43: 349–72.
Gan, S. (2011). *A killer blow to online media. Malaysiakini.* Online. Available at: http://www.malaysiakini.com/news/154538, 26 January (accessed 12 September 2011).
Gaonkar, D. P. (2002). Toward New Imaginaries: An Introduction. *Public Culture,* 14.1: 1–19.
Gaonkar, D. P. and Lee, B. (2002). New Imaginaries. *Public Culture,* 14.1: ix–xi.
Geertz, C. (1963). The Integrative Solution: Primordial Sentiments and Civil Politics in the New States. In: C. Geertz (ed.), *Old Societies and New States: The Quest for Modernity in Asia and Africa,* New York: Free Press.

Geertz, C. (1998). The World in Pieces: Culture and Politics at the End of the Century. *Focaal,* 32: 91–117.
Gellner, E. (1995). *Do Nations have Navels?* The Warwick Debate. Online. Available at: http://members.tripod.com/GellnerPage/Warwick2.html (accessed 15 May 2002).
Gellner, E. (1996). The Coming of Nationalism. In: G. Balakrishnan (ed.), *Mapping the Nation,* London: Verso.
George, C. (2005). The Internet's Political Impact and the Penetration/Participation Paradox in Malaysia and Singapore. *Media, Culture & Society,* 27: 903–20.
Gibson, W. (1984). *Neuromancer,* New York: Ace Books.
Gilder, G. (1989). *Microcosm: The Quantum Revolution in Economics and Technology,* New York: Touchstone.
Gilder, G. (1996). The Gilder Paradigm. 2004. *Wired.* Online. Available at: http://www.wired.com/wired/archive/4.12/gilder.html, December (accessed 20 October 2004).
Gilley, B. (2005). Political Legitimacy in Malaysia: Regime Performance in the Asian Context. In: L. White (ed.), *Legitimacy: Ambiguities of Political Success or Failure in East and Southeast Asia,* Hackensack, NJ: World Scientific Publishing.
Global Bersih 2.0 (2011). Global Bersih. Online. Available at: http://www.globalbersih.org/locations/global-bersih-2-0/ (accessed 9 December 2012).
Global Bersih 3.0 (2012a). The Molitor. Online. Available at: http://www.globalbersih.org/ (accessed 24 April 2012).
Global Bersih 3.0 (2012b). Global Bersih. Online. Available at: http://www.globalbersih.org/locations/global-bersih-3-0/ (accessed 9 December 2012).
Göle, N. F. (2002). Islam in Public: New Visibilities and New Imaginaries. *Public Culture,* 14: 173–90.
Gomez, E. T. (2007). Resistance to Change: Malay Politics in Malaysia. In: E. T. Gomez (ed.), *Politics in Malaysia: The Malay Dimension,* New York: Routledge.
Gomez, J. (2012). Govt sues Bersih. Kuala Lumpur: *NST Online.* Online. Available at: http://www.nst.com.my/top-news/govt-sues-bersih-1.87188, 24 May (accessed 12 December 2012).
Gong, R. (2010). Internet Politics and State Media Control: Candidate Weblogs in Malaysia. Networking Democracy Conference. Cluj-Napoca, Romania/Stanford University.
Gooch, L. (2011). In Malaysia, Freedom of the (Virtual) Press. Kuala Lumpur: *New York Times.* Online. Available at: http://mobile.nytimes.com/article;jsessionid=42D 9149A636619C0A0A8AA088880844E.w6?a=838564&single=1&f=20, 9 September (accessed 9 September 2011).
Gwynne, P. (1993). Directing Technology in Asia's 'Dragons'. *Research-Technology Management,* March/April: 12–15.
Habibu, S. (2010). Ex-candidate for PKR No. 2 post says he's had enough. Petaling Jaya: *The Star Online.* Online. Available at: http://thestar.com.my/news/story.asp?file=/2010/11/15/nation/7430352&sec=nation, 15 November (accessed 12 December 2012).
Hall, J. A. and Ikenberry, J. (1989). *The State,* Milton Keynes: Open University Press.
Hamayotsu, K. (2010). Crises of Identity in PAS and Beyond: Islam and Politics in Post 8 March Malaysia. *The Round Table,* 99: 163–75.
Hambali, S. N., Faruqi, S. S. and Manap, N. A. (2009). *The Development of Education Law Relating to the Public Universities in Malaysia: Towards Liberalisation of the University Governance and Commercialisation of the Academic Activities.* Hanoi: ASEAN Law Association.

Hamid, J. and Azman, S. (2007). *Malaysia's Lina Joy Loses Islam Conversion Case. The Boston Globe.* Online. Available at: http://www.boston.com/news/world/asia/articles/2007/05/30/malaysias_lina_joy_loses_islam_conversion_case/, 30 May (accessed 12 May 2008).

Hand Phone Users Survey (2011). Cyberjaya: Malaysian Communications and Multimedia Commission.

Haque, M. S. (2003). The Role of the State in Managing Ethnic Tensions in Malaysia. *American Behavioral Scientist,* 47: 240–66.

Harper, T. N. (1999). *The End of Empire and the Making of Malaya,* New York: Cambridge University Press.

Harun, J. (1995). IT will speed up development – PM. *Business Times,* 2 November.

Hayles, N. K. (1993). The Seductions of Cyberspace. In: V. A. Conley (ed.), *Rethinking Technologies,* Minneapolis: University of Minnesota Press.

Heidegger, M. (1977). *The Question Concerning Technology and Other Essays,* New York: Garland.

Heim, M. (1995). The Design of Virtual Reality. In: M. Featherstone and R. Burrows (eds.), *Cyberspace/Cyberbodies/Cyberpunk : Cultures of Technological Embodiment,* London: Sage.

Heng, P. H. (1997). The New Economic Policy and the Chinese Community in Peninsular Malaysia. *Developing Economics,* 35: 262–92.

Here In My Home – Malaysian Artistes For Unity (2009). Malaysian Artistes for Unity. Online. Available at: http://www.malaysianartistesforunity.info/?page_id=20 (accessed 8 September 2009).

Hill, H. (1995). Indonesia's Great Leap Forward? Technology Development and Policy Issues. *Bulletin of Indonesian Economic Studies,* 31: 83–123.

Himanen, P. and Castells, M. (2004). Institutional Models of the Network Society: Silicon Valley and Finland. In: M. Castells (ed.), *The Network Society: A Cross-Cultural Perspective,* Cheltenham: Edward Elgar.

Hirschman, C. (1986). The Making of Race in Colonial Malaya: Political Economy and Racial Ideology. *Sociological Forum,* 1: 330–61.

Hirschman, C. (2004). The Origins and Demise of the Concept of Race. *Population and Development Review,* 30: 385–415.

Ho, L. F. (2009). *Civil Society: A Coming of Age?* Singapore. Available at: http://singaporemagazine.sif.org.sg/2009/07/civil-society-a-coming-of-age/ (accessed 1 December 2009).

Household Use of the Internet Survey (2011). Cyberjaya: Malaysian Communications and Multimedia Commission.

Huff, T. E. (2001). Globalization and the Internet: Comparing the Middle Eastern and Malaysian Experiences. *Middle East Journal,* 3: 439–58.

Huff, T. E. (2002). Malaysia's Multimedia Super Corridor and its First Crisis of Confidence. *Asian Journal of Social Science,* 30: 248–70.

Human Rights Watch: Stop harassing Malaysiakini (2009). *Malaysiakini.* Online. Available at: http://www.malaysiakini.com/news/113372, 23 September (accessed 23 September 2009).

Huxley, A. (1977). *Brave New World,* London: Chatto & Windus.

Hwa, Y.-Y. (2012). *The stories of Bersih 3.0. The Nut Graph.* Online. Available at: http://www.thenutgraph.com/the-stories-of-bersih-3-0/, 14 May (accessed 4 June 2012).

Ida, R. (2011). Reorganisation of Media Power in Post-Authoritarian Indonesia. In: K. Sen and D. Hill (eds.), *Politics and the Media in Twenty-First Century Indonesia,* Abingdon: Routledge.

In a quest to upgrade the industries (1996). *New Straits Times.* Online. http://www.nst.com.my/, 28 May (accessed 29 November 2012).

Indergaard, M. (2003). The Webs They Weave: Malaysia's Multimedia Super Corridor and New York City's Silicon Alley. *Urban Studies,* 40: 379–401.

Internet users (per 100 people) (2011). The World Bank. Online. Available at: http://data.worldbank.org/indicator/IT.NET.USER.P2 (accessed 18 October 2012).

Interview with Premesh Chandran of Malaysiakini (Malaysia) on Media Reform (2011). World Movement for Democracy. Online. Available at: http://www.wmd.org/resources/whats-being-done/advocacy-democratic-reform/interview-premesh-chandran-malaysiakini-malays (accessed 12 September 2011).

Jacobs, J. (1997). *Multimedia, The Stalls, The Corridor and Cyberjaya.* Cyberjaya: Business Times. *Factiva.* Online. 9 September (accessed 1 July 2011).

James, P. (2006). Theorizing Nation Formation in the Context of Imperialism and Globalism. In: G. Delanty and K. Kumar (eds.), *The Sage Handbook of Nations and Nationalism,* London: Sage.

Jarman, J. and Chopra, P. S. (2007). Business Services and the Knowledge Economy in Malaysia. *International Journal of Sociology and Social Policy,* 28: 193–203.

Jasin, K. A. K., Heong, Y. S. and Jasin, N. (1998). In Defense of Capital Controls: An Interview with Malaysian Prime Minister Mahathir Mohamed. *Multinational Monitor,* 4.

Jha, P. (2009). Changing Political Dynamics in Malaysia: Role of Ethnic Minorities. *Strategic Analysis,* 33: 117–25.

Joas, H. (1989). Institutionalization as a Creative Process: The Sociological Importance of Cornelius Castoriadis's Political Philosophy. *American Journal of Sociology,* 94: 1184–99.

Jomo, K. S. (1988). Introduction In: K. S. Jomo (ed.), *Mahathir's Economic Policies,* Petaling Jaya: Institute of Social Analysis.

Jones, D. M. (2007). The Southeast Asian Development Model: Non-liberal Democracy with Market Accountability. *Southeast Asian Affairs,* 1: 59–76.

Jong, R. (2010). *Cow's Head Protesters Fined.* Shah Alam: *New Straits Times.* Online. Available at: http://www.nst.com.my/nst/articles/13rjlembu/Article/, 28 July (accessed 28 July 2010).

Jung, J.-Y., Qiu, J. L. and Kim, Y.-C. (2001). Internet Connectedness and Inequality: Beyond the 'Divide'. *Communication Research,* 28: 507–35.

Kakiailatu, T. (2007). Media in Indonesia: Forum for Political Change and Critical Assessment. *Asia Pacific Viewpoint,* 48: 60–71.

Kalyvas, A. (2001). The Politics of Autonomy and the Challenge of Deliberation: Castoriadis Contra Habermas. *Thesis Eleven,* 64: 1–19.

Kamal, S. M. (2011a). *DPM: 'Monitoring system' to replace censorship laws.* Putrajaya: The Malaysian Insider. Online. Available at: http://www.themalaysianinsider.com/malaysia/article/dpm-monitoring-system-to-replace-censorship-laws, 16 August (accessed 12 September 2011).

Kamal, S. M. (2011b). *Reforms possible only if Umno wins GE, says Najib.* The Malaysian Insider. Online. Available at: http://www.themalaysianinsider.com/malaysia/article/reforms-possible-only-if-umno-wins-ge-says-najib/, 28 November (accessed 29 November 2011).

Karim, F. N. (2010). *Clinton says Malaysia a model nation to the world.* Putrajaya: New Straits Times. Online. Available at: http://www.nst.com.my/nst/articles/ClintonsaysMalaysiaamodelnationtotheworld/Article/art_print, 3 November (accessed 3 November 2010).

Karim, K. N. (2010). *Poverty Eradication: Malaysia's Experience and Practice.* International Poverty Reduction Center in China. Online. Available at: http://www.iprcc.org/front/article/article.action?id=1240, 26 May (accessed 31 July 2011).

Katz, J. (1997). *Birth of a Digital Nation. Wired.* Online. Available at: http://www.wired.com/wired/archive/5.04/netizen.html (accessed 6 June 2013).

Keane, J. (2009). Monitory Democracy and Media-Saturated Societies. *Griffith REVIEW.* Online. Available at: https://griffithreview.com/edition-24-participation-society/monitory-democracy-and-media-saturated-societies (accessed 6 June 2013).

Kedourie, E. (1993). *Nationalism,* Oxford: Blackwell.

Khalid, K. M. (2007). Voting for Change? Islam and Personalised Politics in the 2004 General Elections. In: E. T. Gomez (ed.), *Politics in Malaysia: The Malay Dimension,* New York: Routledge.

Khoo, G. C. (2009). Reading the Films of Independent Filmmaker Yasmin Ahmad: Cosmopolitanism, Sufi Islam and Malay Subjectivity. In: D. P. S. Goh, M. Gabrielpillai, P. Holden and G. C. Khoo (eds.), *Race and Multiculturalism in Malaysia and Singapore.* New York: Routledge.

Khor, N. (2011). *The revolution now has a name: Bersih. Malaysiakini.* Online. Available at: http://www.malaysiakini.com/news/169460, 10 July (accessed 11 July 2011).

Kitchin, R. and Kneale, J. (2002). *Lost in Space: Geographies of Science Fiction,* London: Continuum.

Kitley, P. and Nain, Z. (2003). Out of Front: Government Regulation of Television in Malaysia. In: P. Kitley (ed.), *Television, Regulation and Civil Society in Asia,* London: RoutledgeCurzon.

Kitzmann, A. (2001). Pioneer Spirits and the Lure of Technology: Vannevar Bush's Desk, Theodor Nelson's World. *Configurations,* 9: 441–59.

Kline, R. (2003). Resisting Consumer Technology in Rural America: The Telephone and Electrification. In: N. Oudshoorn and T. Pinch (eds.), *How Users Matter: The Co-Construction of Users and Technologies.* Cambridge, MA: MIT Press.

Koh, J. L. (2012). *Not right for gov't to start media council, says don. Malaysiakini.* Online. Available at: http://www.malaysiakini.com/news/199557, 31 May (accessed 1 June 2012).

Koh, J. L. and Zulkifli, Z. (2012). *Students march through KL for 'clean' campus polls.* Kuala Lumpur: *Malaysiakini.* Online. Available at: http://www.malaysiakini.com/news/209067, 16 September (accessed 17 September 2012).

Koh, W. T. H. and Wong, P. K. (2005).Competing at the Frontier: The Changing Role of Technology Policy in Singapore's Economic Strategy. *Technological Forecasting and Social Change,* 72: 255–85.

Kopalan, I. (2006). *Broken Deities and Hammered Faith.* YouTube. Online. Available at: http://www.youtube.com/watch?v=Xvp5cGi4WJY, 6 December (accessed 9 December 2012).

Kreisler, H. (2001). *Identity and Change in the Network Society: Conversation with Manuel Castells.* The Regents of the University of California. Online. Available at: http://globetrotter.berkeley.edu/people/Castells/castells-con4.html (accessed 12 May 2008).

Kuhn, T. S. (1996). *The Structure of Scientific Revolutions,* Chicago, IL: University of Chicago Press.

Kumar, B. N. (2012). *Internal rifts may cost PKR Indian votes. Free Malaysia Today.* Online. Available at: http://www.freemalaysiatoday.com/category/nation/2012/11/23/internal-rifts-may-cost-pkr-indian-votes/, 23 November (accessed 12 December 2012).

Kumar, K. (2006). Empire and English Nationalism. *Nations and Nationalism*, 12: 1–13.
Laffan, M. F. (2003). *Islamic Nationhood and Colonial Indonesia: The Umma Below the Winds*, London and New York: Routledge.
Laws of Malaysia: Act 15, Sedition Act 1948 (2006). The Commissioner of Law Revision, Malaysia.
Laws of Malaysia: Act 301, Printing Presses and Publications Act 1984 (2006). The Commissioner of Law Revision, Malaysia.
Laws of Malaysia: Federal Constitution (2006). Fifteenth edition, University of Richmond.
Laws of Malaysia: Act 736, Peaceful Assembly Act (2012). Percetakan Nasional Malaysia Berhad.
Laws of Malaysia: : Act 747, Security Offences (Special Measures) Act (2012). Percetakan Nasional Malaysia Berhad.
Laws of Malaysia: Act A1436, Printing Presses and Publication (Amendment) Act (2012). Percetakan Nasional Malaysia Berhad.
Lee, J. (2011). Malaysian Dilemma: The Enduring Cancer of Affirmative Action. *Foreign Policy Analysis*. St Leonards, NSW: The Centre for Independent Studies.
Lee, K. Y. (2009). *Dangerous to let highfalutin ideas go undemolished: MM*. Singapore: Straits Times. Online. Available at: http://www.pmo.gov.sg/News/Transcripts/Minister+Mentor/Dangerous+to+let+highfalutin+ideas+go+undemolished+MM.htm, 20 August (accessed 25 August 2009).
Lee, M. Y. (2009). *16 arrested at candlelight vigil*. Kuala Lumpur: The Star. Online. Available at: http://thestaronline.tv/default.aspx?vid=4095, 6 September (accessed 11 September 2009).
Lee, R. L. M. (2004). The Transformation of Race Relations in Malaysia: From Ethnic Discourse to National Imagery, 1993–2003. *African and Asian Studies*, 3: 119–43.
Lee, T. (2001). The Politics of Internet Policy and (Auto)Regulation in Singapore. *Media International Australia incorporating Culture and Policy*, 101: 33–42.
Lee, T. (2010). *The Media, Cultural Control and Government in Singapore*, Abingdon: Routledge.
Lee, W. L. (2007). Net Value: MSC Status but Sleepless Nights. *The Edge Financial Daily*, 29 January.
Leifer, M. (2000). The Changing Temper of Indonesian Nationalism. In: M. Leifer (ed.), *Asian Nationalism*. London and New York: Routledge.
Leiner, B. M., Cerf, V. G., Clark, D. D., Kahn, R. E., Kleinrock, L., Lynch, D. C., Postel, J., Roberts, L. G. and Wolff, S. (2000). *A Brief History of the Internet*. Online. Internet Society (ISOC). Available at: http://www.isoc.org.internet-history/brief.html (accessed 30 July 2000).
Lenhart, A., Horrigan, J., Rainie, L., Allen, K., Boyce, A., Madden, M. and O'Grady, E. (2003). *The Ever-Shifting Internet Population*. Pew Internet Project. Online. Available at: http://pewInternet.org/Presentations/2003/The-EverShifting-Internet-Population.aspx, 16 April (accessed 9 December 2012).
Leong, P. and Yap, S. Y. (2007). Malaysia. *Media Asia*, 34: 156–70.
Leong, S. (2008). Looking through the Corridor: Malaysia & the MSC. In: D. C. L. Lim (ed.), *Overcoming Passion for Race in Malaysia Cultural Studies*, Leiden: Brill.
Leong, S. (2009). *The Hindraf Saga: Media and Citizenship in Praxis*, ANZCA 09, Brisbane, Australia: QUT.

Leong, S. (2012). Sacred Cows and Crashing Boars: Ethno-Religious Minorities and the Politics of Online Representation in Malaysia. *Critical Asian Studies*, 44: 31–56.

Lepawsky, J. (2005a). Digital Aspirations: Malaysia and the Multimedia Super Corridor. *Focus on Geography*, 48: 10–18.

Lepawsky, J. (2005b). Stories of Space and Subjectivity in Planning the Multimedia Super Corridor. *Geoforum*, 36: 705–19.

Lessig, L. (2001). *The Future of Ideas: The Fate of the Commons in a Connected World*, New York: Random House.

Lessing, D. (1980). *The Sirian Experiments*, London: Jonathan Cape.

Lian, K. F. and Appadurai, J. (2011). Race, Class and Politics in Peninsular Malaysia: The General Election of 2008. *Asian Studies Review*, 35: 63–82.

Lim, A. (2001). Intelligent Island Discourse: Singapore's Discursive Negotiation with Technology. *Bulletin of Science, Technology & Society*, 21: 175–92.

Lim, C. W. (2012). *Repeal of ISA is commendable, but provisions in new law that depart from ordinary principles must be reviewed*. The Malaysian Bar. Online. Available at: http://www.malaysianbar.org.my/press_statements/press_release_repeal_of_isa_is_commendable_but_provisions_in_new_law_that_depart_from_ordinary_principles_must_be_reviewed.html (accessed 10 April 2012).

Lim, D. (2008a). *Election results by the streets of Kota Bharu*. Kota Bharu: YouTube. Online. Available at: http://www.youtube.com/watch?v=JQf1JJRcfO0, 6 April (accessed 9 December 2012).

Lim, D. (2008b). *The university of politics*. Kota Bharu: Malaysia Votes. Online. Available at: http://www.malaysiavotes.com/2008/03/04/the-university-of-politics/, 4 April (accessed 9 December 2012).

Lim, D. (18 November 2012). *RE: Introductions and Requests for Information*. Type to S. Leong.

Lim, I. (2012). *Nazri: New law to replace archaic Sedition Act will be tabled next year*. Kuala Lumpur: The Malaysian Insider. Online. Available at: http://www.themalaysianinsider.com/malaysia/article/nazri-new-law-to-replace-archaic-sedition-act-to-be-tabled-next-year, 14 October (accessed 12 December 2012).

Lim, K. S. (2008). *Political Tsunami in General Election*. Online. Available at: http://blog.limkitsiang.com/2008/03/08/political-tsunami-in-general-election/ (accessed 21 July 2011).

Lim, M. (2011). *@Crossroads: Democratization and Corporatization of Media in Indonesia*. Participatory Media Lab, Ford Foundation.

Ling, R. (2004). *The Mobile Connection: The Cell Phone's Impact on Society*, San Francisco: Morgan Kaufmann.

Liu, Y. (2011). Crafting a Democratic Enclave on the Cyberspace: Case Studies of Malaysia, Indonesia, and Singapore. *Journal of Current Southeast Asian Affairs*, 30: 33–55.

Livingstone, S. and Helsper, E. (2007). Gradations in Digital Inclusion: Children, Young People and the Digital Divide. *New Media & Society*, 9: 671–96.

Lotfalian, M. (2004). *Islam, Technoscientific Identities, and the Culture of Curiosity*, Lanham: University Press of America.

Lund, E., Pihl, M. and Sløk, J. (1962). *A History of European Ideas*, Reading, MA: Addison-Wesley.

Macdonald, S. B. and Lemco, J. (2002). Political Islam in Southeast Asia. *Current History*, 101 : 388–92.

Mahathir, M. (1970). *The Malay Dilemma,* Singapore: Asia Pacific Press.
Mahathir, M. (1988). New Government Policies. In: K. S. Jomo (ed.), *Mahathir's Economic Policies.* Petaling Jaya: Institute of Social Analysis.
Mahathir, M. (1991). *Vision 2020: The Way Forward.* United Nations Online Network in Public Administration and Finance. Online. Available at: http://unpan1.un.org/intradoc/groups/public/documents/APCITY/UNPAN003223.pdf, 28 February (accessed 17 April 2007).
Mahathir, M. (1996). *The Opening of Multimedia Asia on Multimedia Super Corridor (MSC).* Prime Minister's Office, Malaysia. Online. Available at: http://www.pmo.gov.my/WebNotesApp/PastPM.nsf/a310590c7cafaaae48256db4001773ea/682f9d3b1112f6614825674a00223bc4?OpenDocument (accessed 19 April 2007).
Mahathir, M. (1997). *The Way Forward.* Prime Minister's Office, Malaysia. Online. Available at: http://www.pmo.gov.my/WebNotesApp/PastPM.nsf/a310590c7cafaaae48256db4001773ea/b8cb14dc894a0fcb4825674a0028dc9c?OpenDocument, 29 April (accessed 1 September 2004).
Mahathir, M. (2002). *The New Malay Dilemma.* Prime Minister's Office, Malaysia. Online. Available at: http://www.pmo.gov.my/WebNotesApp/PastPM.nsf/0/3ee6b68437a12bc848256c0600169e7b?OpenDocument (accessed 27 April 2007).
Mahathir, M. (2011). *A Doctor in the House,* Petaling Jaya: MPH Publishing.
Mahmood, M. (2012). *Rafizi's quit move poser. New Straits Times.* Online. Available at: http://www.nst.com.my/nation/politics/rafizi-s-quit-move-poser-1.97049, 22 June (accessed 12 December 2012).
Malaysia (2012): State aims to control cyberspace (2012). Southeast Asian Press Alliance. Online. Available at: http://www.seapabkk.org/component/content/article/22-seapa-reports/100589-malaysia-state-aims-to-control-cyberspace.html, 3 May (accessed 4 June 2012).
Malaysia beer drink woman's caning sentence commuted (2010). BBC News. Online. Available at: http://news.bbc.co.uk/2/hi/asia-pacific/8598190.stm, 1 April (accessed 12 September 2011).
Malaysia censors Economist article on protest (2011). *The Telegraph.* Online. Available at: http://www.telegraph.co.uk/news/worldnews/asia/malaysia/8650089/Malaysia-censors-Economist-article-on-protest.html, 21 July (accessed 13 December 2012).
Malaysia to Consider Reviewing Law on Print Media (2011). *The Jakarta Globe.* Online. Available at: http://www.thejakartaglobe.com/international/malaysia-to-consider-reviewing-law-on-print-media/459954, 18 August (accessed 12 September 2011).
Malaysia: Continued criminalisation of Hindu Rights Action Force (HINDRAF) and the Human Rights Party (2011). Frontlinedefenders.org. Online. Available at: http://www.frontlinedefenders.org/node/14661, 11 March (accessed 10 October 2011).
Malaysia: End Intimidation of News Website (2003). New York: Human Rights Watch. Online. Available at: http://hrw.org/english/docs/2003/10/08/malays6440.htm, 8 October (accessed 29 April 2007).
Malaysia news portal wins right to start newspaper (2012). Kuala Lumpur: AsiaOne. Online. Available at: http://www.asiaone.com/News/AsiaOne%2BNews/Malaysia/Story/A1Story20121001-374895.html (accessed 1 October 2012).
Malaysia: Public Dialogue on Hindu Temple Relocation After Cow Head Protest Disrupted (2009). YouTube. Online. Available at: http://www.youtube.com/watch?v=/bIEeZ7O7uik, 5 September (accessed 13 September 2009).
Malaysia Replaces Its Worst Law: Najib is barely keeping up with society's demands for change (2012). *Wall Street Journal.* Online. Available at: http://online.wsj.com/

article/SB10001424052702303772904577335223310905892.html, 10 April (accessed 1 June 2012).
Malaysia is Top in Social Networking in Southeast Asia (2011). Kuala Lumpur: Bernama. Online. Available at: http://www.bernama.com/bernama/v5/newsbusiness.php?id=604520, 28 July (accessed 29 July 2011).
Malaysia's Multimedia Super Corridor Proposal (1996). Kuala Lumpur: Asia Pulse. Factiva. Online. 10 July (accessed 20 July 2011).
Malaysia's Racial-Preference Policy: Son versus Sons (2009). The Economist. Online. 2 July. Available at: http://www.economist.com/node/13961677?Story_ID=E1_TPJGTGSS (accessed 23 July 2011).
Malaysian Bar Council Walk for Justice Rally (2007). World News Network. Online. Available at: http://wn.com/malaysian_bar_council_walk_for_justice_rally, 29 September (accessed 10 December 2012).
Malaysian Internet Usage Takes Off in 2010 (2011). NielsenWire. Online. Available at: http://blog.nielsen.com/nielsenwire/global/malaysian-Internet-usage-takes-off-in-2010/, 25 April (accessed 1 August 2011).
Malaysians protest Aussie refinery (2011). Kuala Lumpur: News.com.au. Online. Available at: http://www.news.com.au/business/malaysians-protest-aussie-refinery/story-fn7mjon9-1226059994129, 21 May (accessed 1 July 2011).
Mandarin News Australia (2011). Special Broadcasting Services. Online. Available at: http://www.sbs.com.au/chinese/video/407442/Mandarin-News-Australia-%E6%9C%80%E6%96%B0%E6%BE%B3%E5%A4%A7%E5%88%A9%E4%BA%9A%E6%99%AE%E9%80%9A%E8%AF%9D%E6%96%B0%E9%97%BB/, 9 March (accessed 13 March 2011).
Mandel, K. (2011). *Yahoo! S.E Asia releases study on Internet trends and media consumptions.* Yahoo Asia Pacific. Online. Available at: http://ycorpblog.com/2010/06/09/yahoo-netindex/, 9 June (accessed 27 July 2011).
Mann, M., Nolan, J. and Wellman, B. (2001). Sousveillance: Inventing and Using Wearable Computing Devices for Data Collection in Surveillance Environments. *Surveillance & Society*, 1: 331–5.
Marvin, C. (1988). *When Old Technologies Were New: Thinking about Electric Communication in the late Nineteenth Century*, New York: Oxford University Press.
Mathi, B. (2008). Growing Singapore's Civil Society. *Social Space*, 2011: 80–3.
Mattelart, A. (2003). *The Information Society*, London: Sage.
McGregor, A. (2008). *Southeast Asian Development*, New York: Routledge.
McLuhan, M. (1964). *Understanding Media: The Extensions of Man*, London: Routledge & Kegan Paul.
Media must work for a united Malaysia: PM (2010). Petaling Jaya: *New Straits Times*. Online. Available at: http://www.nst.com.my/Current_News/NST/articles/20100228150636/Article/index_html, 28 February (accessed 1 March 2010).
Mehta, G. L. (1958). Asian Nationalism vis-à-vis Other Asian Nations. *The Annals of the American Academy of Political and Social Science*, 318: 89–96.
Menon, V. (1996). *Put Internet to good use*. Kuala Lumpur: *New Straits Times*. Online. http://www.nst.com.my/, 8 March (accessed 29 November 2012).
Mentor, T. (1986). *The Hacker Manifesto*. Online. Available at: http://www.mithral.com/~beberg/manifesto.html, 8 January (accessed 21 June 2008).
Milner, A. C. (1991). Inventing Politics: The Case of Malaysia. *Past and Present*, 132: 104–29.

Milner, A. C. (1998). Ideological Work in Constructing the Malay Majority. In: D. C. Gladney (ed.), *Making Majorities: Constituting the Nation in Japan, Korea, China, Malaysia, Fiji, Turkey, and the United States.* Stanford: Stanford University Press.

Milner, A. C. (2009). *The Malays,* Malden, MA: Wiley-Blackwell.

Model to be caned for drinking beer in Malaysian bar (2009). *The Guardian.* Online. Available at: http://www.guardian.co.uk/world/2009/aug/20/malaysia-model-alcohol-cane, 20 August (accessed 10 September 2009).

Mohamad, M. (2008). Malaysia – democracy and the end of ethnic politics? *Australian Journal of International Affairs,* 61: 441–59.

Mokhtar, I. L. (2011). *Politicians marshal cyberspace 'forces'. New Straits Times.* Online. Available at: http://www.nst.com.my/nst/articles/04ynac/Article/, 6 February (accessed 7 February 2011).

Morus, I. R. (2000).'The Nervous System of Britain': Space, Time and the Electric Telegraph in the Victorian Age. *BJHS,* 33: 455–75.

Mosco, V. (2004). *The Digital Sublime: Myth, Power, and Cyberspace,* Cambridge, MA: MIT Press.

Moten, A. R. (2009). 2008 General Elections in Malaysia: Democracy at Work. *Japanese Journal of Political Science,* 10: 21–42.

MSC Annual Industry Report. 2009. Multimedia Development Corporation Sdn Bhd.

MSC Malaysia 10 Point: Bill of Guarantees (2008). Multimedia Development Corporation. Online. Available at: http://www.mscmalaysia.my/topic/MSC+Malaysia+Bill+of+Guarantees (accessed 28 July 2011).

MSC Malaysia Impact Survey 2008 (2008). Multimedia Development Corporation Sdn Bhd. Online. Available at: http://www.mscmalaysia.my/codenavia/portals/msc/images/pdf/reports_surveys/impact_survey_2008.pdf (accessed 21 July 2011).

Multimedia Super Corridor: Impact Survey 2004 (2004). Multimedia Development Corporation Sdn Bhd. Online. Available at: http://www.pikom.org.my/docs/hrsig/MSC.pdf (accessed 15 August 2007).

Mumford, L. (1963). *Technics and Civilization,* New York: Harcourt Brace Jovanovich.

Muslim Population of Indonesia (2010). Washington: The Pew Forum on Religion and Public Life. Online. Available at: http://www.pewforum.org/Muslim/Muslim-Population-of-Indonesia.aspx, 4 November (accessed 9 November 2012).

Nagata, J. A. (1979). *Malaysian Mosaic: Perspectives from a Polyethnic Society,* Vancouver: University of British Columbia Press.

Nain, Z. (2000). Globalized Theories and National Controls: The State, the Market and the Malaysian Media. In: J. Curran and M.-J. Park (eds.), *De-Westernizing Media Studies,* London and New York: Routledge.

Nain, Z. (2007). Regime, Media and the Reconstruction of a Fragile Consensus in Malaysia. In: K. Sen and T. Lee (eds.), *Political Regimes and the Media in Asia: Continuities, Contradictions and Challenges,* New York: Routledge.

Nain, Z. (2011). Who Minds the Minders? *Aliran Monthly.* 13 June. Available at: http://aliran.com/5699.html (accessed 1 July 2011).

Najib announces repeal of ISA (2011). *Malaysiakini.* Online. Available at: http://www.malaysiakini.com/news/175949, 15 September (accessed 21 September 2011).

Najib: Measures will help real poor (2012). Kuala Lumpur: AsiaOne. Online. Available at: http://www.asiaone.com/News/AsiaOne%2BNews/Malaysia/Story/A1Story20121001-374748.html, 1 October (accessed 2 October 2012).

Naughton, J. (2000). *A Brief History of the Future: The Origins of the Internet,* London: Phoenix.
Navaratnam, S. (2011). The hypocrisy surrounding Interlok. *The Nut Graph.* Online. Available at: http://www.thenutgraph.com/the-hypocrisy-surrounding-interlok/, 17 January (accessed 4 March 2011).
Nazri uses May 13 riots to justify street protest ban (2011). *Malaysiakini.* Online. Available at: http://www.malaysiakini.com/news/183222, 5 December (accessed 5 December 2011).
NBNetwork (2012).*NBN: Connecting us to a better future.* YouTube. Online. Available at: http://www.youtube.com/watch?v=iaOwxtEgBY8, 3 November (accessed 20 November 2012).
Negroponte, N. (1995). *Being Digital,* London & New York: Hodder & Stoughton.
Neher, C. D. (1994). Asian Style Democracy. *Asian Survey,* 34: 949–61.
Nelson, C. (1995). A clean-cut concept of multimedia super-corridor. *New Straits Times.* Online. http://www.nst.com.my/, 2 November (accessed 1 July 2011).
Ng, E. and Yoong, S. (2012). Tear gas used as 25,000 rally for Malaysia reforms. Kuala Lumpur: *The Independent.* Online. Available at: http://www.independent.co.uk/news/world/asia/tear-gas-used-as-25000-rally-for-malaysia-reforms-7687209.html, 28 April (accessed 3 May 2012).
The Ninth Malaysia Plan: 2006–2010 (2006) 2007: 3–19. Available at: http://www.epu.jpm.my/rm9/english/Mission.pdf (accessed 2 May 2011).
Noor, F. A. (2005).1986 Revisited (Part II): UMNO's Failed Modernist Islamic Project. In: *From Majahapit to Putrajaya,* Kuala Lumpur: Silverfish.
Noor, F. A. (2008). Reformist Muslim Thinkers in Malaysia: Engaging with Power to Uplift the Umma? In: S. T. Hunter (ed.), *Reformist Voices of Islam: Mediating Islam and Modernity,* Armonk, NY: M. E. Sharpe.
Noor, F. A. (2009).The Lost Tribes of Malaysia. In: *What Your Teacher Didn't Tell You: The Annexe Lectures,* Petaling Jaya: Matahari.
Nunziato, D. C. (2009). *Virtual Freedom: Net Neutrality and Free Speech in the Internet Age,* Palo Alto: Stanford University Press.
Okamoto, Y. and Sjöholm, F. (2001). Technology Development in Indonesia. Working Paper. Stockholm: The European Institute of Japanese Studies.
Ong, A. (1999). *Flexible Citizenship: The Cultural Logics of Transnationality,* Durham, NC: Duke University Press.
Ong, A. (2004). The Chinese Axis: Zoning Technologies and Variegated Sovereignty. *Journal of East Asian Studies,* 4: 69–96.
Ong, A. (2005). Ecologies of Expertise: Assembling Flows, Managing Citizenship. In: A. Ong and S. J. Collier (eds.), *Global Assemblages: Technology, Politics, and Ethics as Anthropological Problems,* Malden, MA: Blackwell.
Ong, A. (2006). *Neoliberalism as Exception: Mutations in Citizenship and Sovereignty,* Durham, NC: Duke University Press.
Ong, A. (2009). *Temple demo: Residents march with cow's head.* Shah Alam: *Malaysiakini.* Online. Available at: http://www.malaysiakini.com/news/111628, 28 August (accessed 12 December 2012).
The Online Citizen to be listed as political association (2011). Singapore: *The Straits Times.* Online. Available at: http://www.straitstimes.com/BreakingNews/Singapore/Story/STIStory_623167.html, 12 January (accessed 12 September 2011).
Ooi, K. B., Saravanamuttu, J., Lee, H. G. and Institute of Southeast Asian Studies (2008). *March 8: Eclipsing May 13,* Singapore: Institute of Southeast Asian Studies.

Orwell, G. (1954). *Nineteen eighty-four: A Novel,* Harmondsworth: Penguin Books in association with Secker & Warburg.

Othman, A. F., Zain, H. M. and Lateh, M. F. (2011). *Hisham: ISA may be used against organisers.* Hulu Selangor: *NST Online.* Online. Available at: http://www.nst.com.my/nst/articles//03kaol/Article/, 26 June (accessed 27 June 2011).

Oudshoorn, N. and Pinch, T. (eds.) (2003). *How Users Matter: The Co-Construction of Users and Technologies,* Cambridge, MA: MIT Press.

Oudshoorn, N. and Pinch, T. (2008). User-Technology Relationships: Some Recent Developments. In: E. J. Hackett, O. Amsterdamska, M. Lynch and J. Wajcman (eds.), *The Handbook of Science and Technology Studies,* Cambridge, MA: MIT Press.

Overseas M'sians can apply to vote by post in next GE soon (2012). Petaling Jaya: *The Star Online.* Online. Available at: http://thestar.com.my/news/story.asp?file=/2012/10/21/nation/12204581&sec=nation – 1351010095186117&if_height=589, 21 October (accessed 23 October 2012).

Overseas Malaysians file suit against EC (2011). *Malaysiakini.* Online. Available at: http://www.malaysiakini.com/news/180033, 31 October (accessed 1 November 2011).

Paasonen, S. (2008). What Cyberspace? Traveling Concepts in Internet Research. In: G. Goggin and M. McLelland (eds.), *Internationalizing Internet Studies: Beyond Anglophone Paradigms,* New York: Routledge.

Pacey, A. (1990). *Technology in World Civilization: A Thousand-Year History,* Oxford: Blackwell.

Pathmawathy, S. (2012a). *Media council: Nazri okay with PPPA abolition. Malaysiakini.* Online. Available at: http://malaysiakini.com/news/201251, 19 June (accessed 20 June 2012).

Pathmawathy, S. (2012b). *We will not be cowed, says Bersih.* Kuala Lumpur: *Malaysiakini.* Online. Available at: http://www.malaysiakini.com/news/198566, 21 May (accessed 21 May 2012).

Pathmawathy, S. and Zakaria, H. (2012). *PPPA amendments get nod after much acrimony.* Kuala Lumpur: *Malaysiakini.* Online. Available at: http://www.malaysiakini.com/news/195514, 20 April (accessed 20 June 2012).

Peaceful Assembly Bill comes under UN fire (2011). *Malaysiakini.* Online. Available at: http://www.malaysiakini.com/news/183516, 8 December (accessed 9 December 2011).

Peaceful Assembly Bill mala fide, says ex-top cop (2011). *Malaysiakini.* Online. Available at: http://www.malaysiakini.com/news/183215, 5 December (accessed 6 December 2011).

Penetration rates at a glance (2011). Malaysian Communication and Multimedia Commission. Online. Available at: http://www.skmm.gov.my/attachment/Statistics/Penetration_rate.pdf (accessed 5 August 2011).

'People-oriented' IT agenda required (1996). Kuala Lumpur: *New Straits Times.* Online. http://www.nst.com.my/, 19 December (accessed 25 July 2011).

PeoplePower (2012). *Do you think netizens should make anonymous postings? – PM Lee.* Singapore: AsiaOne. Online. Available at: http://forums.asiaone.com/showthread.php?t=54363–1, 26 September (accessed 28 September 2012).

PM Lee meets bloggers, netizens for tea at Istana (2012). Singapore: Yahoo. Online. Available at: http://sg.news.yahoo.com/pm-lee-meets-group-of-bloggers-and-netizens-for-tea-at-istana.html, 31 August (accessed 13 December 2012).

Port Set to be World's Busiest (2004). Singapore: Singapore Economic Development Board. Online. Available at: http://www.edb.gov.sg/edb/sg/en_uk/index/news_room/publications/singapore_investment04/singapore_investment2/port_set_to_be_world.html, 1 February (accessed 17 December 2007).

Portwood-Stacer, L. (2012a). *How We Talk About Media Refusal, Part 1: 'Addiction'. Flow TV.* Online. Available at: http://flowtv.org/2012/07/how-we-talk-about-media-refusal-part-1/, 29 July (accessed 8 October 2012).

Portwood-Stacer, L. (2012b). *How We Talk About Media Refusal, Part 2: 'Asceticism'. Flow TV.* Online. Available at: http://flowtv.org/2012/09/media-refusal-part-2-asceticism/, 10 September (accessed 8 October 2012).

Portwood-Stacer, L. (2012c). *How We Talk About Media Refusal, Part 3: 'Aesthetics'. Flow TV.* Online. Available at: http://flowtv.org/2012/10/how-we-talk-about-media-refusal-part-3-aesthetics/, 14 October (accessed 1 December 2012).

Poster, M. (1995a). *CyberDemocracy: Internet and the Public Sphere.* Online. Available at: http://www.hnet.uci.edu./mposter/writings/democ.html (accessed 24 August 2001).

Poster, M. (1995b). *The Second Media Age,* Cambridge: Polity Press.

Postill, J. (2006). *Media and Nation Building: How the Iban Became Malaysian,* New York: Berghahn Books.

Postman, N. (1993). *Technopoly: The Surrender of Culture to Technology,* New York: Vintage Books.

Poverty in Malaysia 1957–2002. The Ministry of Information, Communications and Culture, Malaysia. Online. Available at: http://www.malaysiamerdeka.gov.my/v2/en/achievements/economy/123-kadar-kemiskinan-di-malaysia-1957–2002 (accessed 27 July 2011).

Pragalath, K. (2011). *Join us! Ambiga tells BN parties.* Free Malaysia Today. Online. Available at: http://www.freemalaysiatoday.com/2011/06/20/join-us-ambiga-tells-bn-parties/, 20 June (accessed 20 June 2011).

Press statement: Launch of Perhimpunan BERSIH 2.0 (2011). bersih.org. Online. Available at: http://bersih.org/, 19 June (accessed 20 June 2011).

Price, M. (1995). The Nation-State and Global Media. In: *Television, the Public Sphere and National Identity,* Oxford: Clarendon Press.

Publishing permit a 'privilege', not a right (2011). Malaysiakini. Online. Available at: http://www.malaysiakini.com/news/175976, 16 September (accessed 21 September 2011).

Quirk, J. J. and Carey, J. W. (1989). The Mythos of the Electronic Evolution. In: J. W. Carey (ed.), *Communication as Culture: Essays on Media and Society.* Boston: Unwin Hyman.

Rahman, A. S. (1996). *MSC to have special legal framework. New Straits Times.* Online. http://www.nst.com.my/, 25 July (accessed 29 November 2012).

Ramasamy, B., Chakrabarty, A. and Cheah, M. (2003). Malaysia's Leap into the Future: An Evaluation of the Multimedia Super Corridor. *Technovation,* 24: 871–83.

Ramasamy, P. (2004). Nation-Building in Malaysia: Victimization of Indians? In: L. Suryadinata (ed.), *Ethnic Relations and Nation-Building in Southeast Asia: The Case of the Ethnic Chinese,* Singapore: Institute of Southeast Asian Studies.

Razali, N. (2009). *Trends in Malaysia's e-Learning Policies and Projects.* Smart School Department, Multimedia Development Corporation. Online. Available at: http://www.mscmalaysia.my/codenavia/portals/msc/images/articles/smartschool/e-Learning_Asia_Conference_Korea.pdf, 3–4 September (accessed 31 July 2011).

Reid, A. (2009). *Imperial Alchemy: Nationalism and Political Identity in Southeast Asia*, New York: Cambridge University Press.

Reid, A. (2011). *To Nation by Revolution: Indonesia in the 20th Century*, Singapore: NUS Press.

Renan, E. (1990). What is a Nation? In: H. K. Bhabha (ed.), *Nation and Narration*. Abingdon: Routledge.

Repressive Laws (2000). Human Rights Watch. Online. Available at: http://www.hrw.org/campaigns/malaysia/2000/laws.htm (accessed 1 August 2007).

Rheingold, H. (1993). *The Virtual Community: Homesteading on the Electronic Frontier*, Reading, MA: Addison Wesley.

Rheingold, H. (2000). *Tools for Thought: The History and Future of Mind-Expanding Technology*, Cambridge, MA: MIT Press.

Rousseau, J.-J. (2001). The Social Contract: The Origin of Inequality; and The Government of Poland. In: V. P. Pecora (ed.), *Nations and Identities: Classic Readings*, Oxford: Blackwell.

Rudra, G. (2012). A new regime of media control taking shape. Kuala Lumpur: *Malaysiakini*. Online. Available at: http://www.malaysiakini.com/news/199309, 29 May (accessed 30 May 2012).

Ryan, N. J. (1962). *The Cultural Background of the Peoples of Malaya*, Kuala Lumpur: Longman.

Ryan, N. J. (1976). *A History of Malaysia and Singapore*, Kuala Lumpur: Oxford University Press.

Sabri, A. R. (2012). 'Those thinking hudud unimportant are confused'. *Malaysiakini*. Online. Available at: http://www.malaysiakini.com/news/214243, 15 November (accessed 16 November 2012).

Said, E. W. (1978). *Orientalism*. New York: Pantheon Books.

Sani, M. A. M. (2005). Media Freedom in Malaysia. *Journal of Contemporary Asia*, 35: 341–67.

Saravanamuttu, J. (1988). The Look East Policy and Japanese Economic Penetration in Malaysia. In: K. S. Jomo (ed.), *Mahathir's Economic Policies*. Petaling Jaya: Institute of Social Analysis.

Saravanamuttu, J. (2009). MALAYSIA: Political Transformation and Intrigue in an Election Year. *Southeast Asian Affairs*, 2009: 173–92.

SarDesai, D. R. (2003). *Southeast Asia: Past & Present*, Boulder, CO: Westview Press.

Saw, S.-H. (2007). *The Population of Malaysia*, Singapore: ISEAS Publishing.

Schivelbusch, W. (1980). *The Railway Journey: Trains and Travel in the 19th Century*, Oxford: Blackwell.

Schottmann, S. A. (2011). The Pillars of 'Mahathir's Islam': Mahathir Mohamad on Being-Muslim in the Modern World. *Asian Studies Review*, 35: 355–72.

Schutz, A. (1972). *The Phenomenology of the Social World*, London: Heinemann Educational.

Schutz, A. and Luckmann, T. (1974). *The Structures of the Life-World*, London: Heinemann.

Science and Technology in the OIC Member Countries – Executive Summary (2006). Ankara: Statistical, Economic and Social Research and Training Centre for Islamic Countries.

Science, Technology and Enterprise Plan 2015 (2011). Department, P. a. P. (ed.), Singapore: Agency for Science, Technology and Research (A*STAR).

Second Malaysia Plan (1971). In: Malaysia, O. O. T. P. M. O. (ed.), Putrajaya.

Section 15 (5) (a) UUCA: Federal Court dismisses appeal (2011). Putrajaya: NST Online. Online. Available at: http://www.nst.com.my/latest/section-15-5-a-uuca-federal-court-dismisses-appeal-1.175136, 22 November (accessed 12 December 2012).

Segal, A. and Naughton, B. (2001). *Technology Development in the New Millennium: China in Search of a Workable Model*, Cambridge, MA: MIT Press.

Selvaraj, V. (2007). *Responding to Globalization: Nation, Culture and Identity in Singapore*, Singapore: Institute of Southeast Asian Studies.

Selwyn, N. (2003). Apart from Technology: Understanding People's Non-Use of Information and Communication Technologies in Everyday Life. *Technology in Society*, 25: 99–116

Selwyn, N. (2006). Digital Division or Digital Decision? A Study of Non-Users and Low-Users of Computers. *Poetics*, 34: 273–92.

Selwyn, N., Gorard, S. and Furlong, J. (2005). Whose Internet is it Anyway? Exploring Adults' (Non)Use of the Internet in Everyday Life. *European Journal of Communication*, 20: 5–26.

Shamsul, A. B. (1998). Bureaucratic Management of Identity in a Modern State: 'Malayness' in Postwar Malaysia. In: D. C. Gladney (ed.), *Making Majorities: Constituting the Nation in Japan, Korea, China, Malaysia, Fiji, Turkey, and the United States*, Stanford: Stanford University Press.

Shamsul, A. B. (2001). A History of an Identity, an Identity of a History: The Idea and Practice of 'Malayness' in Malaysia Reconsidered. *Journal of Southeast Asian Studies*, 32: 355–66.

Shankar, A. (2009). *Solve the stateless dilemma, gov't told*. Malaysiakini. Online. Available at: http://www.malaysiakini.com/news/113217, 18 September (accessed 5 December 2012).

Sharif, M. N. (1986). Technological Considerations in National Planning. *Technological Forecasting and Social Change*, 30: 361–82.

Shariffadeen, D. T. M. A. (1995). New Communication Era: Economic, Social, and Cultural Consequences for Developing Nations. *Media Asia*, 22: 79–84.

Shariffadeen, D. T. M. A. (1996). *Articulating our concept of civil society*. Kuala Lumpur: *New Straits Times*. Online. http://www.nst.com.my/, October 1996 (accessed 20 July 2011).

Shariffadeen, D. T. M. A. (1997). *Leading Asia into the Information Superhighway*. MIC Annual Conference on Skyways, Highways and Corridors: Asia's Communication Challenges. Kuala Lumpur: Singapore, Asian Media Information and Communication Centre.

Shariffadeen, M. A. (2006). *Developing a Knowledge Society based on Islamic Principles – A Systems View of Maqasid al Shari'ah*. Kuala Lumpur: International Islamic University of Malaysia.

Shariffadeen, D. T. M. A. (2009). *The Role of Culture and Values in Enabling Transformation towards Knowledge Economies: Lessons from Two Countries*. High Level International Conference on Building Knowledge Economies for Job Creation, Increased Competitiveness, and Balanced Development. Carthage: Tunisian Government and ISESCO.

Shariffadeen, M. A. (2012). STI for Socio Economic Transformation – Bridging the Gap, Moving Ahead. Kuala Lumpur. Available at: http://asmic.akademisains.gov.my/download/YM_Tg_Azzman.pdf (accessed 8 December 2012).

Sheldon, P. (2012). Profiling the Non-Users: Examination of Life-Position Indicators, Sensation Seeking, Shyness and Loneliness among Users and Non-Users of Social Network Sites. *Computers in Human Behavior*, 28: 1960–5.

Shelley, M. (1973). *Frankenstein: or, the Modern Prometheus*, London: Arrow Books.

Sheriff, N. (2011). *Malaysia's 'Silent' Awakening. The Nation*. Online. Available at: http://www.thenation.com/article/162835/malaysias-silent-awakening, 17 August (accessed 24 August 2012).

Sim, R. (2012). *Using social media to reach the Chinese. New Straits Times*. Online. Available at: http://www.nst.com.my/opinion/columnist/using-social-media-to-reach-the-chinese-1.53850, 1 March (accessed 2 March 2012).

Singaporeans Can't Get Enough of Digital Media: Nielsen (2011). Nielsen. Online. Available at: http://sg.nielsen.com/site/NewsReleaseJuly112011.shtml, 11 July (accessed 1 August 2011).

Sivanandam, H. (2011). *PM: Very important for Umno, BN to be re-elected. The Sun Daily*. Online. Available at: http://www.thesundaily.my/news/222097?utm_medium=twitter&utm_source=twitterfeed, 28 November (accessed 29 November 2011).

Smith, A. D. (1991). *National Identity*, Reno: University of Nevada Press.

Smith, A. D. (2006). Ethnicity and Nationalism. In: K. Kumar and G. Delanty (eds.), *The Sage Handbook of Nations and Nationalism*, London: Sage.

Smith, J. (2009). *Science and Technology for Development*, London: Zed Books.

Smith, P. (1999). What Does it Mean to be Modern? Indonesia's Reformasi. *The Washington Quarterly*, 22: 47–64.

Spread Multimedia: Bersih 2.0 (2011). Bersih 2.0. Online. Available at: http://bersih.org/?page_id=4342 (accessed 11 July 2011).

Steele, J. (2009). Professionalism Online: How Malaysiakini Challenges Authoritarianism. *The International Journal of Press/Politics*, 14: 91–111.

Stephen, T. and Rose, D. (2011). *We will not allow demonstrations to bring down the Govt here, says PM*. Miri: The Star Online. Online. Available at: http://thestar.com.my/news/story.asp?file=/2011/2/7/nation/8015268&sec=nation, 7 February (accessed 7 February 2011).

Sterling, B. (1993). *Internet (A Short History of the Internet)*. Electronic Frontier Foundation. Online. Available at: http://www.eff.orf/Misc/Publications/Bruce_Sterling/FSF_columns/fsf.05, February (accessed 25 September 2003).

Street demo will bring more bad than good, says King (2011). Kuala Lumpur: *The Star Online*. Online. Available at: http://thestar.com.my/news/story.asp?file=/2011/7/4/nation/9025585&sec=nation – 13510110115488&if_height=567, 3 July (accessed 4 July 2011).

Student Says Sorry for Negarakuku Rap (2007). New Straits Times, 15 August. *Factiva*. Online. http://www.nst.com.my/ (accessed 19 December 2007).

Suaram 20 Years (2010). YouTube. Online. Available at: http://www.youtube.com/watch?v=KO4RwDEUwz4&feature=plcp, 29 January (accessed 11 September 2012).

SUARAM 2011 Human Rights Report Launched (2011). Suaram. Online. Available at: http://www.suaram.net/?p=3714, 28 August (accessed 11 September 2012).

Sun, G. (2007). How Does Asia Mean? In: K.-H. Chen and B. H. Chua (eds.), *The Inter-Asia Cultural Studies Reader*. New York: Routledge.

Suryanarayana, P. S. (2007). Hindraf Leaders Arrested under Tough Law. 14 December. Available online at: http://www.thehindu.com/2007/12/14/stories/2007121450160100.htm (accessed 3 January 2008).

Tan, S. B. C. (2006). *Demonstrators cause Article 11 Forum to end abruptly.* Penang: The Malaysian Bar. Online. Available at: http://www.compassdirect.org/english/country/malaysia/2006/newsarticle_4424.html, 28 June (accessed 9 December 2012).

Tarling, N. (2004). *Nationalism in Southeast Asia: If the People are With Us,* Abingdon: RoutledgeCurzon.

Taylor, C. (1989). *Sources of the Self: The Making of the Modern Identity,* Cambridge: Cambridge University Press.

Taylor, C. (2004). *Modern Social Imaginaries,* Durham, NC: Duke University Press.

Taylor, C. (2007). *A Secular Age,* Cambridge, MA: Belknap Press.

Taylor, K. (2011). *Arab Spring really was social media revolution. TG Daily.* Online. Available at: http://www.tgdaily.com/software-features/58426-arab-spring-really-was-social-media-revolution, 13 September (accessed 26 November 2012).

Tengku, A. T. N. S. (2011). *ISA still relevant, says Singapore DPM Teo.* Singapore: Malaysiakini. Online. Available at: http://www.mysinchew.com/node/65403, 19 October (accessed 20 October 2011).

Teoh, S. (2011). *Armed for cyberwar, Umno Youth wants ammo from Putrajaya. The Malaysian Insider.* Online. Available at: http://www.themalaysianinsider.com/malaysia/article/armed-for-cyberwar-umno-youth-wants-ammo-from-putrajaya/, 18 July (accessed 18 July 2011).

Thee, K. W. (2006). Policies Affecting Indonesia's Industrial Technology Development. *ASEAN Economic Bulletin,* 23: 341–59.

Thomas, G. T. and Wyatt, S. (1999). Shaping Cyberspace: Interpreting and Transforming the Internet. *Research Policy,* 28: 681–98.

Thompson, J. B. (1999). The Media and Modernity. In: H. Mackay and T. O'Sullivan (eds.), *The Media Reader: Continuity and Transformation,* London: Sage.

Thompson, M. R. (2000). The Survival of 'Asian Values' as 'Zivilisationskritik'. *Theory and Society,* 29: 651–86.

Three Per Cent More Broadband Penetration To Reach Target – Rais (2011). Bernama. Online. Available at: http://www.bernama.com/bernama/v5/newsgeneral.php?id=567415, 28 February (accessed 1 August 2011).

Thung, J. L. (2012). Contesting the Post-Colonial Legal Construction of Chinese Indonesians as 'Foreign Subjects'. *Asian Ethnicity,* 13: 373–87.

Tidd, J. and Brocklehurst, M. (1999). Routes to Technological Learning and Development: An Assessment of Malaysia's Innovation Policy and Performance. *Technological Forecasting and Social Change,* 62: 239–57.

Ting, H. (2009). Malaysian History Textbooks and the Discourse of *ketuanan Melayu.* In: D. P. S. Goh, M. Abrielpillai, P. Holden and G. C. Khoo (eds.), *Race and Multiculturalism in Malaysia and Singapore,* Abingdon: Routledge.

Toh, M. H. (ed.) (1998). *Competitiveness of the Singapore Economy: A Strategic Perspective,* Singapore: Singapore University Press.

truthbetoldSir (29 November 2007). *The Malaysian Indian Dilemma,* parts 1–6. Available at: http://www.youtube.com.

Tsun, H. T. (2008). Confining the Freedom of the Press in Singapore: a 'Pragmatic' Press for 'Nation-Building'? *Human Rights Quarterly,* 30: 876–905.

Turkle, S. (1995). *Life on the Screen: Identity in the Age of the Internet*, New York: Simon & Schuster.

Turnbull, C. M. (1989). *A History of Malaysia, Singapore and Brunei*, Sydney: Allen & Unwin.

Turner, B. S. (2007). Islam, Religious Revival and the Sovereign State. *The Muslim World*, 97: 405–18.

Turner, G. (2009). *Ordinary People and the Media: The Demotic Turn*, London: Sage.

Uimonen, P. (2003). Mediated Management of Meaning: On-line Nation Building in Malaysia. *Global Networks*, 3: 299–314.

US Department of State (2011). *U.S. Relations with Malaysia*. Online. Available at: http://www.state.gov/r/pa/ei/bgn/2777.htm (accessed 25 July 2011).

van Dijk, Jan A. G. M. (1999). The One-Dimensional Network Society of Manuel Castells. *New Media and Society*, 1: 127–38. Available at: http://www.thechronicle.demon.co.uk/archive/castells.htm (accessed 13 July 2008).

Verstraete, G. (2002). Railroading America: Towards a Material Study of the Nation. *Theory, Culture & Society*, 19: 145–59.

Vines, S. (1997). '*Unscrupulous' Soros fires a broadside at Mahathir the 'menace'*. *The Independent*. Online. Available at: http://www.independent.co.uk/news/business/unscrupulous-soros-fires-a-broadside-at-mahathir-the-menace-1240660.html, 22 September (accessed 2 January 2013).

Wachowski, A. and Wachowski, L. (dirs.) (1999). *The Matrix*. Film. USA: Roadshow.

Wachowski, A. and Wachowski, L. (dirs.) (2003a). *The Matrix Reloaded*. Film. USA: Roadshow.

Wachowski, A. and Wachowski, L. (dirs.) (2003b). *The Matrix Revolutions*. Film. USA: Roadshow.

Wain, B. (2009). *Malaysian Maverick: Mahathir Mohamad in Turbulent Times*, Basingstoke: Palgrave Macmillan.

Wang, G. (1976). Nationalism in Asia. In: E. Kamenka (ed.), *Nationalism: The Nature and Evolution of an Idea*. London: Edward Arnold.

Wanted – Pact to Check Internet Smut (1996). *The Straits Times*. Online. http://www.straitstimes.com/, 4 April (accessed 29 November 2012).

Wee, M. C. (dir.) (2007). *Negarakuku*. Online video. Taiwan: YouTube.

Weiss, M. L. (2005). *Protest and Possibilities: Civil Society and Coalitions for Political Change in Malaysia*, Palo Alto: Stanford University Press.

Weiss, M. L. (2009). Edging Towards a New Politics in Malaysia. *Asian Survey*, 49: 741–58.

Wellman, B. (2004). The Three Ages of Internet Studies: Ten, Five and Zero Years Ago. *New Media & Society*, 6: 123–9.

Wellman, B. and Haythornthwaite, C. (eds.) (2002). *The Internet in Everyday Life*, Malden, MA: Blackwell.

Welsh, B. (2008). *Election post-mortem: Top 10 factors*. *Malaysiakini*. Online. Available at: http://www.malaysiakini.com/news/79677, 12 March (accessed 18 October 2012).

Welsh, B. (2012). *Popular populism? Najib's Budget 2013 gamble*. *Malaysiakini*. Online. Available at: http://www.malaysiakini.com/news/210383, 1 October (accessed 2 October 2012).

Wertheim, M. (2002). Internet Dreaming: A Utopia for All Seasons. In: D. Tofts, A. Jonson and A. Cavallaro (eds.), *Prefiguring Cyberculture*. London: MIT Press.

What is the MSC Malaysia? (2011). MDeC. Online. Available at: http://www.mscmalaysia.my/topic/12073057908129 (accessed 30 July 2011).
Whiting, A. (2011). *Malaysia – Assembling the Peaceful Assembly Act*. Australia National University. Online. Available at: http://asiapacific.anu.edu.au/newmandala/2011/12/06/malaysia-assembling-the-peaceful-assembly-act/, 6 December (accessed 13 December 2012).
Williams, R. (2003). *Television: Technology and Cultural Form*, London: Routledge.
Winner, L. (1986). Do Artifacts Have Politics? In: L. Winner (ed.), *The Whale and the Reactor: A Search for Limits in an Age of High Technology*. Chicago: University of Chicago Press.
Winstedt, R. (1966). *Malaya and its History*, London: Hutchinson University Library.
Wong, T. C. (2012). *Fresh anti-Lynas campaign with polls focus. Malaysiakini*. Online. Available at: http://www.malaysiakini.com/news/216476, 12 December (accessed 13 December 2012).
Woolgar, S. (2002). Five Rules of Virtuality. In: S. Woolgar (ed.), *Virtual Society? Technology, Cyberbole, Reality*. Oxford: Oxford University Press.
Woon, L. (2012). *Gov't classifying stateless Indians as 'foreigners'. Malaysiakini*. Online. Available at: http://www.malaysiakini.com/news/195991, 25 April (accessed 5 December 2012).
Wyatt, S. (2003). Non-Users Also Matter: The Construction of Users and Non-Users of the Internet. In: N. Oudshoorn and T. Pinch (eds.), *How Users Matter: The Co-Construction of Users and Technologies*. Cambridge, MA: MIT Press.
Wyatt, S. (2008). Technological Determinism is Dead: Long Live Technological Determinism. In: E. J. Hackett, O. Amsterdamska, M. Lynch and J. Wajcman (eds.), *The Handbook of Science and Technology Studies*. Cambridge, MA: MIT Press.
Wyatt, S., Thomas, G. and Terranova, T. (2002). They Came, They Surfed, They Went Back to the Beach: Conceptualizing Use and Non-Use of the Internet. In: S. Woolgar (ed.), *Virtual Society? Technology, Cyberbole, Reality*. Oxford: Oxford University Press.
Yatim, H. (2011). *Court rules UUCA's Section 15 unconstitutional*. Kuala Lumpur: *Malaysiakini*. Online. Available at: http://www.malaysiakini.com/news/180024, 31 October (accessed 31 October 2011).
Yeoh, O. (2008). *Where secondary access prevailed*. The Star Online. Online. Available at: http://thestar.com.my/columnists/story.asp?col=wikimedia&file=/2008/8/28/columnists/wikimedia/22185331&sec=Wikimedia, 28 August (accessed 29 August 2008).
Yoga, S. S. (2011). *Overseas Malaysians want their vote counted*. The Star Online. Online. Available at: http://thestar.com.my/lifestyle/story.asp?file=%2F2011%2F4%2F25%2Flifefocus%2F8090281&sec=lifefocus, 25 April (accessed 2 July 2011).
Yúdice, G. (2003). *The Expediency of Culture: Uses of Culture in the Global Era*, Durham, NC: Duke University Press.
Zahild, S. J. Z. (2009). *Police arrest Uthayakumar, 15 others in aborted candlelight vigil*. Kuala Lumpur: *The Malaysian Insider*. Online. Available at: http://www.themalaysianinsider.com/litee/malaysia/article/Police-arrest-Uthayakumar-15-others-in-aborted-candlelight-vigil/, 6 September (accessed 13 October 2011).

Zeynep, T. (2008). Grooming, Gossip, Facebook and Myspace: What Can We Learn About These Sites From Those Who Won't Assimilate? *Information, Communication and Society,* 11: 544–64.

Zhao, S. (2006). Do Internet Users Have More Social Ties? A Call for Differentiated Analyses of Internet Use. *Journal of Computer-Mediated Communication,* 11: Article 8..

Zurairi, A. R. (2012). *PAS dials down on hudud, concedes it can't rule alone.* Kota Bharu: *The Malaysian Insider.* Online. Available at: http://www.themalaysianinsider.com/malaysia/article/pas-dials-down-on-hudud-concedes-it-cant-rule-alone, 18 November (accessed 12 December 2012).

Index

activism 11, 88, 91, 95, 102
adopt, adopters, adoption 2–4, 15, 24, 46–7, 51, 64–5, 68, 73, 92–3, 113, 115, 124
Aliran (*Aliran Kesedaran Negara*, National Consciousness Movement) 96, 117, 129
Aliran Monthly 96
apostasy 96, 116
Arab Spring 11, 67, 111
ASAS, *see* Islamic Academy of Science
ASEAN (Association of Southeast Asian Nations) 112
assimilate 4, 88
awareness 3, 6, 20, 41, 58, 111, 124

Badawi, Abdullah 1, 88, 97, 110, 115
Bangsa Malaysia 72, 88, 124–5, 129–30, 133
Barisan Nasional (BN) 9, 59
Bernama (Malaysia National News Agency) 112
Berners-Lee, Tim 26, 64
Bersih xiv, 10, 15–16, 19–20, 92, 96, 98–100, 102, 108–11, 116, 119, 122, 124, 128, 130
Bill of Guarantees 2, 80, 86, 119, 129
blogs, blogging 1, 6, 11, 13, 19, 66, 68, 108, 110, 117, 122–3
BN, *see Barisan Nasional*
British Empire 39
broadband network 50
broadcast media 2, 58–9, 91, 100, 106, 120, 128
Bumiputera (son of the soil) 47–8, 72, 80, 84, 86
business 5, 28–9, 55, 71, 80–1, 84–5, 87, 94

capitalist-led development model 52
Castoriadis, Cornelius 7–8, 16–18, 22–4
censorship 2, 11, 58, 80, 86–7, 119, 122, 126
China 11, 32, 38, 40–3, 49, 57, 80, 113, 124, 129
Chinese 9, 33, 39–43, 46–8, 100, 114, 123, 126, 130
citizenship 23–4, 46, 80, 112
CMIO (Chinese, Malay, Indian and Others) 72
coalitional capital 110
colonialism, colonization 5, 33–4, 36–7, 49, 51–2
communication xiv, 49–50, 53, 57, 60–1, 67–9, 91, 98, 106, 116, 127–8
communist threat 33, 58
communitarianism 107
Computer Crimes Act (1997) 86
computers 6, 56, 63, 104
consociates 17, 31, 92, 97, 99, 101–3, 105–6, 127
contemporaries 8, 17, 31, 92, 99–100, 102–3, 105–6, 127
cow's head protest 123
cultural knowledge 7
culture 14–17, 23, 31, 35, 40, 44, 47, 57, 62–3, 66, 76–8, 85, 93, 107, 120, 130
Cyberjaya 5, 80
Cyberlaws 80, 86
cyberpunk 62, 64
cybertroopers 1, 104

DAP (Democratic Action Party) 110
Datuk T Trio 118
democracy 12, 19–20, 29, 44, 56, 65, 75, 78–9, 81, 109, 113, 116–18, 121, 125, 128, 131–2

Index

developed nation status 68, 71, 86, 95, 131, 133
developmentalism 127
diaspora 99, 107; *see also* migrants
discrimination 9
Dutch, The 5, 34, 36, 38–9, 41, 43–4, 47, 51

E-Commerce Act (2006) 86
e-government 83
East Asian Miracle 56, 72, 75
East India Company (VOC) 36
Economic Development Board (Singapore) 29
economic growth 2, 52–3, 56–7, 67, 71, 88
economic policy 48, 52, 71, 81, 112, 114
Economic Transformation Programme (ETP) 53
Economist, The 114
election 1, 9, 19–20, 23–4, 102–4, 109–10, 112, 115–16, 121–2, 125, 129
electoral fraud 102, 122
email 6, 93
ethno-communalism 9, 86
ethno-linguistic categories 40

Facebook 11, 66–7, 97–8, 108, 112, 126
federalism 47
Finland 76, 78
foreign direct investment (FDI) xiv, 55, 85
foreign investment 80
framework 6–8, 11–2, 15–18, 29, 32–5, 48, 71, 73, 77–8, 100, 105, 127
Free and Open Source Software (FOSS)1, 61

GDP, *see* Gross Domestic Product
Global Movement of Moderates (GMM) 115
Google 12, 108
government 5, 9–11, 15, 41, 46–8, 71–2, 82, 87–8, 100–1, 108–17, 119–22, 125–6, 128–30
Gross Domestic Product (GDP) 29, 82

Hacker Manifesto, The 6
Here In My Home 124
Hindraf (Hindu Rights Action Force) 9–10, 92, 96–8, 101–2, 109–11, 116
human capital 77–8
human rights 96–7, 113, 117–18
Human Rights Watch 118

Ibrahim, Anwar 81, 91, 108, 112, 114, 118
ICT 34, 68–9, 73, 76, 80, 84, *see* information and communication technologies
immigrants, outsiders, strangers 8, 20, 46, 102
imperialism 33
implicated user 94
Indian (ethnic group) 9, 31, 33, 35–6, 40–2, 72, 88, 97, 101–2, 108, 111, 114, 123, 130, 133
Indonesia 5–6, 16, 36–7, 41, 43–4, 46–9, 51–2, 54, 56–60
Indonesian aircraft industry company (IPTN) xiv, 54–5
industrialization 51–3, 55, 71
information and communication technologies xiv, 60, 127
instant messaging 6, 87
intellectual property (IP) 21, 86
inter-communal riots 48–9, 52, 58, 67, 108, 120, 122
intermarriage (interracial) 42
Internal Security Act (ISA) 59, 82, 96, 121
Internet 1–6, 26, 53, 55, 57, 59–71, 76, 80–4, 86–8, 90–9, 103–9, 117–19, 121–3, 131
Internet penetration 5, 87, 90–1, 118
IP, *see* intellectual property
IPTN xiv, 54–5, *see* Indonesian aircraft industry company
ISA Internal Security Act 59–60, 82, 96, 121
Islam 9, 33–7, 47–8, 70, 72–3, 96, 110, 114–16
Islam Hadhari 115
Islamic Academy of Science (ASA) xiv, 74
Islamic law 37, 73, 75
Islamic Religious Council of Singapore xiv, 36
Islamization 112, 115–16
IT literacy 95

Japanese occupation 33, 49; *see also* Pacific War
JARING (Joint Advanced Research Integrated Networking) xiv, 67
Joy, Lina 116

Ketuanan Melayu, *see* Malay paramountcy
knowledge society 70, 74, 79, 82, 86–7, 95, 107

knowledge-based economy 69, 75, 107
Koran, The 73, 130
Kuala Lumpur 14, 37, 48, 80, 97

Lee Hsien Loong 122
Lee Kuan Yew 75, 113
Lim Kit Siang 110
Look East policy 54

Mahathir, Mohamad 3, 53–5, 67–8, 70–6, 80–1, 87–8, 95, 101, 107, 113–15, 135, 138
Majlis Ugama Islam Singapura (Islamic Religious Council of Singapore, MUIS) xiv, 36
Malacca (*Melaka*) 36–8, 40, 118
Malay Dilemma, The 72, 101, 126
Malay paramountcy 9–10, 46, 75, 101, 133
Malaysia xiv–xv, 1–6, 8–12, 15–24, 26, 28, 30, 32–44, 46–60, 62, 64, 66–92, 94–104, 106–33
Malaysia Plans 71
Malaysiakini 59, 87, 97–8, 101, 104, 117–8, 126, 128–9
Malaysian Chinese Association (MCA) 114
Malaysian Indian Congress (MIC) 9, 114
Malaysian Indian Dilemma, The 101
Malaysian society 1, 4, 15, 86, 90, 92, 96, 101, 114
Malaysians 1, 3, 9, 23–4, 35, 40–2, 87, 91–2, 97–101, 103–4, 108–12, 114, 116, 122–5, 128, 130
Maqasid al Shari'ah (objectives of Islamic law) 75
MCA, *see* Malaysian Chinese Association
McKinsey and Associates 71, 83
MDeC, *see* Multimedia Development Corporation
Media Council 120, 126
Media Development Authority 122
media, mass 2, 11, 58
media refusal 4, 93
mediascape 5, 109, 122
Melaka, *see* Malacca
Melayu Baru (new Malay) 75
Merdeka Centre for Opinion Research 117
Merdeka day 12, 29, 133
MIC, *see* Malaysian Indian Congress

migrants, Chinese, Indian 8, 40–1, 107; *see also* diaspora
mobile phone 91, 98, 118
monitory democracy 12, 109, 116–18, 121, 125, 128
MSC, *see* Multimedia Super Corridor
MUIS, *see Majlis Ugama Islam Singapura*
multi-ethnic 124
Multimedia Development Corporation (MDeC) xiv, 76, 82–3, 114
Multimedia Super Corridor (MSC) xiv, 1–2, 4–6, 12, 55, 67–77, 79–90, 95, 107–8, 119, 127, 129
MyKad 83, 89
Myoverseasvote 23

Namewee, *see* Wee Meng Che
nation, nationhood 5, 45, 49, 57–8, 107
nation-building 10, 49–50, 53, 57–60, 67, 69, 71, 119, 125
National Economic Policy (NEP) 48
National Harmony Act 121
National Information Technology Council (NITC) xiv
National IT Agenda (NIA) 74
National Science and Technology Board (NSTB) xiv, 55
National Vision Policy (NVP) 71
nationalism, patriotism 8, 30–1, 40, 43–6, 52, 54, 56–7, 72
NDP, *see* New Development Policy
NEM, *see* New Economic Model
New Development Policy (NDP) 71
New Economic Model (NEM) xiv, 71, 110
New Economic Policy (NEP) 48, 71, 81, 112, 114
new media 1–7, 10–12, 54, 58, 60, 62, 64, 66, 68–89, 91–8, 100, 102–4, 106, 108–10, 112, 114, 116, 118, 120, 122, 124, 126–32
New Order (Suharto) 55
newly industrialized countries (NIC) xiv, 54
Newspaper and Printing Presses Act, 1974 (NPPA) xiv, 59
NITC, *see* National Information Technology Council
non-bumi 84
non-use, non-users 1, 3–13, 17, 88, 90–7, 99, 101, 103–7, 109, 119, 127, 131
NPPA, *see* Newspaper and Printing Presses Act

NSTB, *see* National Science and Technology Board
NTT (Japanese Corporation) 79
NVP, *see* National Vision Policy

objectivation 25–6, 28
Official Secrets Act 59
Ohmae, Kenichi 71
Ong, Aihwa 39, 70, 80–1
Online Citizen, The (TOC) 122
outsiders, *see* immigrants, outsiders, strangers
Overseas Malaysians 24, 99

Pacific War 5, 33, 43, 49, 51, 54
Pakatan Rakyat (People's Alliance) xiv, 110–1
Pan-Malaysian Islamic Party xiv, 73, 110–11, 114–15
Parti Islam Se Malaysia 110
Parti Keadilan Rakyat (PKR) xiv, 110–1
PAS, *see* Pan-Malaysian Islamic Party
patriotism, *see* nationalism
Peaceful Assembly Act (2012) 120
peaceful rallies 109
peer groups 99
Penal Code and Evidence Act (2012) 121
Penang 13, 38, 96
PKR, *see Parti Keadilan Rakyat*
Police Watch 97
politics and religion 37
Portuguese 36, 38
potentiality 22, 29–32, 60, 73
poverty 9, 83, 114
power 9–10, 16, 19, 22, 32, 36, 39–40, 43, 46, 49–50, 59, 62–3, 88, 94, 99, 108, 111–12, 114–17, 119, 131–2; Colonial 34, 38, 47; people 9
PPPA, *see* Printing Presses And Publications Acts
Pragmatic Islam 72–3
predecessors xv, 8, 17, 31, 59, 92, 101–2, 105–6, 127
Press Publication Enterprise Permit xv, 59
Printing (or Publishing) Permit (SIT) xv, 59
printing press 58, 119
Printing Presses and Publications Act xiv, 59–60, 119–20
public culture 14–17, 23, 31
Putrajaya 5, 80, 129, 131

racial riots, *see* inter-communal riots
Radio Television Malaysia (RTM) xiv, 58

Raffles, Stamford 38–9
Razak, Najib xiv, 11, 16, 71, 82, 87, 89, 104, 110, 121, 125
red tape 83
reformasi 88, 114
religion 6, 9–10, 29, 32–7, 39–41, 43, 45–9, 52, 69, 72–4, 96, 114
ritual 35
RTM, *see* Radio Television Malaysia

Sabah 26, 46, 129
Sarawak 46, 96, 129
Schutz, Alfred 7–8, 16–18, 24–7, 92, 95–7, 99, 101–3, 105
science fiction 61, 70, 93, 130
Science, Technology and Enterprise Plan (STEP) xv, 23, 55, 87, 104, 121, 125
secondary (proxy) use of Internet 91, 103–6
Security Offences (Special Measures) Act 2012 121
Security Offences Act 60
Sedition Act 59, 82, 121
Sepet (Chinese Eyes) 130
Shah Alam 118
Shared Services And Outsourcing (SSO) 84–5
Shariffadeen, Tengku Mohd Azzman 55, 69–70, 72, 74–6, 79–80, 85, 87, 95, 107
SIC, *see* printing permit
Silicon Valley 76–80, 85
SINDA (Singapore Indian Development Association) xv, 36
Singapore 5–6, 32–4, 36, 38, 42–4, 46–9, 51–3, 55–60, 75, 87, 112–13, 119, 121–2, 131
Smart Schools 83
SMS (short message services) 12, 94, 97–8, 103, 128
social etiquette 14, 22
social imaginaries 6–8, 12, 14–25, 27–35, 38–9, 41, 44–5, 48–51, 60, 67–8, 73, 86, 105, 130–1
social networking (sites) 66, 87, 92, 98, 104, 119, 128
social stock of knowledge 7, 24–9
socio-economic inequalities 114
socio-political acts 20
sousveillance 12, 109, 116–18
Southeast Asia 2, 34–7, 40, 44–5, 48, 51–2, 56, 58, 75, 87, 112
sovereignty 15, 19, 47

Statistical, Economic and Social Research and Training Centre for Islamic Countries 56
STEP, *see* Science, Technology and Enterprise Plan
strangers, *see* immigrants, outsiders
Suaram (*Suara Rakyat Malaysia*, Voice of the Malaysian People) 96, 117, 129
successors 17, 31, 92, 101–2, 105–6, 127
Sukarno, President 16, 44, 59
surat layang (flying letters) 128

Taylor, Charles 7–8, 16–25, 32
techno-laggards 90
techno-nationalism 56–7, 72
technological determinism 2
technology 2–8, 10, 12, 49–58, 61–4, 66–9, 71, 74, 80–1, 87–90, 92–5
technophobia 93
technopole 78, 85
Telehealth 83
Teo, Peter 112
Torvald, Linus 64, 76
tiger economies 107, 113
training 3–4, 14, 43, 51–2, 56, 76, 85, 93, 96

trans-ethnic sodalities 12, 109, 123–4, 126
Treaty Of London 38
Treaty Of Malayan Union 35
Twitter 6, 11, 66, 98, 104, 112, 126

UMNO, United Malays National Organisation xv, 1, 59, 73, 108, 112–15, 119
Universiti Kebangsaan Malaysia 121
Universities and University Colleges Act, (UUCA) 82, 100, 120

venture capital 77
Vision 2020 67–8, 70–2, 79, 95, 107–8, 133

Way Forward, The 72, 95
Wee Meng Che (Namewee) 100–1
Wikileaks 111
World Bank 1, 56
World Wide Web 6, 26, 60, 64, 93, 99, 111

zoning technologies 70, 79–81

Want to stay one step ahead of your colleagues?

Sign up today to receive free up-to-date information on books, journals, conferences and other news within your chosen subject areas.

Visit
www.tandf.co.uk/eupdates
and register your email address, indicating your subject areas of interest.

You will be able to amend your details or unsubscribe at any time. We respect your privacy and will not disclose, sell or rent your email address to any outside company. If you have questions or concerns with any aspect of the eUpdates service, please email eupdates@tandf.co.uk or write to: eUpdates, Routledge, 2/4 Park Square, Milton Park, Abingdon, Oxfordshire OX14 4RN, UK.

ROUTLEDGE INTERNATIONAL HANDBOOKS

Routledge International Handbooks is an outstanding, award-winning series that provides cutting-edge overviews of classic research, current research and future trends in Social Science, Humanities and STM.

Each *Handbook*:

- is introduced and contextualised by leading figures in the field
- features specially commissioned original essays
- draws upon an international team of expert contributors
- provides a comprehensive overview of a sub-discipline.

Routledge International Handbooks aim to address new developments in the sphere, while at the same time providing an authoritative guide to theory and method, the key sub-disciplines and the primary debates of today.

If you would like more information on our on-going *Handbooks* publishing programme, please contact us.

Tel: +44 (0)20 701 76566
Email: reference@routledge.com

www.routledge.com/reference